Disability and Aging

Disability in Society

Ronald J. Berger, series editor

Disability and Aging

Learning from Both to Empower the Lives of Older Adults

Jeffrey S. Kahana
Eva Kahana

LYNNE
RIENNER
PUBLISHERS

BOULDER
LONDON

Published in the United States of America in 2017 by
Lynne Rienner Publishers, Inc.
1800 30th Street, Boulder, Colorado 80301
www.rienner.com

and in the United Kingdom by
Lynne Rienner Publishers, Inc.
3 Henrietta Street, Covent Garden, London WC2E 8LU

Library of Congress Cataloging-in-Publication Data
Names: Kahana, Jeffrey Steven, 1967– author. | Kahana, Eva, author.
Title: Disability and aging : learning from both to empower the lives of
  older adults / by Jeffrey S. Kahana and Eva Kahana.
Description: Boulder, Colorado : Lynne Rienner Publishers, Inc., 2017. |
  Series: Disability in society | Includes bibliographical references and
  index.
Identifiers: LCCN 2016054971 (print) | LCCN 2017009780 (ebook) | ISBN
  9781626375901 (hardcover : alk. paper) | ISBN 9781626376519 (e-book)
Subjects: LCSH: Older people with disabilities. | Aging. | Disabilities.
Classification: LCC HV1568 .K335 2017 (print) | LCC HV1568 (ebook) | DDC
  362.4084/6—dc23
LC record available at https://lccn.loc.gov/2016054971

British Cataloguing in Publication Data
A Cataloguing in Publication record for this book
is available from the British Library.

Printed and bound in the United States of America

The paper used in this publication meets the requirements
of the American National Standard for Permanence of
Paper for Printed Library Materials Z39.48-1992.

5 4 3 2 1

But our machines have now been running for 70 or 80 years, and we must expect that, worn as they are, here a pivot, there a wheel, now a pinion, next a spring will be giving way: and however we may tinker them up for awhile, all will at length surcease motion. . . . [Still] I steer my bark with Hope in the head, leaving Fear astern.

—Thomas Jefferson to John Adams,
July 5, 1814, and April 8, 1816

Contents

Preface

Disability can feel like a tidal wave. When it enters someone's life, it becomes the central focus for the person living with disability, as well as for the disabled person's family members. Those whose lives have been touched by disability—including such writers as Nancy Mairs, Wendy Seymour, and Robert Murphy—have described the experience with great insight. In their self-understanding, they serve as a bridge between the world of disability and the rest of society—but their words also highlight the deep divide that separates those two worlds.

We have no standard measure or test to classify a person as "disabled" or "not disabled." Disability comes in many shapes and sizes, and it affects all age groups. While it is a manifestation of physical and psychological changes in a person, it is also a social concept. Disability is marked by fluidity and gradations, making it hard at times to categorize who is and who is not disabled for public policy purposes. But despite all this variation and ambiguity, for most people disability comes as a permanent change to the status quo—a disruptive force that redefines not only the disabled individual, but that person's family life and relationships with work and social networks. Disability also upends many basic functions that we take for granted: eating, sleeping, hearing, seeing, walking, and talking. And it can make the most basic self-care—dressing, washing, and toileting—much more difficult and time consuming.

Against this background of unremitting challenges, we must ask: What benefits could possibly come from being disabled? Can disability, in fact, be empowering? The point of our book is to make the case that disability in old age need not define a person—as many elders fear it does—but can actually be a source of empowerment. This counterintuitive assertion applies not only to the older person, but also to society, including its able-bodied members.

To be clear, we are not calling for people to abandon health-promoting lifestyles and thereby make themselves more vulnerable to the impairments that can lead to disability. We encourage all older people to follow a healthy diet, to remain socially and civically engaged, and (if they can) to walk and engage in other exercise that fosters physical and psychological well-being.

Nevertheless, even when older people pursue such health-enhancing lifestyles, they will experience incidents of disability as they age. The body is a machine and, even with the greatest of care, things tend to break down in the course of aging. Many older people are terrified that this breakdown will happen to them. But at some point, it will happen to all of us. What then?

To answer this question, we looked at the literatures of both gerontology and disability studies to see if we could find some common ground that would help us to address the experience of aging with disability. We discovered that, although these two fields have developed in different directions, with little overlap between them, we can learn from each discipline. Our aim is to propose ideas and strategies that will enable older people to live good, meaningful lives, even if they become disabled; and to promote better public policies that will support and empower older people who are living with disabilities.

This effort requires more than interdisciplinary dialogue among academic experts and senior and disability services professionals. It requires that we all work to break down the cultural boundaries that separate generations and to encourage greater integration between the young and the old. Often this generational divide stems from biases that frame our expectations of where the old and young fit into society. Everyone—whether elderly, disabled, or both—needs to feel useful and valued. No one wants to be considered obsolete on the basis of false and limiting stereotypes.

When we see elderly or younger individuals living with disability, we need not see them as persons with limitations because they are near the end of life or because they are unable to do certain things that others can do. Instead, we should see them as exemplars of courage who have overcome some of life's greatest challenges and who possess knowledge and practical wisdom that they can share with others. The experience of the elderly—and specifically, how they choose to face disability—can be instructive for younger people.

By examining disability in old age, we realize that some aspects of the disability experience are unique for people who have lived a large portion of their lives as nondisabled persons. The challenges of early-life activities— such as education, job placement, marriage, and child-rearing—are largely absent for the disabled older person. But other challenges exist, and they can be formidable to individuals with little experience as disability insiders. Unfamiliar with navigating the disability terrain—and faced with an idealized model of successful aging that is predicated on the absence of disability—older persons living with disability can become deeply isolated and depressed. Nevertheless, many elderly people who live with disabilities manage to retain their sense of meaningfulness and life satisfaction as they adapt to a shrinking life space and approach the end of life. They draw on psychological and social resources and exercise proactivity in their efforts to marshal informal and formal supports.

* * *

This book is motivated by both scholarly and personal interest in the topics of disability and aging. We are a somewhat unusual mother-son team of coauthors with differing academic backgrounds: Jeffrey Kahana trained as a lawyer and historian, while Eva Kahana trained as a sociologist and gerontologist. We decided to explore this topic together because our life experiences have led us to appreciate the challenges and the gifts of caring for a loved one living with a disability.

Specifically, we share a great love for two family members whose lives have been touched by disability. Our family cared for the late Sari Frost, Jeffrey's grandmother and Eva's mother, during an extended period of disability that began in old age. In 1984 at the age of seventy-five, Sari was diagnosed with diabetes, a disease that led to the successive amputations of her legs. Although Sari had expressed the wish to die if she ever needed an amputation or had to be placed in a nursing home, her positive spirit prevailed and she celebrated life—even as a double amputee and a nursing home resident who lived with dementia during her final years of life. Sari died at the age of eighty-five.

In 2009 Jeffrey's firstborn son and Eva's second grandchild, Zeke Kahana, was diagnosed with autism at the age of two. Caring and advocating for his son has become a central and valued activity in Jeffrey's life. It has also shown him the difference between core disabilities, like Zeke's, and age-related disabilities, like Sari's. Eva has assumed the role of a supportive grandmother in Zeke's life. Jeffrey and Eva have often debated the meaning of disability as a real-world lived experience that is distinct from the jargon of the professional literature. Observing and caring for Sari and Zeke have given each of us an appreciation for using such experiences to inform our academic research and writing.

Throughout her long career as a sociologist specializing in aging, Eva has focused on micro-level phenomena, studying individual adaptations by older adults who encounter stressful life circumstances. As a legal historian whose work has lately focused on social policy, Jeffrey has examined the macro-level implications of assumptions about disabilities and how they affect the welfare of the disabled. These two perspectives closely mirror the contrasting orientations of gerontology and disability studies. While gerontologists have probed the secrets of successful aging since the 1980s and continue to pine for a future of extended disability-free life expectancy, the social model of disability studies views disability as a function of societal failure to accept and support persons with disabilities. Our collaboration has allowed us to embark on an intellectual journey that explores the reasons for the current disconnect between gerontology and disability studies—a disconnect that affects us personally and intrigues us professionally. Through this book, we hope to bring our conversations, debates, and new understandings into the public sphere.

Our book focuses on aging into disability, rather than aging with an existing disability acquired at birth or at an early stage in life. The chapters cast a wide net. We consider late-life disability from the perspectives of first-person narratives by the disabled and their caregivers and of scholarly explorations by researchers and policy analysts. Throughout the book, we acknowledge that no one has all the answers and that we all have a lot to learn by being open-minded about empirical findings that derive from differing theoretical positions. We are committed to removing the barriers that prevent gerontologists and disability advocates from recognizing the intersections of scientific research, lived experience, professional practice, and public policy. Understanding these crossroads can illuminate our understanding of the graying of disability.

Our work on this book has benefited from the supportive environment for research on aging at Case Western Reserve University and Mount Saint Mary College. We began the project in 2010, when Jeffrey was on a sabbatical at the Mandel School of Applied Social Sciences (MSASS) at Case Western. This opportunity was facilitated by Dean Cleve Gilmore and was made productive by so many faculty members at MSASS who are engaged in studying policies and practices concerning aging and disability. A special debt of gratitude goes to David E. Biegel, a colleague and friend and an exemplary scholar and teacher. Sharon Milligan and Terry Hokenstad at MSASS and Kenneth Ledford and David Hammack in the Case Western History Department, all went out of their way to be helpful, welcoming, and encouraging.

At Mount Saint Mary College, this project received enthusiastic support from former president Kevin Mackin and former vice president for academic affairs Iris Turkenkopf. Continued support has been provided by Presidents Anne Carson Daly and David Kennett and Vice President for Academic Affairs Ilona McGuiness. The codirector of the Center on Aging and Policy, Lawrence T. Force, has been a collaborator and friend, and his work and example in the field of caregiving has informed this work in many ways.

Throughout the process, we also benefited from support at the Case Western Elderly Care Research Center from Dale Dannefer, chair of the Sociology Department, and Dean Cyrus Taylor of the College of Arts and Sciences. We also appreciate able assistance by the enthusiastic student research team at the Elderly Care Research Center.

Case Western graduate student Alicia Smith-Tran contributed to Chapter 4, which focuses on the life course. Boaz Kahana, professor of psychology at Cleveland State University, made substantive contributions to Chapter 5, which focuses on the adventurous older traveler. Case Western graduate student Michael R. Slone made valuable additions to Chapter 9, which focuses on policy. These individuals are noted in the book as coauthors of their respective chapters. We also acknowledge the valuable editorial support of graduate students Kaitlyn Barnes Langendoerfer and Christine Schneider and of professional editor Pam Ozaroff. In addition, Richard Liang, our Zotero expert, led a group of helpful undergraduate students who worked on the endnotes: Maritess Escueta, Benjamin Wu, and Siyue Xu.

1

The World of
Late-Life Disability

Disability can be stigmatizing—or it can be liberating. Such are
the opposite connotations of a term that is immensely difficult to define and
is so broadly inclusive as to encompass those with profoundly different
impairments and levels of impairment. The first description derives from
Erving Goffman's 1963 anthropological work *Stigma;* the second from
Irving Zola's 1982 memoir, *Missing Pieces.*[1] That Goffman was writing
from the outside looking in, and Zola from the inside looking out, bears noting. When those who are not disabled define and analyze *disability,* they
often reach quite different conclusions than the descriptions and meanings
that people with disabilities give to the term.

What accounts for such opposite definitions of the term *disability*? It
is not simply the vantage point of the observer, although that surely colors
the perception of disability and its personal and social meaning. Rather, it
is culture and policy—and the shifting ways that time affects perception—
that determine the meaning of disability and the social place of people living with disability. Society does not create the physical and psychological
impairments that are associated with disability. But whether society perceives people living with disability as outside the prevailing norm or as
different but within the norm can make all the difference between stigma
and liberation. In his 1993 historical account of the disability rights movement, *No Pity,* Joseph Shapiro captures a key feeling that to be disabled is
not to be pitied, but to live—and demand the right to live—in the fullness
of life.[2]

In this book, we are concerned with disability in old age—and with the
processes that shape the understanding and experience of disability in late
life. A key theme animating our work is that people experience disability
differently in old age than they do in youth or middle age. Moreover, disability for the young-old (ages sixty-five to seventy-five) and the old-old
(ages eighty-five and over) represent distinct experiences—which is why
we focus separately on each period, drawing different conclusions about

the challenges of the adventurous traveler versus the courageous resident of the nursing home.

Disability and Aging

Growing numbers of older adults worldwide are living well notwithstanding varied physical and cognitive impairments. These individuals have the potential to reshape how society views and understands the concept of disability. Old age brings with it a higher incidence of chronic illness, impairments, and limitations in functioning. Despite such conditions, many elderly persons live robust lives. They manage their illnesses and impairments, enjoy good-to-satisfactory health, and retain an optimistic outlook.[3]

What does this new old-age paradigm portend for the rapidly growing aged population that no longer fits within a narrow and medicalized notion of disability? What does this paradigm mean for how sociologists and gerontologists define the life stage or stages of aging? And what are the political and social implications for countries with a growing population of disabled elders? These questions lie at the heart of the social transformation that is the graying of disability.

In our common language and culture, we are surrounded with the terms *old age* and *disability.* Yet these terms, and the social identities they signify, tend to remain separated based on age cohorts. We tend to reserve the term *disabled* for young and middle-aged people and instead use *sick* or *ill* when we talk about older individuals. And that is how old people view themselves; rarely do they accept the identity—and social personae—of persons living with a disability.[4]

Understanding the divide between disability and old age is the overarching goal of this book. But our path forward is complicated by our very terminology. Like *disability,* the words *aging, old age,* and *the aged* are not easy to define. What—and whom—do we mean when we use these terms? When we speak of "the aged," are we referring to people over a certain age or to people over a certain age whose specific characteristics—health, retirement status, socioeconomic status, gender, family role, or some other social factors—define them beyond their chronological age alone as "old"? Thus, to analyze our terminology is to raise the question of whether old age is a social role rather than a chronological milestone.

For much of the twentieth century, chronological age defined the onset of old age—largely because this milestone was linked to Social Security (and later Medicare) as well as employer-mandated retirement policies. Beginning around the new millennium, however (but with earlier roots, as we will discuss), commentators on aging began to reappraise the social and cultural meaning of growing old. They discovered that they had to view old age in a new light, as it had been transformed by a "longevity revolution"[5] and a new cohort of seniors who were redefining the social expectations and political agenda around aging. It is no coincidence that the new gerontology—with its vision of aging as a time of growth, productivity, happiness, and fully articulated success—emerged just about the time that baby boomers were reaching mature adulthood or early old age.

This new vision of aging was that it could be done without disease or disability. The architects of the new aging viewed the idea of retirement with suspicion; even AARP (formerly the American Association of Retired Persons) removed the word from its organizational name. The new aging did not entail a path to sunny senior communities—replete with bingo, horseshoes, and days of endless relaxation. Most importantly, it equated a longer life with a more youthful one. Personal development through activities and engagement—travel, learning, work, new careers, and new romantic relationships—was a theme that scholars studied and the press popularized. The baby boomers were, after all, a generation with a penchant for being part of an age—whether of Aquarius in the 1960s or the Third Age in the twenty-first century—but not part of *old age,* and certainly not an old age lived with the limitations imposed by disability.

Disability in Old Age

Our specific interest in this book is the graying of disability—the contemporary societal transformation that is taking place as people live to older ages and experience the varied physical and psychological impairments that lead to disability. Disability in old age is an issue that could theoretically unite two distinct communities: those who are aging and those who are disabled, plus the scholars who study these communities and the activists who advocate for their rights. Yet so far, this has not happened. We hope our book will begin to make that connection.

Alzheimer's and Parkinson's disease leave no ambiguity about the effects that aging can have on the body. These diseases are associated with old age, but there are many others—cancer, heart disease, diabetes, arthritis—that disproportionately impact older people. And it is not just disease that causes impairment in old age. The body experiences physiological losses of function that are compounded by other nonphysical losses, including diminished social and financial resources as well as new barriers to enjoying past fixtures of comfort and independence (such as the family home and car).

Our efforts to understand disability in late life should begin with an appreciation of the individual person—and specifically, how the later stages of life are more than just a period of loss. Instead, they are a highly significant part of the life course that gives meaning to the previous stages of life.

The forty-one essays in Phillip Berman's *Courage to Grow Old* poignantly explore this idea, allowing the reader to see how people address multiple layers of loss throughout old age. Berman notes in his introduction:

> Unless we are very lucky, aging inevitably entails increasing physical disabilities, whether it's the slow shift, as Henry Heimlich puts it, from a "cane, to a walker, then to a wheelchair," or the more rapid decline of an individual suffering from Alzheimer's. But whether we age slowly or rapidly, none of us can escape decline. . . . What we can control is the way we choose to deal with our infirmities, and this is where courage—and a healthy dose of humor—works wonders.[6]

The essays in Berman's volume are a window into the world of old age as a time of greater proximity to, and awareness of, death. Yet this concern with death does not diminish the other dominant aspect of the aging experience in late life—that is, the desire to continue, to propel forward, to banish fear, and to embrace what is left of life. Along with adopting a more spiritual orientation, many older people find strength in practicing gratitude. This is especially true for those with disability. In this framework, appreciation and contentment are not merely well-worn sentiments, but can actually become buffers that moderate the effects of loss and disability. During this period of late life, people's subjective understanding of their own health—and their attitude in the face of health challenges—is a predictor of future well-being. A positive attitude and continuous social engagement improve the quality of an older person's remaining life.[7] Disabled persons of all ages can benefit from appreciating how those who are aging with disabilities have adapted over time to changes in their life circumstances.

Gerontology and the New Aging

Readers of the series in which this book is included are well aware of the trends and trajectories in the rich field of disability studies. Works by Ronald J. Berger, Rosalyn Benjamin Darling, Dana Lee Baker,[8] and others in the series—along with output from other publishers and periodicals—highlight the dynamism of disability studies. Yet few books or articles have sought to connect disability and aging—perhaps because of the different languages and cultures that define the respective disciplines. We do not see our project as attempting to reconcile the two different approaches, as much as to begin a dialogue between them.

Most work in disability studies emphasizes the positive aspects of life lived in the context of disability. Gerontology, in contrast, has focused on the negative aspects of disability in the context of an idealized course of healthy aging. Indeed, disability is often treated as undermining a newer vision of old age as a time of productivity, happiness, and rejuvenation. Gerontology as an interdisciplinary field has been built on discrediting an older view of aging as a period of decline, illness, and isolation. On college campuses, young people are drawn to study this new aging. They are intrigued by, and wish to learn more about, the final stages of life. A generation in search of meaning, millennials want to understand how time impacts us all—so that they can plan how to live meaningful lives.[9]

This positive redefinition of old age has many implications, the first of which is that people need not fear growing old. By celebrating old age, we may even discover an answer to the question posed by Robert N. Butler in his Pulitzer Prize–winning *Why Survive?*[10] However, this reinvigorated version of old age has located the aging experience away from disability. The term *disability* has negative connotations in the aging literature and is used to describe an undesirable condition that, at best, should be limited in scope and compressed in time. In this revised formula for a well-centered old age, disability is simply a burden. There is little emphasis on how to live well—and seek support—as a disabled older person.

Survey data may help explain the dearth of professional interest in the topic: they show that older individuals are reluctant to view themselves as having disabilities. The labels *disability* and *disabled* threaten their core identity as empowered and autonomous individuals. Many older people simply eschew *disability* as a label, category, or specific consciousness. And because they do not self-identify as disabled, older persons with disabilities are not disposed to advocate for themselves. Thus, they make limited claims for specialized programs.[11]

The divergence between disability studies and gerontology goes beyond how to characterize disability. Disability advocates and scholars have been most interested in the subject of rights—specifically, how to breach the barriers to social, political, and economic inclusion. The issues of health and sickness are not considered central to the disability experience.[12]

For gerontologists, however, disability does tend to be associated with disease—and thus poses a threat to health, which is considered an aging person's greatest asset. For this reason, gerontology scholarship has focused on the loss of health in old age. Writing from an epidemiological perspective, Christina Victor notes that "the importance of health is a key feature of many studies of the experience of age and ageing, and health is seen as central to the experience of and maintenance of quality of life in old age."[13]

Disability thus poses a challenge to the field of gerontology as people live longer and therefore may spend a greater part of their elder years managing disability.[14] Few older persons have any prior experience living with a disability—and with its emphasis on health, the field has provided little in the way of guidance about how the disabled elderly can lead a rewarding life. In his preface to *The Cambridge Handbook of Age and Ageing,* British gerontologist Malcolm Johnson acknowledges this trend: "From its inception the core area of gerontology has been health," with the leading concern of the past thirty years being "apocalyptic demography." What this focus has obscured, Johnson reports, are studies "on the social features of life in the Third and Fourth stages" that "explore the positive potentialities of being an older person." Even when such studies appear, he argues, they "are overwhelmed by the sheer weight of inquiries about illnesses—physical and psychological— and the interventions that might ameliorate their consequences."[15]

The origins of aging research as a social science may help explain the way gerontology engages—or does not engage—disability. The field began largely as a multidisciplinary project in the years after World War II, with an aim to approach aging as a topic worthy of scientific investigation and a cultural phenomenon appropriate for social and philosophical theorizing.[16] Its main growth came after 1960, and by 1976 it had matured to the point at which the first of many *Handbooks of Aging* were published to showcase the new discipline's accomplishments. Given gerontology's early focus on the social aspects of aging and how they influenced the aging process, the issue of disability might have been expected to attract the attention of scholars. However, this has not been the case.

In the first edition of the *Handbook of Aging and the Social Sciences* (1976), the sociological domains of structure (e.g., population, stratification) and systems (e.g., family, work) received careful attention, as did modes of social intervention (e.g., politics, research).[17] Yet from the first edition through the eighth edition in 2015,[18] the subject of disability has been studied only as a minor note—and chiefly as it relates to the loss of health and rarely from the standpoint of the personal experience of those living with disabilities or caring for persons who have disabilities.[19]

To understand this orientation within the field, it is useful to explore the paradoxical issue of ageism. On the one hand, the term *ageism* suggests grounds upon which to seek common cause with the disability rights movement in fighting discrimination and securing a protected minority status for the aged. On the other hand, ageism has spurred a movement to reject old age as a time of limits imposed by either society or physiology. One might say that ageism has led to a curious antiaging stance on the part of the aged and those who study them.

The Problem of Ageism

To appreciate the development of the field of gerontology and the relatively low priority of disability as one of its concerns, it helps to consider the field's intense concern with ageism. "Beginning in the late 1960s," writes Thomas

Cole, "America witnessed a formidable effort to eliminate negative stereo-types of and prejudice toward older people."[20] But unlike disability advocates who embraced the lived experience of disability, these advocates for the aged took their project to be debunking myths about old age. In the process of doing so, however, they created new myths centered on an antiaging ideal.

This project of reassessing the meaning of old age was built on an older research foundation that saw limits in studying aging as a function of age alone. Since the 1940s, some gerontologists had been arguing that age itself was a poor indicator or predictor of behavior and that older people adjusted to late life and its challenges in many different ways.[21] Increasingly, the key question in gerontology turned on the issue of personal adjustment in old age—with the individual's ability to adapt to his or her environment seen as the centerpiece of the aging experience.[22] The field recognized from an early date that society structures the life prospects for the elderly—and that it was the responsibility of these older persons to optimize their responses to these conditions and social limitations.[23]

Gerontologists did not view the problems of aging in terms of "changes in physical and mental capacities but in changes in social opportunity."[24] Thus, understanding the shrinking of social opportunities—what would later be called "ageism"—became central targets for the field of gerontol-ogy in its early days. But unlike the disability rights movement, the aging community did not make gaining rights its chief priority. Rather, it focused on finding ways for individuals to adapt to and integrate with their environ-ment—a largely personal act of evolution and coping.

One form of adaptation that goes beyond the individual is gerontol-ogy's effort to reframe the aging experience so that age itself is less rele-vant as a category of analysis. This movement to minimize the relevance of age was a response to an earlier period's definition of old age as a key marker for disengagement from economic and social activities. From the 1930s through the 1960s, age itself had assumed a high degree of impor-tance. The bookended policies of Social Security (1935) and Medicare (1965) provided older persons with a guaranteed income and access to medical care on the basis of age alone. Retirement also emerged as a new period in the life cycle, when workers were required to leave work and seek fulfillment in other (often less fulfilling, leisure-based) activities.

But almost as soon as age cemented its relevance in policy and social consciousness, a reaction against age as a category of analysis found a ready audience amid the cultural changes of the late 1960s and 1970s. The genera-tional tide of the baby boomers, with their attendant challenge to authority structures and normative behavior, began a shift in outlook toward an old age that was diverse and youthful—a view that may be seen in retrospect as sanc-tioning the social current of the times. In 1976, prominent University of Chicago gerontologist Bernice Neugarten and Norwegian sociologist Gunhild

O. Hagestad surmised that we "seem to be moving in the direction of what might be called an age irrelevant society; and it can be argued that age, like race or sex, is diminishing in importance as a regulator of behavior."[25]

At around the same time, Butler also was questioning the utility of thinking about aging according to chronological age. In *Why Survive?* he argued that "the idea of chronological aging (measuring one's age by the number of years one has lived) is a kind of myth." Butler, of course, was not denying that age has physiological consequences, but he contended that the differences in how old people aged were more significant than their actual ages. "Physiological indicators show a greater range from the mean in old age than in any other age group. . . . Older people actually become more diverse rather than more similar in advancing years."[26]

Butler addresses this issue in a section of his book called "Myths and Stereotypes About the Old" in which he enumerates a series of negative but unfounded societal attitudes toward the elderly—attitudes that promote ageist conclusions. These myths and stereotypes include "unproductivity," "disengagement," inflexibility," "senility," and "serenity." After considering each, Butler notes that "insufficient contact" with older persons was one cause of these myths, but he maintains that "there is another powerful factor operating—a deep and profound prejudice against the elderly which is found to some degree in all of us." Butler explains that he "coined the word 'ageism'" to describe this prejudice, defining the term to mean "a process of systematic stereotyping of and discrimination against people because they are old, just as racism and sexism accomplish this with skin color and gender."[27]

Rejecting the social meaning of chronological age had a lasting impact on gerontology. If being old means many different things, then what does it mean to engage in a study of older persons? The diversity of the aged as a group has led Richard A. Settersten, a specialist in life course studies, to worry that although "gerontologists now assume that there is [great] variability among old people, . . . only rarely do we consider the things that old people may have in common."[28]

This attitude is in contrast to the approach of disability studies, which unites many impairments and social environments under the broad umbrella of disability. Aging has presented less of a common experience. As we show in this book, disability in old age is marked by variability and disparities rather than by a common consciousness or unifying policy agenda. The many typologies of disability are thus grafted onto the multiple scaffolding of the aging experience.

The work of social historian and gerontologist Tamara Hareven points to the need to integrate life course research with an understanding of the family and its relationships over time. In the social contexts of aging and disability, the role of the family is central—specifically, whether the family is available to support an elder or child with a disability. Few families are untouched by either aging or disability—and our own lived experiences show the connections across three generations in this regard. It is often a person's social networks, within and beyond the family, that define what it means to be "disabled," as much as any impairment or public policy.[29]

If old age is to become a more meaningful signifier of a period of change in the life course, the impact of disability must figure prominently in our analysis of the aging process. Understanding how age intersects with disability on the individual level will also help us see how disability impacts the cross-generational role of the entire family in late life. Today, an entire generation of middle-aged and young-old persons (mostly women) are providing unreimbursed care for parents, grandparents, and even siblings whose lives are affected by disability.[30]

Disability in old age not only matters at the individual and family levels, but it may also lead to a shift in the way that gerontologists think about aging. Many leaders in the aging field, including Powell Lawton and Malcolm Johnson, have observed that the field is rich in empirical knowledge but limited in theoretical perspectives. There are, to be sure, varied theories that have dominated the field (e.g., successful aging, stress and coping, continuity, activity, and quality of life). Yet according to Elias Cohen, an elder statesman in the field, we are "in need of some kind of theory about aging, at least some kind of social theory."[31] To generate such a theory will require substantive dialogue among academics across the disciplinary lines of aging and disability. It will also require input from those whose lives are affected by both aging and disability as well as from those who are engaged in what Cohen describes as the "public administration of services designed to mitigate the insults of old age."[32]

Such a new theory of aging and disability may, in part, find support in an older framework called "disengagement theory," which posits a view of old age as a time of slowing down and withdrawing—disengaging—from previous social interactions.[33] Few gerontologists have been willing to embrace this theory since its introduction in 1961—and one can see how it runs counter to the ideal of an active and sustained lifestyle for those who are aging. But disengagement need not be considered in only this narrow way. There may be, as Cohen suggests in his forthcoming monograph, a process of "successful disengagement," especially in very old age.[34]

A theory of aging and disability would examine how individuals can continue to live long and meaningful lives—especially as the long-term processes of disability in late life take effect—even if these lives are different from what they were in middle life and young old age. This new theory would address the reality that, in old age, the previous organizing framework of life recedes as people exit the workforce, lose their spouses, have fewer ties that bind them to place, and experience more difficulty getting out and making new ties. Such a theory would not need to reject activity—and could even be pro-activity. It would, however, need to offer a vision of activity on a smaller scale, addressing the challenges of maintaining life and managing the tasks of day-to-day living that can be daunting to elders, especially when they are living with disability.

How Age Matters

Ironically, the acceptance of disability as part of the aging process may serve to bolster the significance of age as a scholarly construct within the discipline of gerontology. Few people would discount the importance of old age as a time with its own special meaning. In the past half-century, however, this traditional meaning has increasingly been called into question—and as we have seen, the field of gerontology has challenged the very idea that old age qua old age matters.[35]

Attention to disability offers gerontology a way of looking at old age as both a diverse and a discrete period in life. Acknowledging the role of disability in old age reveals the ways in which disability restructures how people see themselves and are viewed by others throughout the aging process. Recognizing old age as a key life period reveals the dynamic ways in which disability is accepted (or rejected), internalized (or externalized), and managed (or not managed). For many disabled younger people, disability has always been part of their lives or has been from an early age. For older people, however, the transition from a state of not being disabled to one of being disabled is a process that provides a valuable window into a lesser-understood aspect of the human life course experience.

In addition, disability may unlock the mystery of why and how age matters. The fear of losing health and experiencing disability is a dominant concern for older persons, even outpacing their fear of death. This mindset—the fear of loss—is central to the consciousness of being old and distinguishes this period of life from earlier ones. This consciousness delineates a time frame when individuals find themselves changing gears and refocusing their attention on how to survive in late life. Yet this period also presents unique opportunities to develop the self by attaining a level of wisdom and peace that may allow for the journey forward—and permit many years of continued growth, though not necessarily by any conventional standard of success or productivity.

This point of view recognizes that we cannot defy age indefinitely; we will all grow old. The question is how we can retain our sense of self—who we are—while accepting changes in health and the inevitable disabilities and barriers that come with advanced age. This recognition and acceptance of aging broadens gerontology's well-known focus on healthy lifestyles to include support for all older persons and those who care for them. As Malcolm Johnson urges, such support should be in the form of a public-private partnership that values individual autonomy—the opportunity to exercise control over one's own life.[36]

But even with government and private entities working together to provide this support, older people need something more: they need to find a community. The role of community—as both a place and a group of people who care for one another—can play a key role in minimizing disability. Elders who participate in community programs (e.g., senior centers), who volunteer to help others, and who retain a group of friends are more likely to continue to manage independently as they age and encounter disability. In contrast, older people who are not integrated into a community, who have not cultivated a practice of helping others, and who have few friends are more likely to find themselves isolated and without support in late life. Even if these individuals do not have many or significant physical impairments, they are at great risk for losing their independence.

Bodies and Minds in Time and Place

Old age and disability exist in a relational framework. Both the young and the old may experience disability—it cannot be defined by age alone. In this sense disability is analogous to space, its contours constantly shifting and uncertain. Similarly, we are all suspended between states of living and dying in a broad continuum of life. The idea that disability is not a state that is distinct from normal life was a prime claim for sociologist Irving Zola. He believed that disability is not an external and unnatural state, but one that at some point in time affects all people, though in degrees that can be as varied as the population itself.[37]

The present reality is that disability is more often framed as a particular situation whose relevance is given meaning in relationship to others. This is why historians—who are the scholars most focused on time and context—have in recent years championed disability as an example of the "other" and what it means to speak of historical "otherness."[38]

This notion of the relational other has resonance for gerontologists' views of aging and disability. What we mean by "health" and "wellness" in old age is often constructed in relation to those who are ill; how we construe "old" is often in relation to those who are young or young-old; and seniors we view as "disabled" are considered so in relation to seniors we perceive as able and capable. In each case, the strength of the positive modifier—the healthy old, the young-old, and the able old—is given meaning by an often unmentioned other, and this is the negative modifier: the sick old, the old-old, and the disabled old.

The concepts of aging and disability are not only relational, but also quite inclusive. Both are social categories with core and noncore members. In the first category, that core group consists of people over age eighty-five, who are considered by gerontologists to make up the old-old. In the second category, that core group consists of people whose disabilities have long been recognized by society as markedly distinguishing (as real or core disabilities): those who are totally blind, those who experience fundamental mobility impairments, and those who are deemed mentally impaired. In both the aging and disabled categories, the noncore groups are more varied in functional abilities as well as self-perceptions.[39]

Navigating the borders of what we mean when we speak of someone as "aged" or "disabled" is not merely about semantic constructions. These are also categories that enlist claims on the public, its resources, and the social expectations of those currently neither aged nor disabled. The very old and those persons with core disabilities share certain common themes in public policy, including society's paternalistic attitude toward them. These groups are viewed with sympathy and pity—such that they are deemed worthy of support and assistance. For much of our history, the old-old and the core disabled were indeed set apart. The very old and the very disabled often found themselves in special institutions, where their days were subjected to disciplined regimes designed to promote order and stability. Neither group had much prospect for inclusion in society writ large. Their world was—and, in the case of many, still is—an other world.

The story of modern disability policy has been the breakdown of the separate silos that had previously marked each of these groups as distinct. The impulse toward democratization at the turn of the twentieth century, during the Progressive Era, led to a typology approach to disability. New policies in special education and rehabilitation, along with alternating fears and hopes for those deemed disabled, started a course of state interest in addressing differences based on dependency and ability. Although the resulting policies were often confused and oppositional, they focused on addressing an ever wider range of issues—educational, work related, medical, and financial—that surfaced in a new society, economy, and polity. The typology approach to disability—with its distinct groups of the blind, the deaf, the crippled, and the mentally impaired—increasingly gave way to viewing disability as a larger social and economic issue. A broader spectrum of disability emerged that occupied policymaking at the state and, beginning with the New Deal, federal level. This elastic notion of disability as a broad catchall would find its most complete statement in the 1990 Americans with Disabilities Act (ADA).

The understanding that aging posed a similar set of issues that mattered to the public also has its roots in the Progressive years—albeit during the seemingly immoderate Roaring Twenties. Many states organized commissions to consider the "problem of aging" as the percentage of older people grew in relative and absolute terms.[40] The modernizing economy—and the transformation that new technologies and efficiency systems promised to bring about—won the approbation of many who praised the "divinity of machinery."[41] This was a decade when "labor-saving methods" were imposed through "what Thomas P. Hughes has called 'Networks of Power'"[42] and older workers had a harder time keeping up. In this environment, policymakers increasingly focused on the issues posed by superannuated workers as well as older people who had worked throughout their lives and in old age found themselves without work, resources, or family. The fear was that, without the help of the state, these individuals could not survive.

The concepts of disability and old age retain core elements that are based on this similar history of dependency and need (framed within a compass of public virtue) that distinguishes the plight of each group's members and makes them attractive recipients of assistance.[43] But this support diminishes when the rights and privileges that are granted to a blind person or a person who requires a wheelchair or an individual with profound mental challenges are extended to the malleable lists of disabling conditions that are recognized under law. In such instances, it seems that the very meaning of *real* disability is diluted in a sea of special interests.[44] A similar diminution in attitude toward programs for the aged has been ongoing since the late 1970s and early 1980s. As the size of the federal budget devoted to aging—through Social Security and Medicare—continues to increase and as many beneficiaries of these programs receive far more than they have contributed, those older persons who are not truly needy are increasingly eroding society's sympathy for the senior cause.[45]

The futures of disability policy and aging policy are thus caught in a paradox. As these policies have become more generalized and greater numbers of individuals are included in benefit programs, the specialness of the disabled and the aged—as dependents who are deserving of support based on their unique conditions—has diminished. There is much talk of benefit seekers who abuse the classification of disability and of greedy geezers who receive disproportionate benefits. How can public policies for these groups evolve in response to a twenty-first-century society that will both be older and experience higher rates of disability for all age groups? How can these policies best serve an inclusionary model that fosters dignity, promotes care, and avoids the excessive benefit seeking that imperils public support? As we contemplate the growing number of seniors who will age with disabilities in the coming decades, these questions demand our attention. We can begin to answer them by understanding the interconnections between the concepts of aging and disability.

Notes

1. Erving Goffman, *Stigma: Notes on the Management of Spoiled Identity* (Simon and Schuster, 2009); Irving Kenneth Zola, *Missing Pieces: A Chronicle of Living with a Disability* (Temple University Press, 1982).
2. Joseph P. Shapiro, *No Pity: People with Disabilities Forging a New Civil Rights Movement* (Three Rivers Press, 1994).
3. Gerontologists have studied this process of age-associated disease within the framework of the "cascade of disability." See Lois M. Verbrugge and Alan M. Jette, "The Disablement Process," *Social Science and Medicine* 38, no. 1 (1994): 1–14.
4. These words resonate with most people, yet most of us do not realize that *old age* and *disability* relate not just to others, but also to ourselves—if not now, then at some point in our lives. We are all aging, and we all fear the loss of ability—although we do not always feel these fears at a conscious level.
5. Robert N. Butler, *The Longevity Revolution: The Benefits and Challenges of Living a Long Life* (PublicAffairs, 2010).
6. Phillip L. Berman, *The Courage to Grow Old* (Ballantine Books, 1989), xii.
7. Eva Kahana, Tirth Bhatta, Loren D. Lovegreen, and Boaz Kahana, "Altruism, Helping, and Volunteering: Pathways to Well-Being in Late Life," *Journal of Aging and Health* 25, no. 1 (2013): 159–187.
8. Ronald J. Berger, *Introducing Disability Studies* (Lynne Rienner, 2013); Rosalyn Benjamin Darling, *Disability and Identity: Negotiating Self in a Changing Society* (Lynne Rienner, 2013); Dana Lee Baker, *The Politics of Neurodiversity: Why Public Policy Matters* (Lynne Rienner, 2011).
9. Not too long ago, few undergraduates showed any interest in older persons. Today, classes in aging-related subjects—even courses on death and dying—are quite popular, and the Gerontological Society of America (GSA) has a burgeoning student membership. The *millennial generation* is defined broadly as those born after 1980. See William Strauss and Neil Howe, *Generations: The History of America's Future, 1584 to 2069* (William Morrow, 1991); Neil Howe and William Strauss, *Millennials Rising: The Next Great Generation* (Vintage Books, 2009).
10. Robert Butler, *Why Survive? Growing Old in America* (Harper and Row, 1975).
11. An adverse view of disability is not without foundation in experience. A leading historian argues that in Western cultures, social "hierarchy depends on the threat of disability always lurking as the ultimate living catastrophe." See Catherine J. Kudlick, "Disability History: Why We Need Another 'Other,'" *American Historical Review* 108, no. 3 (2003): 765. It should be noted that disability scholars view the concept of disability as "a key defining social category on a par with race, class, and gender" rather than as "an individual characteristic." Ibid., 764–765. Disability also serves an emancipatory function as "an effective weapon in contests over power and ideology." See Kim E. Nielsen, *A Disability History of the United States* (Beacon Press, 2012), xiii.
12. It should be noted, however, that internal stigmas have existed toward people whose disability includes a degenerative component, as opposed to those whose disability is in conjunction with stable health. Sociologist Irving Zola explores this notion in his account of Het Dorp, a residential community for adults with severe physical disabilities in the Netherlands. Zola observed the distinctions that community members drew between the "diseased" and the "handicapped." As one longtime resident told him: "To be handicapped is to be stabilized, to be diseased is *not*"

[emphasis in original]. Irving Kenneth Zola, *Missing Pieces: A Chronicle of Living with a Disability* (Temple University Press, 1982), 53.

13. Christina Victor, "The Epidemiology of Ageing," in *The Cambridge Handbook of Age and Ageing,* ed. Malcolm L. Johnson, with Vern L. Bengtson, Peter G. Coleman, and Thomas B. L. Kirkwood (Cambridge University Press, 2005), 95. A natural corollary to this focus on health is the imperative to avoid disability in old age. John W. Rowe and Robert L. Kahn, "Successful Aging," *The Gerontologist* 37, no. 4 (1997): 433–440.

14. The view that longer life entails a greater period of more severe disability is suggested by Michael Marmot, *Status Syndrome: How Your Social Standing Directly Affects Your Health and Life Expectancy* (Bloomsbury, 2004). The exact relationship between extended life and disability is not clear—specifically, whether disability will constrict or expand as people live longer. For a review of the literature on population trends and late-life disability, see Vicki A. Freedman, "Disability, Functioning, and Aging," in *Handbook of Aging and the Social Sciences,* 7th ed., ed. Robert H. Binstock and Linda K. George, with Stephen J. Cutler, Jon Hendricks, and James H. Shulz (Elsevier/Academic Press, 2011), 66–68.

15. Malcolm Johnson notes that research on health and illness in old age "is more methodologically and technically proficient" than it was in the past but "there is no parallel development in our conceptualising. Theoretical work remains a remarkably neglected area of gerontological work." See Malcolm L. Johnson, "Preface," in *The Cambridge Handbook of Age and Ageing,* ed. Malcolm L. Johnson, with Vern L. Bengtson, Peter G. Coleman, and Thomas B. L. Kirkwood (Cambridge University Press, 2005), xxi–xxiii. W. Andrew Achenbaum, the respected historian of old age and gerontology, has likewise shown how physical decline and its connection to old age are the preeminent concerns of the field. See W. Andrew Achenbaum, *Crossing Frontiers: Gerontology Emerges as a Science* (Cambridge University Press, 1995).

16. Achenbaum, *Crossing Frontiers;* see also W. Andrew Achenbaum, *Old Age in a New Land: The American Experience Since 1790* (Johns Hopkins University Press, 1978).

17. Robert H. Binstock and Ethel Shanas, with Vern L. Bengtson, George L. Maddox, and Dorothy Wedderburn, *Handbook of Aging and the Social Sciences* (Van Nostrand Reinhold, 1976).

18. Linda George and Kenneth Ferraro, *Handbook of Aging and the Social Sciences,* 8th ed. (Academic Press, 2015).

19. Another factor that has anchored aging research in health has been the funding mechanisms established by the National Institute on Aging (NIA), which is part of the larger National Institutes of Health (NIH). Funding in the basic sciences of aging has been health oriented—how to promote a biology of wellness in old age, largely through clinical trial research designs—and projects that are more socially based generally must show a connection with the goals of health promotion and disease prevention. There is limited funding to explore how life with disability in old age can be made more meaningful or satisfactory to those living with disability. See Timothy J. O'Leary, Jean R. Slutsky, and Marie A. Bernard, "Comparative Effectiveness Research Priorities at Federal Agencies: The View from the Department of Veterans Affairs, National Institute on Aging, and Agency for Healthcare Research and Quality," *Journal of the American Geriatrics Society* 58, no. 6 (2010): 1187–1192.

20. Thomas R. Cole, *The Journey of Life: A Cultural History of Aging in America* (Cambridge University Press, 1992), 227.

21. Ralph Linton, "Age and Sex Categories," *American Sociological Review* 7 (1942): 589–603; L. S. Cottrell Jr., "Adjustment of the Individual to Age/Sex Roles," *American Sociological Review* 7 (1942): 617–620.

22. See Otto Pollack and Glen Heathers, "Social Adjustment in Old Age: A Research Planning Report," *Sociological Practice* 11, no. 1 (1993): 33–39. See also George Lawton, *New Goals for Old Age* (Columbia University Press, 1945); Nathan Wetherill Shock, *Trends in Gerontology* (Stanford University Press, 1951).

23. Often trained in social work, a cadre of gerontology researchers and professionals soon emerged who would serve as guides to the elderly in how to manage their lives effectively in the later years. See Carroll L. Estes, *The Aging Enterprise* (Jossey-Bass, 1979).

24. Irving Rosow, *Socialization to Old Age* (University of California Press, 1974), 12.

25. Bernice L. Neugarten and Gunhild O. Hagestad, "Age and the Life Course," in *Handbook of Aging and the Social Sciences,* ed. Robert H. Binstock and Ethel Shanas, with Vern L. Bengtson, George L. Maddox, and Dorothy Wedderburn (Van Nostrand Reinhold, 1976), 52.

26. Butler, *Why Survive?* 7.

27. Ibid., 11–12.

28. Richard A. Settersten Jr., "Aging and the Life Course," in *Handbook of Aging and the Social Sciences,* 6th ed., ed. Robert H. Binstock and Linda K. George (Academic Press, 2006), 8. Settersten offered his colleagues a corrective to gerontology's emphasis on variability among the aging by asking them to "be as open to things that are shared by old people, experiences that may persist across time and context, as we are to the things that make old people different and may vary across time and context." Ibid.

29. "Collective family requirements and strategies" are central to the study of the life course and have functioned in many capacities throughout history. See Tamara K. Hareven, "The History of the Family and the Complexity of Social Change," *American Historical Review* 96, no. 1 (1991): 106. For example, families have helped secure work and fostered adaptation to the workplace; see Tamara K. Hareven, *Family Time and Industrial Time: The Relationship Between the Family and Work in a New England Industrial Community* (Cambridge University Press, 1982). In rural societies, families have provided for family members in old age as part of an inheritance contract "in which sons agreed to support aging parents in exchange for inheriting property"; see Hareven, "The History of the Family and the Complexity of Social Change," 116. More recently and closer to home, families have helped secure appropriate education for disabled children. What makes the family's place special and deserving of attention is "its bond of 'love' and 'altruism' not generally thought to be found in other groups in our society"; see Hareven, "The History of the Family and the Complexity of Social Change," 117.

30. Robyn Stone, Gail Lee Cafferata, and Judith Sangl, "Caregivers of the Frail Elderly: A National Profile," *The Gerontologist* 27, no. 5 (1987): 616–626.

31. Elias S. Cohen, personal communication with the authors, 2015.

32. Elias S. Cohen, forthcoming work, in possession of the author.

33. See Elaine Cumming and William Earl Henry, *Growing Old: The Process of Disengagement* (Basic Books, 1961).

34. Elias S. Cohen, manuscript in possession of the authors. See also Elias S. Cohen, "The Last 2000 Days," *The Gerontologist* 57, no. 1 (2017): 116–120.

35. Indeed, the newest movement in the field sees the earlier life course as integrated into old age, so that aging is considered more of a lifelong process than a dis-

crete period. According to such a measure, it is the earlier period of the life course that informs much of our understanding of what comes later.

36. Malcolm Johnson, "Dependency and Interdependency," in *Ageing in Society,* ed. John Bond and Peter G. Coleman (Sage, 1993).

37. Zola, *Missing Pieces.*

38. Catherine L. Kudlick argues that the discovery of disability by scholars in the fields of anthropology, sociology, and literature has allowed historians of disability "to rethink what we do." Kudlick, "Disability History," 763–764.

39. The case of the deaf is more complex. See Douglas C. Baynton, *Forbidden Signs: American Culture and the Campaign Against Sign Language* (University of Chicago Press, 1996).

40. Achenbaum, *Old Age in a New Land,* 115–116.

41. Carroll Pursell, *The Machine in America: A Social History of Technology* (Johns Hopkins Press, 2007), 230.

42. Ibid. Pursell is referring to Thomas Parke Hughes's *Networks of Power: Electrification in Western Society, 1880–1930* (Johns Hopkins University Press, 1983).

43. See Harlan L. Lane, *When the Mind Hears: A History of the Deaf* (Random House, 1984).

44. On disability as a special category, see Richard K. Scotch, "Disability Policy: An Eclectic Overview," *Journal of Disability Policy Studies* 11, no. 1 (2000): 6–11.

45. Robert H. Binstock, "The Emergence of the Oldest Old: Challenges for Public Policy," in *The Future of Age-Based Public Policy*, ed. Robert B. Hudson (Johns Hopkins University Press, 1997), 56–73.

2

Contextualizing
Aging and Disability

In this chapter, we highlight orientations of gerontological research and theory to understanding disability in later life. Pointing to the different realities and options of older adults who acquire disability in late life, we consider the alternative meanings of disability at different stages in the life course.[1] Specifically, we call attention to older adults' desire and right to opt out of a disability identity, even in the face of significant physical impairments. Older adults may benefit from *disability cognizance,* or a conscious awareness of their disabilities, even without embracing a disability identity. The wisdom of the elderly is important to recognize, as elders contextualize their disabilities, informed by a long journey through the life course. Longitudinal studies that were framed outside the ideological and activist traditions of the disability rights movement should also be considered in discussing the context of aging and disability.

Over half of individuals (63 percent) who are classified as having at least one functional limitation are adults over the age of sixty-five.[2] Older adults with disabilities include those who developed disabilities late in life as well as increasing numbers of persons who are aging with long-term disabilities and are now surviving to reach old age.[3] Given the high rates of disablement among older adults, gerontology and disability studies can undoubtedly complement one another. Gerontologists have primarily focused on individuals whose disabilities emerged in late life. In contrast, disability studies scholars have greater experience and expertise in understanding the unique needs of those who are aging with long-term disabilities.[4] Gerontologists' expertise in disability in later life can serve to extend contributions that scholars of disability studies have made in looking at physical and intellectual limitations during early life.[5]

Before delving more deeply into understanding late-life disability, we take a step back to consider how onset of disability at different points during the life course can influence research approaches and salient features of the disability experience. We do so by offering a schematic presentation of a matrix of disability in a life course context. Following the presentation of this matrix, we discuss patterns of late-life disability. We then shift our focus toward a discussion of how gerontology can contribute to issues addressed by disability studies.

A Life Course Matrix of Disability

The matrix presented in Table 2.1 offers examples of normative characteristics of disabilities experienced at different stages of the life course. The matrix can provide a useful guide for our subsequent discussions of disability in adulthood versus late life. However, we note that each example masks important variability and offers only a glimpse into the complex characteristics of disability at each life stage. To keep the matrix parsimonious and easy to follow, we only include brief references to literature that corresponds to each life stage. Research evidence is discussed in detail as we refer to the characteristics designated in our matrix throughout the book.

The matrix distinguishes three life stages that are relevant to understanding distinctions based on the time of onset of the disability. These are: (1) childhood onset; (2) young to middle adult onset; and (3) late-life onset. Of course, the focus throughout this book is on disability in late life—specifically, the onset of disability during this stage in the life course. Gerontologists largely focus on disabilities that arise in old age and these are often limited to the final stage of life. Disability scholars, on the other hand, generally focus on disabilities acquired in early to mid-adulthood and

Table 2.1 Matrix of Disability in a Life Course Context

Disability	Childhood Onset	Young to Middle Adult Onset	Late-Life Onset
A. Type	Intellectual/severe sensory	Mobility	Functional limitations, memory and mild sensory
B. Trajectory	Stable	Stable	Progressive
C. Identity	Acceptance	Pride	Rejection
D. Model	Medical/social	Social	Medical
E. Institutional Context	Schools	Work	Retirement
F. Intervention	Educational	Rehabilitation	Medical/prosthetic
G. Formal Support	Teachers	Attendants	Service staff
H. Informal Support	Family members (parents, siblings, grandparents)	Self, friends, family members	Caregiver (spouse, adult child)
I. Type and Source of Research Data	Educational testing, parents, teachers, advocates, and children	Auto-ethnography, person with disability, advocates	Survey, quantitative, self or proxy reports, ethnography, qualitative observers

place limited emphasis on the life experiences of those living with disabilities after they reach old age.[6]

Many of the comparisons throughout this book relate to the second and third columns in our matrix (Table 2.1). Our book does not address the life course journey of individuals with congenital or childhood onset disabilities and their experiences of aging with a disability.[7] Nevertheless, it is important to recognize that these individuals may face different types of experiences, challenges, and socialization or identity processes.[8]

Our matrix depicts several key aspects of the disability experience and corresponding models in the study of disability that may be linked to the timing of disability onset in rows A through I of Table 2.1.

Row A: Disability Type

This row highlights the types of disabilities focused on in the literature for each life stage. It is important to recognize that our matrix depicts ideal types and there can be significant overlap in types of disability acquired at different points during the life course. Research and literature on childhood onset disabilities often involve intellectual or severe sensory impairments such as blindness or deafness.[9] Disabilities in young adulthood often relate to sudden accidents posing challenges of mobility limitations. These mobility limitations are a focus of the disability studies movement and are depicted in the universal sign of a wheelchair for denoting disability.[10] Late-life onset disability is typically characterized by functional limitations, memory impairments, and mild sensory impairments.[11]

Row B: Disability Trajectory

Regarding the trajectory of disability at each life stage, we note that the trajectory of both childhood onset and young to middle adult onset of disability tends to be stable. For instance, blind and deaf children exhibit what has been termed "core disabilities" and often retain their disability throughout their life course.[12] Similarly, victims of accidents in young adulthood tend to retain their disabilities. In contrast, the trajectory of late-life onset disabilities is often progressive resulting in frailty and dependency and is often accompanied by cognitive impairments that ultimately signal the nearing of the end of life.[13]

Row C: Disability Identity

Disability identity is a key feature in the experience of disability.[14] The life stage of when an individual becomes disabled can greatly shape their identity. In terms of the literature, childhood onset disabilities are generally characterized by acceptance and at times by limited awareness of a disability identity. Young to middle adult onset disabilities have served as an impetus for redefining disability as a social movement that is characterized by pride and full identification with disability.[15] In striking contrast, late-life disability is often actively rejected by many older adults who want to maintain their lifelong nondisabled identity.[16]

Row D: Disability Model

Consideration of models of disability is linked with the understanding of the lens through which the disability is studied. While earlier studies of childhood disability espoused elements of a medical model, more recently there has been a shift toward bringing children with disabilities more into center stage and closer to the social model.[17] The disability studies movement is typically focused on the young or middle adult onset disabilities and exemplars of disabilities acquired in adulthood. Disability studies that espouse a social model of disability and consider the disabled as a minority group are generally focused on the young to midlife onset disabilities.[18] In contrast, late-life onset disabilities are often studied in the context of a medical model.[19]

Row E: Institutional Context

Salient institutional contexts refer to the environments where individuals spend most of their time and may have to lobby for accommodations for their needs. For childhood onset disability, the key institutional context is a school setting.[20] For young to middle adult onset disabilities, the institutional context is typically a work-related setting.[21] Late-life onset disability generally occurs after individuals are retired and no longer a part of the workforce.[22]

While we link disability at different points in the life course to specific institutional contexts, it is important to note that the broader environment impacts persons with disabilities across the life course.[23] Accordingly, the Americans with Disabilities Act involves legislation that benefits all persons with disabilities.

Row F: Intervention

Consideration of interventions relate to the disability model being followed and the life course stage when disability occurs. Within the medical model, the goal of interventions are usually to improve or maintain functioning and social competence that allow for successful participation in society.[24] Within the social model of disability, interventions are focused on offering accommodations with the goal of achieving social inclusion. Such accommodations have been viewed as preferable to traditional bureaucratic approaches of rehabilitation.[25]

Row G: Formal Support

As interventions for children tend to be educational and administered in school settings, teachers typically serve as the major formal providers of support. There is also participation by health care professionals and physical, occupational, and speech therapists.[26] For adult onset disabilities, the older rehabilitation model called for medically oriented therapists.[27] However, the social model seeks independence with subsidies for hiring patient-directed attendants.[28] Therapeutic interventions for late-life onset disabilities are mostly delivered by trained service staff. For those older adults who can no longer remain in the community, formal services tend to be custodial rather than therapeutic and often involve long-term care.

Row H: Informal Support

For childhood onset disabilities, informal social support is generally provided in the context of the family. Sources of such support are primarily the parents and may also include siblings and grandparents.[29] Those experiencing young adult or midlife onset disabilities focus on independence and self-reliance. Nevertheless, friends and family members do play a role as potential sources of social support, especially for those living with severe disabilities.[30] Informal social supports to older adults who live in the community and require assistance in late life are usually spousal or adult child caregivers.[31] Even among older adults requiring long-term care, family members are a source of important support through visitations and oversight of staff.[32]

Row I: Type and Source of Research Data

Our matrix also notes striking differences in the types and sources of research data that comprise the foundation for our understanding of disability during different stages in the life course. Many studies of childhood onset disabilities are based on medical or educational testing of children.[33] Some studies also focus on perspectives of parents and teachers and use their observations or evaluations of the child as their data. It should also be recognized that the voices of children with disabilities and their understanding of their disability have often been excluded from research studies.[34]

Studies of disability in young or mid-adulthood are typically conducted in the context of disability studies frameworks. These studies are often based on autoethnography or first-person accounts of persons with a disability.[35] Generally, the writers of autoethnographies are professional social scientists. Finally, research on late-life onset disabilities is often conducted by researchers based on surveys with older persons.[36] When the disability involves cognitive impairments, information may be obtained through proxy data from caregivers.[37] At times, ethnographic observations are used as study data. This approach has mostly been used in research focused on residents of nursing homes or other long-term care institutions.[38]

We are hoping that the introduction of a schematic life course matrix will offer a useful reminder that the issues we discuss represent only a truncated view of a more complex and textured life course matrix of disability. In the remainder of this chapter we direct the searchlight on the distinct, but potentially interconnected, issues of disability and aging.

Patterns of Late-Life Disability

Due to an exponential increase in the prevalence of chronic disease in late life, along with increasing life expectancy, it is anticipated that there will be growing numbers of older adults living with disabilities. Since chronic illnesses increase rates of disability, there has been a general anticipation of the graying of disability. These expectations about increasing rates of disability over time have been tempered by countervailing trends. The majority of adults over age sixty-five do not experience major disabilities. There has also been a compression of morbidity reflected in an increase in disability-free life expectancy over time.[39]

A 2014 NIA-sponsored report by the US Census Bureau on older Americans with disability found that during the period 2008–2012 there were 40.7 million people over age 65 and 38.7 percent of these older adults reported at least one disability. This was based on physical impairments and functional limitations that were included in this standard national survey as components of disability. Six types of disability were measured in this report: difficulty with hearing, difficulty with vision, cognitive difficulty, ambulatory difficulty, self-care difficulty, and independent living difficulty. The first four of these categories include physical impairments while the latter two incorporate social functioning. Notably, they were all subsumed under the label of disability.

In the report, 66.5 percent of those reporting a disability referred to ambulatory difficulties with walking or climbing stairs. Difficulty with independent living and hearing difficulties were second and third in prevalence (47.8 percent and 40.4 percent, respectively). Whereas most older adults reported only one type of disability, a notable 14.7 percent reported three or more types of disability. Multiple disabilities were most common among the very old, with 41.5 percent of those age eighty-five and older reporting three or more disabilities. Further, Wan He and Luke J. Larsen confirm earlier findings indicating that the oldest old (age eighty-five-plus) are at greatest risk for multiple disabilities.[40]

Two important factors are likely to contribute to the graying of disability. First, there has been an increase in the proportion of old-old persons in the overall US population from 8.8 percent in 1980 to 13.6 percent in 2010. Second, the entry of the baby boomer cohorts into the ranks of the elderly started in 2011 and is expected to persist for the next twenty years, adding substantially to the numbers of older adults with disabilities. Even with anticipated reduction in rates of disability, the numbers of older adults needing assistance and the demands for caregiving placed on families are likely to rise. Thus, the needs of older adults with disabilities are likely to impact the aging network with growing demand for services. This will also pose challenges for the family, and particularly for members of the sandwich generation.[41] Researchers note that due to social mobility and the lack of close ties between grandparents and grandchildren, the middle generation shoulders much of the informal caregiving responsibilities.

Demographic and Social Correlates of Late-Life Disability

It is noteworthy that the oldest old age group is stratified in terms of the demographics that are more heavily affected by disability. Race and socioeconomic status play important roles in the disability patterns among elders. In a study on the trends of disability-free life expectancy from 1991 to 2001,[42] findings showed gender, race, and education to be crucial for increasing life expectancy among the older population (ages sixty to ninety). However, the study shows that disability-free life expectancy increased only among white men during the 1990s. In addition, the discrepancy between black men and black women was wider than the discrepancy between white men and white women. Socioeconomic differences in disability-free life expectancy were also found. Rates of disability were significantly higher among women than among their male counterparts.[43] Notably, there was a ratio of 69 men for every 100 women reporting a disability. Ambulatory difficulties were most frequently reported. Similarly, there were disparities found in rates of disability based on race, with African Americans showing higher rates. These findings illustrate that we need to further investigate the social determinants of disease and disability to understand the graying of disability.[44]

The importance of social determinants of disability suggest that it may be useful to place gerontological perspectives in the broad context of stress studies, which we discuss in greater detail in Chapter 3. Accordingly, we might also consider the lived experience of older people as they encounter disability.[45] This can include stressful life events such as a diagnosis of chronic illness, perceptions and appraisals of disability, utilization of resources and coping strategies to deal with physical impairments, and outcomes of good quality of life and psychological well-being among those living with disabilities. In Chapters 5, 6, and 7, we offer some personal accounts of these lived experiences.

Organizational Divides and Rapprochement

Although disability is part of the lives of a number of older adults, advocates for the elderly and those concerned with disability have seldom combined forces. There have been some recent breakthroughs, such as the establishment of the US National Coalition on Aging and Disability that includes organizations from both communities in an effort to merge appropriate services. On the front of scientific inquiry, there has also been relatively little interaction between researchers in the field of disability studies and gerontological scholars. For instance, the American Sociological Association (ASA) has had a long-standing section on Aging and the Life Course. However, a new section on Disability and Society was first established in 2011 and interaction between the sections had initially been limited. This picture is changing for the better with more cosponsored conference sessions by the two sections. Such sessions garnered a modest, but enthusiastic, audience at the 2015 and 2016 ASA meetings.

Efforts to enhance quality of life for the disabled often lack knowledge pertaining to the special needs of older adults. For example, design of barrier-free environments may presuppose muscle strength and may have only limited usefulness to frail elderly who have multiple disabling conditions. Advocacy in the disability rights movements also requires energy expenditure that is beyond the capabilities of many elderly persons with disabilities. Furthermore, offering rehabilitation services to improve job skills may have little applicability for retired older adults.

To foster a fruitful dialogue between gerontology and disability studies, we must recognize the importance of structural barriers in the lives of older adults living with disabilities and work toward translating needs and desires of persons with disabilities into social policy that can impact the lives of older persons with disabilities. Thus, there would be great value in integrating gerontological, rehabilitation, and disability studies perspectives based on a greater understanding of the special needs, preferences, and orientations of older adults who develop disabilities in late life.

There are potential benefits that could accrue to the disability studies movement by considering orientations from the field of gerontology. In this context, we are placing emphasis on human agency and individual differences, offering an orientation that is divergent from views of disability studies advocates who seek accommodations rather than "pity."[46] While this emphasis is part of the dialogue that is the focus of this book, we remain cognizant that environmental and social accommodations are key factors in the lives of all individuals living with disabilities.[47]

The field of gerontology identifies aging as having social and cultural reference points. The initial focus of gerontological orientations was laid out in Clark Tibbits's introduction to the first edition of the *Handbook of Social Gerontology:* "Aging is usually thought of in terms of changes occurring in the individual."[48] This is not to say that pioneers in gerontology bypassed the social aspects of aging. An entire field of social gerontology emerged concerned with these issues. Early on, Tibbits notes that "changes in any aspect of the environment, including the culture, may affect the status or position of the older persons within the society."[49] Still, the individual played the major role and society was seen as merely a supporting part of the aging process. This informed the legacy of gerontological research whose primary focus was the aged person. In terms of causal inference, the impact of aging on the individual was considered the independent variable while their social role in society was the dependent variable. This helps explain why disengagement theory postulated a mutual withdrawal between society and the aged person.[50] This theory posited a natural desire by the elderly to disengage from social interactions and social involvements in late life. Disengagement theory reflected early gerontological thinking about role restrictions in late life that may be associated with the disablement process. Later gerontological theorists rejected the disengagement model in favor of activity theory, arguing that there is a continued desire by older adults for engagement and that continued activity yields positive well-being outcomes.[51]

From an early stage in gerontological studies, disability was seen as an attribute of the individual that caused them to leave the workplace and retire. Disability offered a natural marker for when one's work life was over, and a new phase of retirement would begin. From the 1950s through the 1970s, gerontologists devoted attention to studying retirement and the role of leisure in later life. In contrast, there was little focus on living with disability in later life and how to maintain quality of life with disability.

The meaning of disability for gerontologists has been anchored to issues associated with health, even as the disability rights movement was pushing for a social or nonmedical theory of disability. This is illustrated in the classic reference work, the *Handbook of Aging and the Social Sciences*.[52] Upon perusing the index for the entry on "disability," readers are directed to "health and aging." The most relevant chapter notes that health and illness were social concerns because "impairment and disability increase the probability of failure in carrying out personal tasks and social concerns" and this condition of "dependency . . . challenges widely shared personal and social expectations and preferences for independence."[53] This divergence between gerontologists and disability studies scholars in talking about the health—or in the case of disability studies, avoiding tying health to disability—highlights the ways in which the two are different in their focus.

Most revealing, however, is the way disability was conceptualized as a combination of "pathological process" and "impairment of function." This idea that disability is linked to a clinical assessment and functional fitness helps us understand that, for gerontologists, disability was best viewed as a process of general diminishment of both health and function. But it should also be noted that, from an early stage, gerontologists emphasized functionality to a greater degree than the biological or medical nature of disability. This led them to distinguish between an *impairment* and a *disability*. The former has been defined as "a physiological and psychological abnormality that does not interfere with the normal life activities of the individual" and the latter as "a condition which results in partial or total limitation of the normal activities of the individual."[54]

Explicit Gerontological Paradigms of Disablement

The Disability Cascade

Since the 1990s, the prevalent paradigm in gerontology for understanding late-life disability has been based on the notion of the "disability cascade," proposed first by Saad Z. Nagi and further elaborated by Lois M. Verbrugge and Alan M. Jette.[55] This theory is based on the idea that increasing incidence of chronic illnesses in late life results in physical impairments such as pain or sensory losses. It is argued that active disease pathology causes organ-level impairment and subsequent functional limitations. These may progress toward generalized disability in the performance of personal care and social functions. Impairments translate into limitations in the performance of daily activities. Such functional limitations are considered to be the building blocks of late-life disability.

There is consensus in the literature dealing with late-life morbidity that meaningful distinctions exist between organ-level physical impairments and the personal or social disability that develops as a consequence of such impairments. Physical impairments appear to be closely linked to physiological and structural changes in the body due to the underlying pathology of chronic illness. Disabilities, on the other hand, are linked to task demands of daily living and social functioning. The degree of disability shown for a given level of physical impairment will depend on the level of environmental demand and the resources and adaptations of the person experiencing impairment.[56]

Gerontological researchers recognize that, in the cascade from disease to organ system impairment to functional limitations, disability is not inevitable and may be reduced or buffered by a number of factors. Understanding the natural history of this cascade and the factors used by the old-old to adapt to decline has useful implications for health planners and those providing services to older adults living with disabilities. Verbrugge and Jette note that medical interventions have their greatest potential in preventing disease from progressing to organ-level impairment and that social supports and psychological coping mechanisms may be most effective in buffering the progression from impairment to social disability.[57] Medical care has traditionally focused on preventing and treating disease pathology. However, in the elderly population where disease has already led to organ-level impairments, the greatest impact of efforts to decrease disability may be felt from interventions that enhance resources and adaptations. Often, interventions can slow down the cascade from physical impairment to disability.[58]

This gerontological formulation presupposes the reality of physical impairments and links them directly to functional limitations that lead to disability. There is limited focus on environmental factors and oppressive social realities postulated by disability scholars.[59] While recent critiques of a fully constructionist view of disability advocate for assigning a greater valence to physical impairments,[60] gerontologists have been unapologetic about considering functional limitations as the fundamental sources of disability.[61] Some may argue that this gerontological orientation reflects a medicalized view of disability. Yet such a view is not far removed from the perceptions and appraisals of older adults who typically acquire disabilities gradually in late life and who seek personal, rather than social, solutions to living with impairments. Older adults try hard to disentangle their illness and disability from normal aging and attempt to cope by strategies ranging from information gathering to medication management and effective communication with their physicians.

Qualitative studies of disability among the elderly offer a different perspective and represent the lived experiences of older people who encounter disabilities in late life. For example, Samantha Solimeo's in-depth anthropological study describes older adults living with Parkinson's disease as "Parkinson's Disease sufferers."[62] This is aimed to denote "living with a burdensome physical, spiritual and social condition."[63] It is notable that patients who were older at the time of diagnosis in Solimeo's study found it easier to normalize living with their degenerative chronic illness. A focus on the lived experience of late-life disablement allows for a broader appreciation of social context and the role of social networks and supports in shielding older persons with disabilities from the depersonalizing aspects of the onslaught of chronic illnesses and their sequelae.

Research in gerontology has frequently used the disability cascade as a point of departure. Studies based on this formulation have consistently demonstrated linkages among elements of the cascade and declines in psychological well-being and social functioning.[64] For example, older adults reporting greater functional limitations manifest loss of psychological well-being in the absence of buffers of social support and proactive coping strategies.[65]

The Sick Role and Related Medical Models

Gerontological research focused on disability generally reflects a top-down orientation. Researchers or clinicians thus determine the number of chronic illnesses, the types and levels of impairment, and the number of functional limitations that are ultimately used to define disability.[66] While the vast majority of people over the age of sixty-five have at least one chronic medical condition, there is wide variation among those with specific illnesses in levels of disability.[67] The rapidly growing old-old segment of the population uses a disproportionate amount of health care resources as it confronts frailty, illness, and disability during the last years of life. Indeed, the lives of some seriously ill older adults, such as dialysis patients, have been characterized as assisted survival that involves ongoing medical intervention.[68] Consequently, medical models of disability have readily been applied to this group.

Theorizing and studying late-life disability has been the domain of gerontologists, geriatricians, social workers, and others focused on health-related challenges of late life. Most of these scholars and practitioners have been comfortable with medical models described in Talcott Parsons's influential work related to the "sick role."[69] Originally formulated as an acute care model of illness behavior, the sick role emphasizes obligations of patients to seek professional help and to comply with medical advice for alleviating illness-related symptoms. The sick role absolves the patient from social role obligations.

Parsons's notions of the sick role have been criticized for disregarding social context and for applying an acute care model to chronic illness.[70] Yet the medical model persists. The traditional rehabilitation paradigm may be viewed as a variant of the medical model as it focuses on professional interventions, such as medical care or therapy, which can assist individuals to improve their functioning in the face of impairments.[71] Goals of rehabilitation for late-life disabilities include increased social participation and reduced depressive symptoms.

Older adults generally turn to health care providers as the first line of defense to deal with chronic illnesses and attendant physical impairments and functional limitations. There are vocal sociological critiques of the medical model lamenting the situation of older adults with disabilities as being neglected by the health care system. Those requiring long-term care are viewed as banished to a "no-care zone"[72] where older persons grappling with disabilities find few, if any, pathways for improving their life experiences. Environmental approaches that we describe below reflect one useful set of alternatives seeking to substitute environmental interventions for medical treatment and rehabilitation.

Ecological Models

Disablement is gradual and incremental for many older adults. Older adults may be living with chronic illnesses for long periods of time before the attendant physical limitations seriously interfere with daily functioning. Once older adults experience disabilities that pose serious threats to independent living, attention to person-environment transactions can offer a promising framework for promoting better quality of life. The environmental docility hypothesis has long been the dominant paradigm for understanding environmental influences on frail or impaired aged.[73] Based on this view, the greater the frailty or impairment, the more likely the aged person is to be constrained by his or her environment. Thus, good person-environment fit becomes an important influence for older adults living with disabilities.[74] Accordingly, living in a home where getting to bedrooms or bathrooms requires stair-climbing can create difficult challenges for older adults who develop mobility impairments. Environmental interventions or prosthetics can improve quality of life outcomes by compensating for personal infirmity through environmental supports.

Gerontologists have also recognized that even frail elders can play an important role in shaping their environments. As the life space of the impaired older person may shrink and they are increasingly confined to their homes, there may be an increase in control of the remaining spaces in the home environment. Older persons experiencing impairments often reorganize their home environments to create a command center that includes a comfortable chair, reading materials, telephone, and other articles that enhance their sense of control and comfort.[75] The elderly can thus engage in meaningful goal-directed behaviors that are designed to shape their environment so that it better fits with their needs. Older adults could thus be viewed as proactive agents who are no longer passive victims of illness and impairment.

Ecological perspectives allow for a complementary set of individual accommodations for late-life disabilities. The ecological paradigm can also be well-suited to professional and societal accommodations to help persons with disabilities enhance their comfort and social functioning. The ecological model in gerontology would be compatible with the contextual interactionist framework proposed by Tom Shakespeare in his revision of the social model of disability.[76] The latter revision recognizes social determinants, but does not dismiss the influence of physical aspects of disability. We return to a more detailed discussion of environmental modifications as a useful adaptation to late-life disability in Chapter 6.

Applying Gerontological Perspectives to Benefit All People with Disabilities

Having outlined gerontological paradigms for understanding late-life disability, we next detail four unique contributions of gerontological orientations that can offer fresh perspectives to the field of disability studies.

Freedom to Embrace or Reject a Disability Identity

For many older adults, disablement is gradual and incremental. Having lived a long life without disabling illness, older adults desire to maintain their long-held beliefs about autonomy and self-determination. Maintenance of a nondisabled identity helps define the status of older adults as aging successfully.[77] Such denial of disability may be considered unacceptable from a disability studies perspective. Yet it may also be viewed as constituting freedom from conformity in maintaining an identity that is comfortable and consistent with an individual's prior history, preferences, and value orientations. Indeed, values of autonomy and self-determination suggest that all individuals should be encouraged to decide whether or not they want to think of themselves as disabled.[78]

Gradual changes of late life that constitute pathways to disability contrast dramatically with core disabilities of early life such as deafness, blindness, and intellectual disability. Core disabilities become defining features of an individual's identity.[79] Individuals who experience similar disabilities in childhood may share experiences of schooling designed to acquire life skills and facilitate bonding among individuals facing similar challenges.[80] Individuals with core disabilities and their advocates recognize the importance of collective action to ensure societal facilitation of independent living through accommodations. Individuals with stable core disabilities have readily formed interest groups and associations based on shared disabilities.[81]

The focus of disability studies is on commonalities in problems that can call for shared solutions to be offered by society and its institutions.[82] Social policies can be more readily formulated to deal with the needs of a readily defined and large constituency. The ADA of 1990 addresses broad categories of individuals such as those with mobility limitations who require wheelchair access.

Yet empirical research indicates that there are considerable individual differences among older adults in regard to considering themselves as disabled. Indeed, it is notable that a high proportion of older adults with limitations in activities of daily living (ADL) do not consider themselves to be disabled.[83] In support of this, as part of a panel study of community-dwelling older adults, we explored determinants of assuming an identity as a disabled person.[84] Our findings reveal that assuming an identity as a disabled person is a multidimensional phenomenon. Beyond differences in health status, social factors (e.g., expressive supports received) and psychological factors (e.g., health anxiety) were found to play an important role in older adults self-identifying as disabled.

Gerontological research focused on disability has shared in the self-imposed reluctance of older adults to call attention to a condition they desire to avoid or at least to delay as long as possible. Older adults have been found to be less likely than their younger counterparts to demonstrate disability pride or to be involved in disability activism through advocacy movements.[85] They may be willing to change their home environment, but not their long-held self-image. Such persistence of the self is consistent with the continuity theory of aging advocated by Robert C. Atchley.[86] This theory suggests that in late life there is a resistance to change and a strong desire to maintain long-term habits, associations, and environments.

Many older adults experience disability as gradual and even imperceptible change that some gerontological scholars have referred to as "diminishment."[87] Thus, it is often unclear to patients diagnosed with a chronic illness (e.g., type 2 diabetes) that visual or mobility limitations are in store for them. Gerontology has recently acquired a greater focus on issues of life course development. The timing of a disability in a person's life trajectory has a major influence in the way the disability is assimilated, interpreted, and responded to. Thus, for example, midlife disability may interfere with work-related and family role demands in ways that are no longer as salient for retired older adults who have raised their children. Disability studies can greatly benefit from an expanded view that situates individuals' disability experiences in the trajectory of the life course. This perspective is the subject of Chapter 4.

To the extent that older adults do not assimilate disability into their identity, they are unlikely to self-disclose their functional limitations and to seek the company of others who are living with similar disabilities.[88] To do so, they often reject assistive devices, such as hearing aids, to avoid the external or internal stigma of living with a disability. It is interesting to entertain the possibility that persons of all ages and all types of disabilities may want to have the freedom to decide whether they want to identify as disabled. Their choices can legitimately range from denial or rejection of a disability identity to seeking to obtain help to remediate their disabling conditions. More closely aligned with positions of disability studies, identification with the disability movement and disability advocacy represents one of several legitimate choices.

Recognition of Individual Differences in Impairment Trajectories

Gerontological orientations to disability have also benefited from methodologically sophisticated studies that point to diverse disability trajectories among the elderly. Research based on large samples that examine patterns in functional limitations acquired in late life reveal considerable intraindividual as well as interindividual variation over time.[89]

What can such research tell us about late-life disability? It indicates that substantial segments of older adults who develop functional limitations in late life may actually experience upward trajectories allowing for improved levels of functioning over time. Accordingly, there may be an adaptive value for maintaining a nondisabled identity by older adults. This may offer insights into the paradox of late-life optimism and future orientation among elderly individuals who are actuarially approaching the end of life.[90] These elders plan trips and purchases that they may not actually live to enjoy, but the future orientation allows for the process of planning that can add meaning to their remaining days.

Additionally, findings of interindividual variability suggest that the same chronic illnesses, or even the same physical impairments, may yield differing quality of life and psychological well-being outcomes as well as differing limitations in daily functioning. There is an important influence of additional stressors, such as comorbidities and negative life events, including social losses in the way different older adults adapt to disabilities. Additionally, external and internal resources also play important roles in the impact of disabilities on quality of life outcomes among older adults.

Consideration of individual differences based on gerontological understandings can benefit disabled individuals of all ages. We recognize that early onset core disabilities are less likely to present intraindividual differences in trajectories than are disabilities due to chronic illnesses in late life. Nevertheless, meaningful variations in functional limitations also exist for people with long-term disabilities due to accidents or for people with core disabilities such as autism. Recognition of the different meanings of functional limitations for individuals with disabilities can remove the pressures of uniform expectations for shared desires and shared outlooks by different disabled individuals. The disability studies orientation calls for membership in a community based on shared disabilities. While there are clear benefits of this communitarian orientation, there are also homogenizing influences that counter recognition of the uniqueness of each individual.

Gerontological Focus on Individual Adaptations

Management of disability in late life benefits from active initiatives of individual patients rather than being the domain of only the formal health care system. The traditional rehabilitation paradigms have focused on interventions such as medical care and physical and occupational therapy that can assist elderly individuals to improve their capabilities for self-care in the face of illness-related impairments. In the aging literature, linkages to action for improving the lives of those living with functional limitations are viewed in terms of health promotion, access to medical care, and potential social services.

Various formulations have been advanced to reflect useful adaptations to shrinking energy and physical impairments of late life. The influential late-life theory of adaptation to disability proposed by Paul B. Baltes and Margret M. Baltes is focused on selective optimization with compensation (SOC).[91] This formulation suggests that older adults refocus activities to utilize remaining abilities and find ways of compensating for losses. Research has found support for the role of assimilative and accommodative coping in dealing with disabilities among the elderly.[92] Laura L. Carstensen's theory of socioemotional selectivity addressed the social arena.[93] She argues that older adults tend to refocus their more limited energies to maintain enduring and close social relationships. They do not disengage from their most meaningful interactions, but conserve energy to prioritize the most rewarding social ties. Further, Eva Kahana, Boaz Kahana, and Jeong Eun Lee's proactivity model designates special corrective adaptations that can help older persons cope with chronic illness and disablement. Useful corrective adaptations put forth by this model include environmental and activity modifications, illness adaptations, and active efforts to marshal support.[94]

Each of these theories addressing individual adaptations to aspects of late-life disability can also be relevant to individuals with early onset disabilities. Furthermore, even proponents of the social model of disability recognize that there is value in self-help and behaviors that promote access and accommodations for people with disabilities.[95] Advances in health promotion, medical care, and rehabilitation can open up new options for persons with disabilities. Indeed, research has found support for the value of late-life health promotion in improved physical and mental health outcomes.[96]

Individuals with disabilities who take pride in a disability identity may be reluctant to engage in efforts that could result in relinquishing their identity. The recent availability of cochlear implants that has found lack of acceptance by some within the disability rights community provides a notable example.[97] In contrast, older adults are less hesitant to embrace new technology that can reverse a disabling condition. Older adults readily embraced abandoning their glasses after LASIK and cataract surgery. They did not consider acceptance of such interventions as disloyal to their bespectacled counterparts. The rise of antiaging medicine further documents the willingness of older adults to carry their aversion to disability to the extreme, attempting to reverse the aging process.[98]

Active pursuit of competent medical care also has an important advocacy component. Proactive health care consumers of the Internet age can play active roles in searching for health information, including new treatments and health promotion strategies. The role of the Internet in helping persons with disabilities has recently been recognized in the field of disability studies as well as in gerontology.[99] While a digital divide may place older patients and those with disabilities at a disadvantage, there are encouraging indications about older adults' willingness and ability to embrace the Internet in ever greater numbers. Such older patients place greater demands on doctors to be available by e-mail, thereby facilitating communication that can help them better cope with disabilities.

The diverse coping strategies reviewed here might serve as mediators that delay progression along the disability cascade or improve quality of life outcomes in the face of movement along the cascade. The disability studies approach can benefit from greater recognition of the value of personal adaptations in helping individuals of all ages enhance their quality of life, even as they collectively work for greater societal accommodations.

Recognizing Benefits of Reliance on Informal Caregivers

In the field of gerontology, there has been a great deal of interest in the role of caregivers who play a major role in providing support to older adults with disabilities and help ensure that they can remain at home outside of institutional facilities. As people get older and have increased risk of disability, there is an increase in informal and formal help received.[100] The availability of family and other informal caregivers has been found to decrease reliance on formal caregivers such as utilizing assisted living and nursing homes.

Both young people with disabilities and their elderly counterparts value and seek to maintain autonomy. Younger people with core disabilities are likely to search for autonomy in order to assume developmentally appropriate social roles such as getting a job or establishing a family. Obtaining an entitlement to hire an attendant can serve as an enabling function for young people with disabilities. In contrast, older people are likely to develop functional limitations after retirement and after having fulfilled typical family obligations such as the raising of children. Indeed, disability is most likely to necessitate assistance with ADL among the very old (age eighty-plus). Accordingly, the majority of older adults with disabilities seek to obtain care from informal caregivers. Older adults attempt to avoid formal assistants or other agency-based approaches to receiving assistance to deal with disabilities.

Among older adults living with disabilities, there is a strong preference for turning to family members, including spouses and adult children, for care when such care is required. There is also evidence of mutual assistance among spouses and among elderly friends.[101] Formal caregivers are viewed by older adults as last resort sources of support. Among younger core-disabled individuals, parents are a natural source of care and support during the early years. However, as persons with disabilities reach young adulthood, the desired model of care is that provided by paid attendants. For those needing extensive support, group homes are also a well-regarded alternative. There is an assumption among the young that individuals with disabilities will direct the attendant to provide assistance fitting with the care recipient's wishes. Such direction presupposes the care recipient's ability to clearly articulate his or her desires and needs and the willingness of the attendant to follow directions given by the individual requiring assistance.

Family members or close friends are more likely to be motivated by altruistic attitudes or by norms of obligation and be in a position to offer emotional as well as tangible support. Furthermore, family members can serve as committed and ardent advocates within the health care system. Paid attendants are far less likely to assume advocacy roles in interactions with the health care system. Indeed, research has indicated instances of disregard by paid attendants for wishes and instructions of the person with disabilities whom they assist.[102] Older adults are generally reluctant to entrust their care to strangers and worry about the potential for abuse.[103] Accordingly, there might be some wisdom younger adults with disabilities can gain from marshaling and accepting supports provided by kin, when available.

Help-seeking, or marshaling of support, poses important challenges and present useful opportunities for older adults with disabilities. Our longitudinal research indicates that older adults who have the motivation and skill set to actively marshal social support to help them cope with chronic illnesses and physical impairment maintain greater social participation and better psychological well-being than do their counterparts who are more reluctant to marshal social support.[104] Since most older adults lack paid attendants to help them live with functional limitations, they must reach out to friends, neighbors, and family members to obtain needed help with transportation, errands, and other daily tasks. The disability studies field can gain valuable insights about benefits that can accrue to persons with a disability at all ages by actively seeking help from informal support sources. Consideration of gerontological perspectives on care-getting may also benefit younger persons with disabilities, as it offers an alternative approach to seeking paid attendants. Informal family caregivers may compensate for loss of autonomy by offering higher levels of emotional support and personal commitment.

Lessons from Late Life: Recent Onset Disability

In our discussion of intraindividual variability, we noted that substantial numbers of older adults who develop functional limitations in late life may actually experience improved levels of functioning as time goes on. Accordingly, there may be an adaptive value for maintaining a nondisabled identity by older adults. Additionally, findings of interindividual variability suggest that the same chronic illnesses, or even the same physical impairments, may yield differing quality of life and psychological well-being outcomes as well as differing limitations in daily functioning for different older adults. We now present a brief case study with the disability experience of one of the respondents in our panel study. This respondent experienced mild mobility limitations that are common later in life. Our case study illustrates the sometimes unexpected trajectories among older adults with impairments and functional limitations that are acquired late in life.

Case Study: Susan

Susan was a recent widow and retiree at age seventy-two when we first interviewed her. She was in generally good health and enjoyed going on hiking trips with friends and colleagues. However, she developed significant knee pain and started to find it more difficult to climb stairs while visiting historical sites. Nonetheless, she was readily able to accommodate to this situation by deciding to take less strenuous trips. However, her impairment of pain and stiffness resulted in increasing mobility limitations. She started to find it difficult to use public transportation, feeling insecure in getting on and off buses. She obtained a cane and selected public transportation routes where buses offer low step accommodations.

She visited her primary care doctor, who attributed the problem to arthritis. Susan initiated seeing a specialist and was told that rheumatoid arthritis may be the cause. She was given anti-inflammatory medications, but her pain did not subside. She had to call on her children, who lived nearby, more and more frequently to take her shopping and drive her places. She was reluctant to hire a driver or even take a cab, based on her mistrust of strangers and her desire to have a caring person take her to doctors' appointments.

Susan had gotten used to being less active, but had a few longtime friends who visited her regularly. She did not think of herself as disabled and came up with creative ways to get around her limitations. She rearranged the furniture in her home to make it safer to navigate. She had not established connections with other older people suffering from similar disabilities. Susan used individual adaptations, including activity modifications, to deal with her physical impairments. Interacting more frequently with a limited circle of friends and family represented a form of socioemotional selectivity.[105]

After over a year of pain and increasing functional limitations, Susan encountered some unexpected improvement in her condition. The pain in Susan's knees eased and episodes became more infrequent. The doctor indicated that it is not unusual for anti-inflammatory medications to take a long time before they can take effect. Susan relied on the health care system to try to improve her health condition. She was willing to try new and even experimental medications. Her disability trajectory allowed for almost unexpected improvement that reduced her functional limitations.

Intraindividual Variations in the Trajectory of Disability

The case study of Susan exemplifies gerontological understandings about the cascade of disability.[106] According to Verbrugge and Jette's prominent theory of disablement, older people develop chronic illnesses (e.g., arthritis) that subsequently result in physical impairments (e.g., pain). In turn, physical impairments translate into disability. Verbrugge and Jette's model of the cascade of disability captures interindividual variations in the trajectory of disability in later life.However, to inform practice and policy relevant to disability it is also useful to consider other factors, such as the disabled individual's proactivity and agency, to appreciate intraindividual variations.

Additionally, contextual differences in physical and social environments can lead to important differences in quality of life and psychological well-being outcomes for all individuals with disabilities. This concept has been studied in gerontology in the framework of person-environment fit.[107] Where the environment is not suited to the individual's needs, preferences, and capabilities, environmental change represents a useful adaptation.

Disability scholars are less likely to focus on individual differences in coping with disability and, instead, emphasize factors that persons with disabilities share. The directive to embrace and celebrate one's disability is also part of this collectivistic orientation. Older adults offer a counterpoint to this orientation within the disability studies movement. Our earlier studies of older adults living with disabilities revealed that the majority experienced their disability as an unwelcome burden.[108]

The notion that some people consider their disability as burdensome has been advocated for by Shakespeare, but has not been widely accepted by the disability studies community.[109] Yet older adults frequently articulate their rejection of disability and impatience with the hardships that functional limitations pose for them. They are able to do this because the types of disability they confront does not define them.

Allowing for rejection of functional limitations could also offer a greater measure of freedom to younger people living with disabilities. It can provide for focusing on their areas of strength without having to totally embrace their limitations. Thus, gerontology can help disability studies move beyond identity politics. We agree with Shakespeare's view that the identity politics that served such a useful role in securing rights for persons with disabilities can also become a hindrance to individual self-determination.[110] Individuals in general, and the elderly who are living with disabilities in particular, must be given choices to relate to their disability in accordance with their value system. They should be able to fully embrace a disability identity, or fully reject it. Those who identify fully will become part of an important and effective social movement. Those who want nothing to do with it can enjoy the continuity of self that this rejection affords them.

Conclusion

In considering this dialectic between gerontological and disability studies approaches, it is important to recognize the generational dynamics that may be at play. These include understanding of age-associated stressors, coping strategies, and resource mobilization that might maximally benefit individuals living with disabilities. Young people with disabilities may find a source of social capital, affiliation, and common purpose by joining forces to demand that society recognize their special needs and offer suitable accommodations. It is natural for young people to try to assert their rights along with assuming responsibilities as young adults.[111]

In contrast, older people with late onset disabilities are reluctant to identify themselves as disabled and are likely to engage in individual coping strategies in an effort to acclimate to life with disabilities. Because most older adults do not form natural associations based on their disabilities, they can endorse more diverse orientations and offer greater acceptance of alternative adaptations to disability without taking political stances. Gerontological research places greater focus on physical impairments than do disability studies. It also considers the progression to disability in an interactionist, rather than constructionist, framework. This vantage point may offer a more inclusive orientation to disability studies that can help incorporate the growing numbers of older adults who live with newly acquired disabilities. While we focus on gerontological contributions and insights, we acknowledge that perspectives of older adults with long-standing disabilities are largely absent from gerontological research and call for increased attention as more individuals with long-term core disabilities will be living to old age.

While acknowledging life course–related differences between groups and individuals who experience early versus late onset disabilities, we nevertheless point to important commonalities between these groups. Orientations of gerontologists have been tailored to the needs and propensities of the populations they study. So have the orientations of disability scholars been suited to younger persons with core disabilities.

Notes

1. Tamar Heller and Sarah K. Parker Harris, *Disability Through the Life Course* (Sage, 2011).
2. US Department of Health and Human Services, "Summary Health Statistics: National Health Interview Survey, 2014." (2014). Available at https://ftp.cdc.gov /pub/Health_Statistics/NCHS/NHIS/SHS/2014_SHS_Table_A-10.pdf.
3. Ibid.
4. Suzanne R. Kunkel and Robert A. Applebaum, "Estimating the Prevalence of Long-Term Disability for an Aging Society," *Journal of Gerontology* 47, no. 5 (1992): S253–S260.
5. Sara Green, Christine Davis, Elana Karshmer, Pete Marsh, and Benjamin Straight, "Living Stigma: The Impact of Labeling, Stereotyping, Separation, Status Loss, and Discrimination in the Lives of Individuals with Disabilities and Their Families," *Sociological Inquiry* 75, no. 2 (2005): 197–215.
6. Joseph P. Shapiro, *No Pity: People with Disabilities Forging a New Civil Rights Movement* (Three Rivers Press, 1994).
7 Bryan J. Kemp and Laura Mosqueda, *Aging with a Disability: What the Clinician Needs to Know* (Taylor and Francis, 2004).
8. Lois M. Verbrugge, Kenzie Latham, and Philippa J. Clarke, "Aging with Disability for Midlife and Older Adults," *Research on Aging* (2017): 1–37.
9. Clare Gilbert and Allen Foster, "Childhood Blindness in the Context of VISION 2020: The Right to Sight," *Bulletin of the World Health Organization* 79, no. 3 (2001): 227–232; Christine Yoshinaga-Itano, Allison L. Sedey, Diane K. Coulter, and Albert L. Mehl, "Language of Early- and Later-Identified Children with Hearing Loss," *Pediatrics* 102, no. 5 (1998): 1161–1171.
10. Tom Shakespeare, "Disability Studies Today and Tomorrow," *Sociology of Health and Illness* 27, no. 1 (2005): 138–148.
11. Lois M. Verbrugge and Alan M. Jette, "The Disablement Process," *Social Science and Medicine* 38, no. 1 (1994): 1–14.
12. Paul K. Longmore, "Uncovering the Hidden History of People with Disabilities," *Reviews in American History* 15, no. 3 (1987): 355–364, http://www .jstor.org/stable/2702029.
13. Atul Gawande, *Being Mortal: Medicine and What Matters in the End* (Macmillan, 2014).
14. Michelle Putnam, "Conceptualizing Disability: Developing a Framework for Political Disability Identity," *Journal of Disability Policy Studies* 16, no. 3 (2005): 188–198.
15. Michael Oliver, *Understanding Disability: From Theory to Practice* (St. Martin's Press, 1996).
16. Sheila Riddell and Nick Watson, *Disability, Culture and Identity* (Routledge, 2014).

17. Nick Watson, "Theorising the Lives of Disabled Children: How Can Disability Theory Help?" *Children and Society* 26, no. 3 (2012): 192–202.

18. Mark Priestley, "Childhood Disability and Disabled Childhoods Agendas for Research," *Childhood* 5, no. 2 (1998): 207–223.

19. Verbrugge and Jette, "The Disablement Process."

20. Chris Forlin, Graham Douglas, and John Hattie, "Inclusive Practices: How Accepting Are Teachers?" *International Journal of Disability, Development and Education* 43, no. 2 (1996): 119–133.

21. Mary Blair-Loy and Amy S. Wharton, "Employees' Use of Work-Family Policies and the Workplace Social Context," *Social Forces* 80, no. 3 (2002): 813–845.

22. David Piachaud, "Disability, Retirement and Unemployment of Older Men," *Journal of Social Policy* 15, no. 2 (1986): 145–162.

23. Barbara Altman and Sharon Barnartt, *Environmental Contexts and Disability*, vol. 8 (Emerald Group, 2014).

24. Samuel L. Odom and Scott R. McConnell, *Social Competence of Young Children with Disabilities: Issues and Strategies for Intervention* (Paul H. Brookes, 1992).

25. Gary L. Albrecht, *The Disability Business: Rehabilitation in America,* (Sage, 1992).

26. Fred P. Orelove, Dick Sobsey, and Rosanne K. Silberman, *Educating Children with Multiple Disabilities: A Collaborative Approach* (Brookes, 2004).

27. Guy Dixon, Everard W. Thornton, and Carolyn A. Young, "Perceptions of Self-Efficacy and Rehabilitation Among Neurologically Disabled Adults," *Clinical Rehabilitation* 21, no. 3 (2007): 230–240.

28. Shapiro, *No Pity.*

29. Eva Kahana, Jeong Eun Lee, Jeffrey Kahana, Timothy Goler, Boaz Kahana, Sarah Shick, Erin Burk, and Kaitlyn Barnes, "Childhood Autism and Proactive Family Coping: Intergenerational Perspectives," *Journal of Intergenerational Relationships* 13, no. 2 (2015): 150–166.

30. Craig H. Kennedy, Robert H. Horner, and J. Stephen Newton, "Social Contacts of Adults with Severe Disabilities Living in the Community: A Descriptive Analysis of Relationship Patterns," *Research and Practice for Persons with Severe Disabilities* 14, no. 3 (1989): 190–196.

31. Carlos F. Mendes de Leon, Thomas A. Glass, and Lisa F. Berkman, "Social Engagement and Disability in a Community Population of Older Adults: The New Haven EPESE," *American Journal of Epidemiology* 157, no. 7 (2003): 633–642.

32. Marie-Luise Friedemann, Rhonda J. Montgomery, Bedonna Maiberger, and A. Ann Smith, "Family Involvement in the Nursing Home: Family-Oriented Practices and Staff-Family Relationships," *Research in Nursing and Health* 20, no. 6 (1997): 527–537.

33. James M. Perrin, "Health Services Research for Children with Disabilities," *Milbank Quarterly* 80, no. 2 (2002): 303–324.

34. Nancy A. Murphy, Becky Christian, Deidre A. Caplin, and Paul C. Young, "The Health of Caregivers for Children with Disabilities: Caregiver Perspectives," *Child: Care, Health and Development* 33, no. 2 (2007): 180–187.

35. David A. Karp, *Speaking of Sadness: Depression, Disconnection, and the Meanings of Illness* (Oxford University Press, 1996).

36. Ellen L. Idler, Louise B. Russell, and Diane Davis, "Survival, Functional Limitations, and Self-Rated Health in the NHANES I Epidemiologic Follow-Up Study, 1992," *American Journal of Epidemiology* 152, no. 9 (2000): 874–883.

37. Peter J. Neumann, Sally S. Araki, and Elane M. Gutterman, "The Use of Proxy

Respondents in Studies of Older Adults: Lessons, Challenges, and Opportunities," *Journal of the American Geriatrics Society* 48, no. 12 (2000): 1646–1654.

38. Jaber F. Gubrium, *Speaking of Life: Horizons of Meaning for Nursing Home Residents* (Transaction, 1993); J. Neil Henderson, "The Culture of Care in a Nursing Home: Effects of a Medicalized Model of Long-Term Care," in *The Culture of Long-Term Care: Nursing Home Ethnography*, ed. J. Neil Henderson and Maria D. Vesperi (Greenwood, 1995), 37–54.

39. Eileen M. Crimmins, Yasuhiko Saito, and Dominique Ingegneri, "Trends in Disability-Free Life Expectancy in the United States, 1970–90," *Population and Development Review* 23, no. 3 (1997): 555–572.

40. Wan He and Luke J. Larsen, "Older Americans with a Disability: 2008–2012," US Census Bureau, American Community Survey Reports (US Government Printing Office, 2014).

41. Brenda C. Spillman and Liliana E. Pezzin, "Potential and Active Family Caregivers: Changing Networks and the 'Sandwich Generation,'" *Milbank Quarterly* 78, no. 3 (2000): 347–374.

42. Aïda Solé-Auró, Hiram Beltrán-Sánchez, and Eileen M. Crimmins, "Are Differences in Disability-Free Life Expectancy by Gender, Race, and Education Widening at Older Ages?" *Population Research and Policy Review* 34, no. 1 (2014): 1–18.

43. He and Larsen, "Older Americans with a Disability."

44. Bruce G. Link and Jo Phelan, "Social Conditions as Fundamental Causes of Disease," *Journal of Health and Social Behavior* Extra Issue (1995): 80–94.

45. Samantha Solimeo, *With Shaking Hands: Aging with Parkinson's Disease in America's Heartland* (Rutgers University Press, 2009).

46. Shapiro, *No Pity;* Tom Shakespeare, *Disability Rights and Wrongs Revisited* (Routledge, 2013).

47. Irving Kenneth Zola, "Self, Identity and the Naming Question: Reflections on the Language of Disability," *Social Science and Medicine* 36, no. 2 (1993): 167–173.

48. Clark Tibbitts, *Handbook of Social Gerontology: Societal Aspects of Aging* (University of Chicago Press, 1960), 6.

49. Ibid., 13.

50. Elaine Cumming and William Earl Henry, *Growing Old, the Process of Disengagement* (Basic Books, 1961).

51. Bruce W. Lemon, Vern L. Bengtson, and James A. Peterson, "An Exploration of the Activity Theory of Aging: Activity Types and Life Satisfaction Among In-Movers to a Retirement Community," *Journal of Gerontology* 27, no. 4 (1972): 511–523.

52. Robert H. Binstock and Ethel Shanas, with Vern L. Bengtson, George L. Maddox, and Dorothy Wedderburn, *Handbook of Aging and the Social Sciences* (Van Nostrand Reinhold, 1976).

53. Ethel Shanas and George L. Maddox, "Aging, Health, and the Organization of Health Resources," in *Handbook of Aging and the Social Sciences*, ed. Robert H. Binstock and Ethel Shanas, with Vern L. Bengtson, George L. Maddox, and Dorothy Wedderburn (Van Nostrand Reinhold, 1976), 592–618.

54. Ibid.

55. Saad Z. Nagi, "Disability Concepts Revisited: Implications for Prevention," in *Disability in America: Toward a National Agenda for Prevention*, ed. Andrew Pope and Alvin Tarlov (National Academies Press, 1991); Verbrugge and Jette, "The Disablement Process."

56. M. Powell Lawton, "Residential Environment and Self-Directedness Among Older People," *American Psychologist* 45, no. 5 (1990): 638.

57. Verbrugge and Jette, "The Disablement Process."

58. Alan M. Jette and Julie J. Keysor, "Disability Models: Implications for Arthritis Exercise and Physical Activity Interventions," *Arthritis Care and Research* 49, no. 1 (2003): 114–120.

59. Michael Oliver, *The Politics of Disablement: Critical Texts in Social Work and the Welfare State* (Macmillan, 1990).

60. Shakespeare, *Disability Rights and Wrongs Revisited*.

61. Verbrugge and Jette, "The Disablement Process."

62. Solimeo, *With Shaking Hands*.

63. Ibid., 23.

64. Nancy G. Kutner and Donna J. Brogan, "Assisted Survival, Aging, and Rehabilitation Needs: Comparison of Older Dialysis Patients and Age-Matched Peers," *Archives of Physical Medicine and Rehabilitation* 73, no. 4 (1992): 309–315.

65. Eva Kahana, Jessica Kelley-Moore, and Boaz Kahana, "Proactive Aging: A Longitudinal Study of Stress, Resources, Agency, and Well-Being in Late Life," *Aging & Mental Health* 16, no. 4 (2012): 438–451.

66. Linda P. Fried, Luigi Ferrucci, Jonathan Darer, Jeff D. Williamson, and Gerard Anderson, "Untangling the Concepts of Disability, Frailty, and Comorbidity: Implications for Improved Targeting and Care," *Journals of Gerontology Series A: Biological Sciences and Medical Sciences* 59, no. 3 (2004): M255–M263.

67. Donna Falvo, *Medical and Psychosocial Aspects of Chronic Illness and Disability* (Jones and Bartlett, 2013).

68. Kutner and Brogan, "Assisted Survival, Aging, and Rehabilitation Needs."

69. Talcott Parsons, "The Sick Role and the Role of the Physician Reconsidered," *Milbank Memorial Fund Quarterly: Health and Society* 53, no. 1 (1975): 257–278.

70. David A. Rier, "The Patient's Experience of Illness," in *Handbook of Medical Sociology*, ed. Chloe E. Bird, Peter Contrad, Allen M. Prefont, and Stefan Timmermans (Vanderbilt University Press, 2010), 163–178.

71. A. Horowitz, J. P. Reinhardt, and K. Boerner, "The Effect of Rehabilitation on Depression Among Visually Disabled Older Adults," *Aging and Mental Health* 9, no. 6 (2005): 563–570.

72. Carroll L. Estes and James H. Swan, *The Long Term Care Crisis: Elders Trapped in the No-Care Zone* (Sage, 1992).

73. M. Powell Lawton, "Environment and Other Determinants of Well-Being in Older People," *The Gerontologist* 23, no. 4 (1983): 349–357.

74. Eva Kahana and Boaz Kahana, "Contextualizing Successful Aging: New Directions in an Age-Old Search," in *Invitation to the Life Course: Toward New Understandings of Later Life*, ed. Richard A. Settersten, Jr., and Jon Hendricks (Baywood, 2003), 225–255.

75. Lawton, "Residential Environment and Self-Directedness Among Older People."

76. Shakespeare, *Disability Rights and Wrongs Revisited*.

77. Kahana and Kahana, "Contextualizing Successful Aging."

78. Richard M. Ryan and Edward L. Deci, "Self-Determination Theory and the Facilitation of Intrinsic Motivation, Social Development, and Well-Being," *American Psychologist* 55, no. 1 (2000): 68–78.

79. Zola, "Self, Identity and the Naming Question."

80. Valerie Leiter, "Bowling Together: Foundations of Community Among Youth with Disabilities," in *Disability and Community*, ed. Allison C. Carey and

Richard K. Scotch, Research in Social Science and Disability Series (Emerald, 2011), 3–25.

81. Ronald J. Berger, *Introducing Disability Studies* (Lynne Rienner, 2013).

82. Alan Roulstone and Simon Prideaux, *Understanding Disability Policy* (Policy Press, 2012).

83. Jean A. Langlois, Stefania Maggi, Tamara Harris, Eleanor M. Simonsick, Luigi Ferrucci, Mara Pavan, Leonardo Sartori, and Giuliano Enzi, "Self-Report of Difficulty in Performing Functional Activities Identifies a Broad Range of Disability in Old Age," *Journal of the American Geriatrics Society* 44, no. 12 (1996): 1421–1428.

84. Jessica A. Kelley-Moore, John G. Schumacher, Eva Kahana, and Boaz Kahana, "When Do Older Adults Become 'Disabled'? Social and Health Antecedents of Perceived Disability in a Panel Study of the Oldest Old," *Journal of Health and Social Behavior* 47, no. 2 (2006): 126–141.

85. Rosalyn B. Darling and D. Alex Heckert, "Orientations Toward Disability: Differences over the Lifecourse," *International Journal of Disability, Development and Education* 57, no. 2 (2010): 131–143.

86. Robert C. Atchley, "Continuity Theory, Self, and Social Structure," in *The Self and Society in Aging Processes*, ed. Carol D. Ryff and Victor W. Marshall (Springer, 1999), 121.

87. Elias S. Cohen, "The Elderly Mystique: Constraints on the Autonomy of the Elderly with Disabilities," *The Gerontologist* 28, Suppl. (1988): 24–31.

88. Darling and Heckert, "Orientations Toward Disability."

89. Thomas M. Gill, Evelyne A. Gahbauer, Ling Han, and Heather G. Allore, "Trajectories of Disability in the Last Year of Life," *New England Journal of Medicine* 362, no. 13 (2010): 1173–1180.

90. Jeffrey S. Kahana, Eva Kahana, and Loren D. Lovegreen, *Expanding the Time Frame for Advance Care Planning: Policy Considerations and Implications for Research* (INTECH Open Access, 2012).

91. Paul B. Baltes and Margret M. Baltes, "Psychological Perspectives on Successful Aging: The Model of Selective Optimization with Compensation," *Successful Aging: Perspectives from the Behavioral Sciences* 1, no. 1 (1990): 1–34.

92. Kathrin Boerner, "Adaptation to Disability Among Middle-Aged and Older Adults: The Role of Assimilative and Accommodative Coping," *Journals of Gerontology Series B: Psychological Sciences and Social Sciences* 59, no. 1 (2004): P35–P42.

93. Laura L. Carstensen, "Social and Emotional Patterns in Adulthood: Support for Socioemotional Selectivity Theory," *Psychology and Aging* 7, no. 3 (1992): 331.

94. Eva Kahana, Boaz Kahana, and Jeong Eun Lee, "Proactive Approaches to Successful Aging: One Clear Path Through the Forest," *Gerontology* 60, no. 5 (2014): 466–474.

95. Oliver, *Understanding Disability*.

96. Eva Kahana, Renee H. Lawrence, Boaz Kahana, Kyle Kercher, Amy Wisniewski, Elanor Stoller, Jordan Tobin, and Kurt Stange, "Long-Term Impact of Preventive Proactivity on Quality of Life of the Old-Old," *Psychosomatic Medicine* 64, no. 3 (2002): 382–394.

97. Katrien Vermeire, Jan P. L. Brokx, Floris L. Wuyts, Ellen Cochet, Anouk Hofkens, and Paul H. Van de Heyning. "Quality-of-Life Benefit from Cochlear Implantation in the Elderly," *Otology and Neurotology* 26, no. 2 (2005): 188–195.

98. Robert H. Binstock, "The War on 'Anti-Aging Medicine,'" *The Gerontologist* 43, no. 1 (2003): 4–14.

99. Paul T. Jaeger, *Disability and the Internet: Confronting a Digital Divide* (Lynne Rienner, 2012).

100. Peter Kemper, "The Use of Formal and Informal Home Care by the Disabled Elderly," *Health Services Research* 27, no. 4 (1992): 421.

101. Margaret Denton, "The Linkages Between Informal and Formal Care of the Elderly," *Canadian Journal on Aging/La Revue Canadienne Du Vieillissement* 16, no. 1 (1997): 30–50.

102. Gary R. Ulicny, Glen W. White, Barbara Bradford, and R. Mark Mathews. "Consumer Exploitation by Attendants: How Often Does It Happen and Can Anything Be Done About It?" *Rehabilitation Counseling Bulletin* 33 (1990).

103. Jacki Pritchard, *Male Victims of Elder Abuse: Their Experiences and Needs* (Jessica Kingsley, 2001).

104. Kahana, Kelley-Moore, and Kahana, "Proactive Aging."

105. Carstensen, "Social and Emotional Patterns in Adulthood."

106. Verbrugge and Jette, "The Disablement Process."

107. Lawton M. Powell and Lucille Nahemow, "Ecology and the Aging Process," in *The Psychology of Adult Development and Aging*, ed. Carl Eisdorfer and Lawton M. Powell (American Psychological Association, 1973).

108. Eva Kahana, Jessica Kelley-Moore, and Boaz Kahana, "Social Dimensions of Late Life Disability," in *Aging Well: Gerontological Education for Nurses and Other Health Care Professionals*, ed. May L. Wykle and Sarah H. Gueldner (Jones and Barlett, 2011), 457–468.

109. Shakespeare, *Disability Rights and Wrongs Revisited*.

110. Ibid.; see, also Ryan and Deci, "Self-Determination Theory and the Facilitation of Intrinsic Motivation, Social Development, and Well-Being."

111. Patience H. White, "Access to Health Care: Health Insurance Considerations for Young Adults with Special Health Care Needs/Disabilities," *Pediatrics* 110, no. Supplement 3 (2002): 1328–1335.

3

Learning
from Gerontology

In this chapter, we address gerontological orientations to aging and disability as experienced by a gerontologist, through my (Eva Kahana's) personal account of my lived experience and evolving program of gerontological research over a still active career of fifty years. This chapter is written in an autoethnographic framework.[1] The focus here is on the evolution of my gerontological thinking as it intersects at various points with our personal experiences as a family with my mother, Sari Frost, and her disability. The narrative in this chapter traces my biography and my collaborative research initiatives within the context of historical trends in the field of gerontology.

Our personal and family history frames the gerontological journey that I describe. I was born in 1941 and received my PhD in human development from the University of Chicago in 1967. My husband, Boaz, graduated from the same program in 1966 after practicing for five years as a clinical psychologist. Jeffrey, our older son, was born in 1967 and his brother Michael was born in 1969. Our children were growing up during a large part of my career as described in this chapter. My mother, Sari, who was a central member of our family, regularly took care of our two sons after she retired, as I was immersed in my gerontological career. She was also a significant influence in our lived experiences with late-life disability. The studies I describe were mostly collaborations with my husband and with graduate students and colleagues affiliated with the Elderly Care Research Center (ECRC) that I founded in 1969. In describing these studies, "we" refers to the ECRC research team. This chapter also sets the stage for making connections in the later chapters of this book between alternative approaches of gerontology and disability studies.

Eva's Gerontological Journey

The year was 1961 and I was an eager nineteen-year-old college student with an unusual interest in old people. Having grown up as an only child in the aftermath of the Nazi Holocaust in Hungary, I had spent a lot of time surrounded by older people and always felt comfortable in their company, so I was pleased to get a summer job at a camp for older adults in Essex, Massachusetts. I spent my evenings listening to the campers tell stories about their adventurous lives. There was also a great deal of discussion among the camp's participants about absent children. These children, with their busy schedules, found the long journey to the camp difficult. Instead of visiting, many sent gifts to their parents, including a television that could not receive a signal at that rustic location.

In September 1961, I returned to my senior year at Stern College in New York. I had been a history major, but I was now determined to learn more about the science of aging. Based on my summer experiences at the adult camp, I decided to write a term paper related to the emerging field of gerontology. I did not have much luck finding materials at the public library, but the librarian directed me to a volume on the new books shelf: *Growing Old* by Elaine Cumming and William Henry.[2] The book made fascinating reading, though it did not offer sufficient background for a well-researched term paper. Readers who are well versed in gerontology will realize that my library find was the original formulation of disengagement theory—the first influential social theory of aging. The ideas expressed in this new book about mutual withdrawal between older adults and society seemed to fit well with the stories I had heard from some elderly residents at the summer camp. Yet they didn't seem to dovetail with aspirations of other elderly campers for greater social contact and connectedness.

During the next academic year, I enrolled in psychology courses to prepare for applying to the City College of New York's graduate program in clinical psychology. My decision was also influenced by discussions with my soon-to-be husband, Boaz, who worked as a clinical psychologist and was fascinated by human behavior.

I did not think my chances for acceptance to a psychology graduate program would be very good, but in the spring of 1962 I was invited for an interview. One of the professors on the admission committee happened to be Rose Kushner, a specialist in the study of aging. When I described my interests as being focused on older adults, she exclaimed with amazement, "You are the first student applying to our program with an interest in old age!" Another committee member followed up with a question appropriate for a clinical psychology program: "Do you think you might become depressed by working with old people who may be sick and nearing the end of life?" This question surprised me. I responded that, as a child survivor of the Holocaust, I would consider it a happy task to be surrounded by people who survived to reach old age. Professor Kushner smiled, and I soon learned that I had been accepted into the program in spite of my limited academic preparation in psychology.

At City College, only a few of my classes in clinical psychology had any aging-related content. Nevertheless, I received permission to write my master's thesis on adaptation of frail older people to life in a home for the aged. Through my thesis supervisor, Professor Edward Kelty, I was fortunate to meet two young women researchers who were affiliated with the Hebrew Home for the Aged. Ruth Bennett and Lucille Nahemow were pioneering gerontologists who made seminal early contributions to the study of institutional care of the aged. They helped me understand the important role that environments can play in either facilitating or hindering the well-being of older adults who are dependent on others for their care.[3] While conducting research on my master's thesis, I do not recall hearing the term *disabled* in reference to residents living in the old-age home. The discourse in those times was centered on old people who needed care, almost as part of the natural progression of having reached an advanced age.

In my studies at City College I discovered that my intellectual interests did not lie in the field of clinical psychology, which at that time had strong Freudian influences. When I discussed my reactions with Professor Kushner, she recommended that I continue my studies for a PhD under the tutelage of Bernice Neugarten, one of her close friends at the University of Chicago's Committee on Human Development. After all, the University of Chicago was the place where the study of disengagement, and the book *Growing Old* that so influenced me, had originated. Professor Kushner reassured me that my studies in Chicago would offer much greater focus on social and environmental factors in aging than my clinical master's program. She noted the strong impact of sociologists at the University of Chicago in the field of sociological theory.

I now embarked on a ten-hour journey by Greyhound bus with my new husband, Boaz, to visit Chicago. He too had applied to the same doctoral program. The bus was hot, the trip was exhausting, and I arrived with swollen ankles, walking slowly and feeling pretty old. Once we arrived, no one was surprised by our interest in aging. Apparently, Rose Kushner's recommendation mattered and, to our pleasant surprise, we were both accepted into the human development PhD program and offered fellowships.

The University of Chicago:
Pioneering Optimism in the New Field of Gerontology

The mid-1960s were heady days for gerontology, with this nascent field gaining great momentum. Publications were appearing regularly during this period about the promises and hazards of growing old. I was assigned to work as a research assistant with both Robert Havighurst and Bernice Neugarten.

From the perspectives of these now-legendary social scientists, late life held a great deal of promise. They were interested in debunking long-held views in the medical literature about psychological problems associated with menopause or with old age. I fast-forward forty years to the 2014 special issue of *The Gerontologist* on "successful aging" and note that Havighurst is credited as the gerontologist who coined the term.[4] I can still see the imposing figure of my elderly professor and hear his optimistic depiction of leisure pursuits that older adults actively engage in as they seek "life satisfaction." In retrospect, it seems that the ideas and concepts of disability in later life and the social reaction to people with varied impairments were not a subject of interest or discussion at this early stage of the field of gerontology. Optimism about old age precluded meaningful consideration of the challenges many seniors faced as they grew older.

Such a positive view of aging was echoed in the work of Ethel Shanas, a professor at the University of Illinois. She guest-lectured in our classes and described the encouraging findings of her longitudinal study on the health of older people.[5] There is a single entry about impairments and disability in her book. It highlights the rare occurrence of problems that may interfere with daily function among normal elderly. Shanas's findings were echoed a decade later in the Duke longitudinal studies of normal aging that described high-functioning older people.[6]

We also read the important treatise *Aging: Some Social and Biological Aspects* by Nathan Shock, and James E. Birren's *Handbook on Aging and the Individual*.[7] Disability was not addressed by these early authors. There were debates during our class discussions about debunking the disengagement theory and articulating the activity theory of aging. I honestly do not remember much discussion of illness, frailty, or disability associated with old age during my Chicago days. Perhaps this optimistic perspective on aging also reflected the confidence of America before President John F. Kennedy was assassinated.

However, this upbeat view of late life was incongruent with my personal experience as a summer intern in 1964 at a Chicago area Veterans Administration Hospital, where I was exposed to elderly patients experiencing memory loss and physical ailments. They were housed in segregated units specially reserved for the old and the frail, where they received substandard care by jaded and seldom-present psychiatrists. I was particularly disturbed by my encounter with a newly admitted elderly patient, Mr. Brown. He wandered away from the home he shared with his children in Chicago and later tried to take a cab to go back home. When he could not recall his own address the cab took him to the police station and, based on lack of information about contacting his family, he was sent to the mental hospital. His children ultimately reported him missing and were able to locate him. They came to the hospital to pick him up and take him home, but were dissuaded from doing so in order to have him receive treatment. When I first met Mr. Brown, he was a friendly and well-groomed elderly man. He thanked me for the good care he was going to receive to improve his memory. I visited him on several occasions as he was warehoused with other aged patients and received only custodial care. After spending two months at the hospital, he became incontinent and assumed an unkempt appearance. He no longer seemed to look forward to my visits. When I asked him what seems to be the problem, he responded, "If they treat you like a pig, you become one!" I was shocked by this encounter and soon thereafter I learned that Mr. Brown had passed away. His experience haunted me and I could only wish that his family had insisted on taking him home.

Becoming a Researcher:
Questioning Segregation of the Aged

Following this internship, I began asking questions about the scientific rationale for the practice of segregating older patients in special units that I had observed at the Chicago Veterans Administration Hospital. When no rationale was forthcoming, I decided to investigate the impact of age segregation on elderly psychiatric patients—a topic that would become my doctoral dissertation. My gerontological mentors at the University of Chicago did not find my topic to be of great interest, however. It took considerable effort, including letters of encouragement from nationally known gerontologists Robert Butler and M. Powell Lawton, to persuade Professor Neugarten that I should stake my professional future on a study of mentally ill or "disabled" older adults.

I must acknowledge that my focus was less on the impairments that landed these unfortunate old people at a psychiatric hospital and more on the injustice of their being forgotten by their families and the health care establishment. Why were these people warehoused and segregated? Could I find out if this established mode of treatment carried any benefits?

In the end, I conducted my study on the effects of age segregation on the psychological well-being of elderly patients who were newly admitted to a psychiatric hospital. I was helped in this process by a geriatric psychiatrist, Jerome Grunes. I received permission to randomly assign newly admitted elderly patients either to a geriatric ward (the standard practice) or to a regular ward that included many young patients. Conducting the study without any outside funding was a tall order, and my husband conducted many of the 120 interviews called for in the research design. This was the first of our career-long collaborations. My study took me outside the gerontological comfort zone of the Chicago school, as it focused on older adults with disabilities rather than on the "normal aged" who were the primary concern of gerontological theorizing at the time. I did not realize it until much later, but I was taking my first step into the domain of disability studies focusing on the elderly.

The age segregation study in the psychiatric hospital yielded unequivocal results. Those elderly patients who were assigned to age-segregated wards fared significantly worse than their counterparts who were assigned to age-integrated units. My observations revealed that there were many more social workers and visitors on those wards that were designated for younger patients. Patients on wards housing the young were also far more likely to be discharged after only a brief stay. In contrast, on the geriatric ward, patients were rarely discharged. They were expected to live out their remaining days sitting in rocking chairs, staring into space, and often becoming incontinent due to lack of toileting services. This study also revealed that the hospital found it more convenient to segregate disabled elderly people—and, consequently, made no accommodations to situate these patients into a more humane environment.

My early enthusiasm about the potential benefits of changing the structural features of institutional care was met with disappointment when I encountered the realities of policy and practice. Although my dissertation won an award and the study was published in both the *Journal of Abnormal Psychology* and the *Journal of Orthopsychiatry,* major gerontological publications showed little interest.[8] A few years after my findings were published, I was invited back to give a lecture at the very facility where I had conducted research demonstrating the benefits of age integration. The invitation was based on my "important research" in the field. When I inquired about the current status of elderly patient integration or segregation, I was informed that there was now increased interest in developing new programs for older patients. Consequently, I was told, the psychiatric hospital had hired a geriatric director and staff who specialized in aging. The administration had concluded that dispersing elderly patients throughout the hospital and integrating them with younger patients would undercut the efforts of these newly recruited geriatric specialists. Thus, the hospital continued to segregate elderly patients—and I learned the hard lesson that research findings seldom guide prevailing practice and social policy.[9]

The St. Louis Years: Focus on Humanizing Institutional Care

In 1966, three years after Boaz and I started graduate school, Boaz had almost completed his dissertation and he was offered a job as an assistant professor at Washington University in St. Louis in the Departments of Psychology and Psychiatry. Still writing my dissertation[10] and also expecting our first child, I did not get a tenure-track job. However, through connections and the recommendation of Professor Neugarten, I found a position as a research associate at the Medical Care Research Center at Washington University, working with a highly productive and insightful medical sociologist, Rodney Coe.

Working with Dr. Coe opened up new vistas for me in the field of sociology and medical care and enabled me to continue to study the lives of older people in an environmental context. As part of my job, I also began working at the Ida Rosenblatt Center of the local Jewish home for the aged. There, I discovered that the staff knew little about the past lives and self-conceptions of the older people they cared for. In collaboration with Dr. Coe, I published a paper on the divergence between self and staff conceptions of the institutionalized aged.[11]

Although our findings showed that these older adults typically had both physical and mental infirmities, they seldom referred to these disabilities when articulating their self-concepts. This was the first evidence I had encountered in my research that older adults are not prone to adopt a disability-based identity. Instead, they defined themselves in terms of their previous social roles: "a skillful seamstress "or "a devoted father." On the basis of this research, the facility instituted a program to teach staff about finding out the three most important things that defined the identity of each resident. This knowledge enabled the building of bridges between staff and residents. Staff members would now know that their patients had once held distinct jobs and social roles, and could find examples from their own lives to connect to their patients' experiences. Reflecting my deep concern about the treatment of frail and mentally vulnerable older adults, I published several articles on the humane treatment of older people in nursing homes and other health care institutions.[12] I also received my first NIH-funded grant at this time and established the ECRC.

During this early period, there was a growing stream of research emanating from the medical literature and reflecting the nascent field of geriatric medicine. Much of this work sought to measure physical impairments and medical infirmities of late life. Indeed, this was the era when Sidney Katz, Amasa Ford, and colleagues developed and published in *JAMA* the Index of ADL, a standardized measure to assess functioning in disabled older adults.[13] This index, which measures basic abilities to perform activities of daily living such as dressing and transferring, has later become ubiquitous in gerontological assessments of disability.

Moving to Detroit: Focus on Person-Environment Fit

Although Boaz was well situated at Washington University, he was concerned about my career and thought it was important for me to obtain a tenure-track job. In 1971, after five years in St. Louis, Boaz and I were both offered new positions in Detroit. Our job offers in Detroit stemmed from a chance encounter between psychology faculty members at Oakland University in Rochester, Michigan, where they were searching for a new department chair, and Alvin Rose, chair of the Sociology Department at Wayne State University. After a whirlwind visit, we were offered attractive positions. Boaz was recruited as chair of the Psychology Department at Oakland University. I was invited to join as a tenured associate professor of sociology and move my ECRC to Wayne State University.

My interest in theory developed during this era of my research career when I focused on environmental influences on the well-being of older people. This orientation was anchored in ecological approaches that link human welfare and social behavior in later life to person-environment interactions.[14] My new work recognized that adjustment of older residents in long-term care institutions depended on the congruence between their needs and preferences in salient areas and the environmental features and demands that were either consistent or inconsistent with their needs and preferences.

The initial insight about this theory came through my lived experience in caring for my mother, Sari. She retired from her position as a bookkeeper to help care for our children in 1970. She still maintained a separate home just around the corner, but spent her days immersed in caring for our two sons. Sari was a self-educated Holocaust survivor—a strong independent person. Nevertheless, she experienced great discomfort as she encountered health challenges in later life. When she was briefly hospitalized after our move to Detroit, I tried to secure a private room for her. She vehemently protested that she did not want the private room—she wanted to have a roommate. But why? The answer was unexpected. Sari wanted another person in the room who could be a witness to any mistreatment she might receive from hospital staff. The forced dependency of the patient role, along with her feelings of physical vulnerability, brought back old memories of the Holocaust and the ghetto and of being at the mercy of people she could not trust.

Sari's reaction to hospitalization made me question the conventional wisdom about optimal care environments for all older patients.[15] The standard practice, in both acute and long-term care facilities, did not take into account individual differences in needs and preferences. I began studying the benefits of matching environments to the specific needs of the aged. This research laid the groundwork for my theory of person-environment fit. I termed this new framework the *congruence model of person-environment fit*.[16]

To test my model, I designed an empirical study aimed at identifying and analyzing the most important dimensions of the physical and social environments of long-term care settings—the specific dimensions where a good person-environment fit would be particularly beneficial to residents. With funding from the NIH, I conducted research at three institutions for the elderly and found that maximizing the fit between residents' personal preferences and their environmental setting, particularly in terms of privacy and stimulation, benefited residents by improving morale.[17] Thus, for example, older adults who preferred a quiet environment appeared to become distraught when bombarded with stimulating programs and activities of the institution. Several of my PhD students, including Barbara Felton, Asuman Kiyak, and Zev Harel, developed dissertations related to this framework. Each has subsequently forged productive careers in the field of gerontology. The congruence model of person-environment fit has endured the test of time and remains my most cited theoretical framework.

This work on environmental influences was timely for gerontology in the early 1970s. My research fit within the general interest in the role of environmental design in facilitating the aging process. Housing for the elderly became an important topic, with architects Leon Pastelan, Tom Byerts, and their colleagues using environmental design to facilitate successful aging.[18] Today, I can recognize how close the field of gerontology came during this era to proposing accommodations for persons with disabilities during late life, although we did not consciously relate our efforts to the study of disability. We recognized that elderly persons represented a vulnerable population, and were impressed by the potential of environmental interventions to enable frail older adults to fulfill their human potential and to retain their human dignity. Yet we lacked the indignation that has been palpable in disability studies about the absence of universal design that is so vital to continued independence and identity maintenance among elders with disabilities.

The next thirteen years of our professional careers (1971–1984) were spent in Detroit. With my mother's help, we raised two academically oriented sons and were immersed in our research careers. We did get a taste of the world of gerontological practice and innovation as Boaz and I took university-based study tours to explore innovative programs serving the elderly in Scandinavia and in other Western countries.

The Focus on Informal Caregiving to Help Dependent Elders: A New Gerontology for the 1980s

As the 1970s were coming to a close, the gerontological zeitgeist was increasingly attentive to challenges posed by frail elderly. Elderly persons were considered to be a growing social problem and were being objectified as clients, at times with little sensitivity to their human qualities. The emergence of the aging network (discussed in Chapter 9) had the unintended consequence of seeking outlets for the professional contributions of a new cadre of gerontological experts.[19] Critics of these health care and ancillary aging services began to examine unique power differentials that emerge during late life.[20] The focus of these political economy-based views were on disadvantages arising from race, class, and gender, with limited attention to disability as a source of social stratification.[21]

Dependency models of aging were also prevalent in gerontology at this time. These models centered on demands placed on society by service needs of frail older adults. Curiously, there was little attention to the needs and desires of physically or mentally impaired older adults. Psychologists were focused on developing assessment tools for measuring health, illness, and psychological well-being of older adults. Social workers were conducting needs assessment surveys. This era also generated growing interest from social scientists in professional and informal caregivers.[22] Research during this period was often patronizing of frail elderly clients, people who we might now term *disabled.*[23] Had there been greater communication between the aging and disability constituencies, these problems of objectification and social control may have come to light. In the field of gerontology in the early 1980s, growing attention was given to problems of cognitive impairment in late life. Concurrent with this interest, there was a great upsurge of research focused on perspectives of informal caregivers.[24]

It is important to recognize, through the lens of contemporary disability studies, that the people being cared for were generally not considered to be credible informants about their own disabilities. Social scientists worried that individuals experiencing cognitive impairment would not be able to provide reliable information, and this attitude extended to older adults with physical disabilities. This focus on objective assessments and disregard for lived experience in research in the early 1980s reflects the stigma that was associated with disabilities in late life.[25] Accordingly, caregivers increasingly became the proxies who offered information about the people they cared for. This pattern of learning, mainly through caregivers, about people with cognitive disabilities persists.

During this period, gerontological research also focused on the burdens experienced by caregivers. Our ECRC research team that included Rosalie Young also undertook a number of studies of caregiving.[26] An important theme in our research and conceptual work was the linked lives of caregivers and care receivers. In reviewing the literature on caregiving, we recognized that the dyadic aspects of caregiving were generally neglected. For example, in studies designed to explore spousal caregiving to cancer patients, the *care-*

giver was typically defined as the spouse who didn't have cancer.[27] Similarly, in other studies of patients with heart disease, the *caregiver* was defined as the spouse who didn't have heart disease, even though that person might also be a cancer patient. In other words, an individual might be both a caregiver and a care receiver with their own care needs.

This commonsense observation led me to question the unidimensional and unidirectional nature of the caregiving paradigm.[28] Our new research afforded an opportunity to study caregiving across the life course and to consider the diverse types of disability that may require caregiving. *Family Caregiving Across the Lifespan,* coauthored with David Biegel and May Wykle, documents this journey in evolving understandings about the complex interactions involved in caring for others.[29] Although I was onto something by recognizing the dyadic nature of caregiving, my studies still focused on the caregiver. The field of gerontology did not fully discover the importance of considering the perspectives of the care receiver until some twenty years later. It was much later research that finally gave voice to the lived experience of the disabled individual who is typically the receiver of care.[30]

Ushering in the 1990s: Looking at Coping and Human Agency in Confronting Stressors

In the 1990s, I began to address the problems posed by the limitations that appeared in environmental solutions to address problems of frail older individuals. It became evident that many older adults were being placed in nursing homes by family members, often with the support of professionals, once they could not manage independent living. While greater support to facilitate continued community living would have been optimal, this support typically was not forthcoming. The optimism I had felt as a graduate student about the potential benefits of improving institutional environments for older adults was met with disappointment when I encountered the realities of policy and practice. I saw little evidence that calls to humanize health care institutions would result in major reforms. There appeared to be many impediments to offering humane care in institutional settings, ranging from limited training of staff to high staff turnover and ultimately to cost cutting in the care of "obsolete" human beings.[31]

During this stage in our careers, Boaz and I once again began to collaborate on research. His long-standing interest in psychological coping mechanisms influenced my own thinking about options for older adults who were being poorly served by their informal or professional caregivers and, as a result, were forced to become self-reliant in performing illness-related adaptive tasks.[32] Turning attention from the environment to the individual, we began to explore the efforts of elderly patients to cope with the stressors of institutional living.[33] This approach diverged from the gerontological focus of the 1970s and 1980s, an era when dependency models were popular.[34]

There was growing concern in the 1980s with the biological processes that put the elderly at risk for developing chronic illnesses. Because such illnesses often result in physical impairments, gerontologists during this period engaged in extensive efforts to assess functional limitations in older adults' activities of daily living.[35] The gerontological literature published numerous studies focusing on these disabling limitations and the responsibilities of the growing aging network to provide care for frail and dependent elderly persons.

Following an alternative paradigm, Boaz and I began to focus on human agency in the face of stressful life circumstances and iatrogenic environments. This new emphasis coincided with the ascendancy of stress theoretical formulations, exemplified by the work of Leonard Pearlin on stressful life events that call for adaptation by individuals who confront stressors.[36] This new orientation is reflected in *Stress and Health Among the Elderly*.[37] We conducted a longitudinal study at fourteen health care institutions, with a focus on ways that newly admitted residents cope with the stressors of institutional life. We were interested in identifying individual adaptations that resulted in desirable post-institutional outcomes such as high self-esteem and life satisfaction. Our study revealed that residents who used instrumental adaptations were most likely to maintain their psychological well-being in restrictive institutional environments.

Looking back at these findings with my current understanding of the disability movement, I now realize that disabled older adults living in long-term care facilities had to marshal their social and psychological resources to make their voices heard and at least informally demand some accommodations to make their lives bearable. Thus, it appears clear that older adults living in long-term care facilities are helpless without the broader disability advocacy pioneered by the disability studies movement.[38]

Arriving in Cleveland:
Grasping Challenges of Living with Disability

We undertook our last major career move in 1984. Boaz was offered a position at Cleveland State University and I was recruited by Case Western Reserve University. Our sons, Jeffrey and Michael, started college at Case Western Reserve University at this time. Jeffrey's interests in both gerontology and in policy studies were also influenced during this period by his work with Robert Binstock, which resulted in a coauthored critique of Daniel Callahan's book *Setting Limits*.[39]

My mother, Sari, was getting older and more frail and moved into our home after our relocation to Cleveland. Jeffrey and Michael, who each had a close relationship with Sari, participated eagerly and lovingly in her care. Close association with Sari became a critical influence in our family's insights into the lived experience of older persons with disabilities. Through firsthand encounters with her medical challenges, and later through her life as an amputee, Jeffrey and I (as well as Boaz and Michael) discovered the limitations of our health care system in meeting the needs of older adults with disabilities (a discovery that is discussed in greater detail in Chapter 8). I also witnessed the power of older adults to use their proactivity to lead meaningful lives, even in the face of major disability. Such proactivity was most effective, however, when exercised within environments responsive to the unique needs of the disabled person.

After our arrival in Cleveland, it took the next thirty years to bring together seemingly disparate observations from our research on successful aging among healthy older people with our deeper understanding of the lived experience of late-life disability. After completing college at Case Western Reserve University, Jeffrey and Michael left home and went on to graduate schools. Jeffrey finished law school and earned a PhD in policy history during this period. Michael completed a PhD in psychology. They each embarked on independent careers. Both of our sons married and had families of their own, each family including a child with special needs. This is when Jeffrey and I recognized an important convergence between our separate interests in gerontology and disability studies. But now I return to the chronology of our research endeavors.

Boaz's work and my funded research program in the mid-1980s were centered on the strengths and resilience of older adults, but our daily lives were also increasingly focused on caring for my disabled mother. Additionally, over the years our own encounters with serious illness episodes and disability contributed to evolving our understanding of convergence between gerontology and disability studies. No amount of quantitative gerontological research could inform these understandings. They had to emerge from a deeper level of knowing that can be achieved only through lived experience.[40]

Our forays into the fields of stress, coping, and adaptation were the focus of our funded research during these years. Many of our observations draw on a twenty-year follow-up study of originally healthy older adults. This series of studies resulted in my second major theoretical framework developed in collaboration with Boaz: that of preventive and corrective proactivity (PCP).[41] Parallel to our NIH-funded research, I also describe here a separate line of unfunded but published investigations and observations that were based on my personal experiences during a long period of caring for Sari. They were further informed by challenging illnesses and disability that Boaz, Jeffrey, and I encountered in our own lives. In my narrative I also continue to refer to trends in the field of gerontology that serve as a backdrop to our journey.

Proactivity as the Engine of Successful Aging: Implications for Addressing Disability

During the late 1980s, our research focused primarily on factors that led to wellness in old age and those coping strategies that served to buffer the harmful effects of stress and illness. This appreciation of resilience in the face of stressors was broadly referred to as *successful aging*. Our interest in this line of research was connected to the perception that individuals played a critical role in navigating their environments. The stress paradigm provided a framework to understand how people responded to cumulative stressors across the life course.[42]

This segment of my intellectual journey included studies related to a broad range of stressors. Notable among these studies was a project on late-life adaptation of survivors of the Nazi Holocaust.[43] This study with Boaz and Zev Harel as principal investigators alerted us to the influences of stress and trauma, endured long before old age, on later-life well-being. This research also sensitized us to consideration of lifelong and core disabilities, a topic seldom addressed in the field of gerontology.[44] Cumulative stress, akin to cumulative disadvantage, leaves an indelible mark that accompanies individuals and their families throughout the life course.[45]

Late-life relocation—the decision made by people over age sixty to change their permanent residence, often to a new and unfamiliar environment—represented a new area for Boaz and my research. Our studies of adaptation by individuals to stress extended to consideration of stressors posed by such late-life relocation. Although this research did not directly focus on disability, it played an important role in the evolution of my thinking. We found that voluntary relocation to retirement communities was welcomed by older adults in our study and even improved the health of respondents.[46] The lesson from this research was that self-determination for older people buttressed their overall well-being, a lesson familiar to the disability community. As I described the positive effect of voluntary relocation for older adults, questions were raised about the viability of such new lifestyles for older adults who may become increasingly frail and may experience disabilities.

To answer these questions, I formulated a proposal with Boaz on "Adaptation to Frailty Among Dispersed Elders" that was funded in 1990 as a Method to Extend Research in Time (MERIT) Award study by NIA. Based on the opportunity to conduct annual interviews with the 1,000 older adults recruited for our study, we now had a firsthand opportunity to gain a better understanding of the disablement process.[47] Here we return to the *disability cascade* associated with late life. This formulation describes how chronic illnesses, which reflect normative stressors of late life, result in physical impairments that subsequently translate into functional limitations.[48]

The study of Adaptation to Frailty has been the central focus of my work since the 1990s and has often been referred to as the Florida Retirement Study.[49] The research included several independently funded research projects that afforded me an opportunity to conduct twenty annual follow-ups (1990–2010) with our panel of initially healthy persons age seventy-two or older.[50] A unique feature of the study was the ability to follow participants even if they moved to live closer to their children or entered institutional facilities.

Study participants were interviewed in their own homes by a trained interviewer. A semi-structured questionnaire was used that covered information about demographics; health status, including physical impairments; functional limitations; and subjective rated health. Questions were also asked about early life crises, recent stressful life events, social connectedness and social supports, psychological coping strategies and resources, and indicators of social and psychological well-being. Respondents were also queried about whether they considered themselves to be disabled.

During the initial years of this longitudinal study, it was surprising to learn that respondents remained hale and hearty and portrayed little evidence of new physical impairments or functional limitations. Many older adult amenity movers pursued healthy and active lifestyles at the Florida retirement community. They developed close friendships with their neighbors, initiated healthier diets, and engaged in volunteer activities. Yet with the passing of time, there was increased evidence of chronic illnesses and attendant physical impairments. However, respondents did not follow a clear trajectory leading to increasing disability. For many, periods of ill health were followed by recovery. Others experienced alternating episodes of wellness and frailty. There was a discernible effort by study participants to not focus on their disabilities. Sometimes, even in the face of obvious disabilities, respondents declared that they had good health and did not view themselves as disabled. Most of the participants endeavored to cling to their lifelong identity as a well person.

We began an exploration in collaboration with Elaine Borawski and Jennifer Kinney of physical, psychological, and social determinants of health appraisals.[51] This investigation reflected the gerontological insight that individuals' definition of their health status may be more important for good quality of life than their objective health conditions.[52] Based on open-ended responses that reflected self-appraisals of their health status, we subdivided our sample into health optimists, health realists, and health pessimists. *Health optimists* are individuals who evaluate their health as more favorable than warranted by the number of chronic health conditions, the number of medications, and the degree of pain and shortness of breath experienced.

Health pessimists, on the other hand, overestimated their health problems. *Health realists* showed the greatest congruence between indicators of objective health status and their subjective attributions. Our findings confirmed our expectations that health optimism serves a protective role, as health optimists were significantly less likely to die three years later than were health pessimists given the same level of objective health problems. These data sensitized us to the realization that positive attitudes and self-concepts can go a long way toward protecting older adults from the ill effects of disability. Here, I began to see a point of departure between older adults who develop disabilities in late life and the young disabled who readily adopt a disability identity.[53] Unlike individuals described in the disability studies literature, the older adults in our study did not choose to associate with other persons facing similar disabilities. They also engaged in limited advocacy for themselves and did not generally seek to take advantage of entitlements that their health condition would have merited. It is important to note that the retirement community where respondents lived boasted on big billboards that it was a "community for active seniors." Furthermore, there were no transportation, meal, or household assistance services offered in this setting.

In a paper coauthored with Jessica Kelley-Moore, we further explored what factors contribute to older adults assuming a disability identity. Respondents were asked to rate themselves, based on the extent to which they considered themselves as disabled. These self-appraisals reflected perceived disability. Our studies reflected gerontological interest in linking subjective evaluations of older adults about emerging functional limitations and objectively confirmed disability status.[54]

We found that the number of chronic illnesses, functional limitations, and cognitive impairments served as a significant predictor of developing an identity as a disabled person. Service needs that threaten independent function, such as requiring home care and driving cessation, contributed to considering oneself as disabled. Interestingly, social factors also influenced self-perceptions of disability independent of physical health-related factors. We found that having a dense social network delayed the assumption of disability identity whereas having a high level of health anxiety accelerated this process. These findings point to the complex forces that play a role in older persons' viewing themselves as disabled.

Most of the respondents in our long-term follow-up study managed to retain high levels of life satisfaction and continued to show good psychological well-being over time. Respondents tended to take an active role in dealing with challenges and problem situations that they confronted. It is noteworthy that the vast majority of older adults in our study continued their participation with little loss to follow-up over time. Those who dropped out of the study did so due to severe health decline or mortality.[55] Those individuals who needed more extensive assistance typically received care from their spouses. Some respondents requiring greater assistance moved to live closer to their children or to enter continuing care retirement facilities, assisted living, or, as a last resort, nursing homes.[56]

Overall our findings pointed to a group of older adults who were able to maintain life satisfaction and psychological well-being in the face of increasing social losses and disabling health conditions. We explored the personal and social resources and modes of coping that could contribute to resilience of older adults. Based on following this sample, we developed our theory of Preventive and Corrective Proactivity (PCP).[57]

There are unique and innovative features about the proactive aging model and how it applies to the study of late-life disability. Unlike previous models that define successful aging based on good outcomes, such as being healthy, wealthy, and wise, the proactivity model allows for process-based definitions of success.[58] Accordingly, even older persons who live with disabilities can have a place at the table of successful aging. We argue that, in spite of the stressors of chronic illness and social losses, older persons can maintain psychological and social well-being if they possess and can mobilize needed resources.

The old-age related stressors that we considered include chronic illnesses resulting in physical impairments and disabilities, social losses, and lack of person-environment fit. Absence of person-environment fit is generally a function of disabling health problems that interact with unsuitable environmental characteristics. Thus, for example, older adults living with arthritis experienced a lack of person-environment fit if their housing required walking up stairs.

The major engine of successful aging is based on preventive and corrective behavioral adaptations that older adults engage in to reduce and delay stressors and to ameliorate negative consequences of stressors. Preventive proactive adaptations include health promotion, helping others, and planning ahead. These behaviors can help delay disablement. Corrective adaptations come into play once stressors, including the development of functional limitations, have already occurred. Corrective adaptations include marshaling support and environmental or activity modifications. Thus, maintenance of good quality of life presupposes both social and environmental supports and human agency.

It is important to acknowledge that the necessity of taking action on their own behalf can place the full burden of adaptation on older adults who are encountering disabilities. This conceptual approach is consistent with Paul B. Baltes and Margret M. Baltes's popular model that focuses on the individual's role in accommodating disabilities through selective optimization with compensation.[59] Thus, gerontological theory is focused on the need for accommodations, but does not take the next step of demanding those accommodations through social services or public policy.[60]

In terms of personal resources, we consider external resources based on availability of finances and social supports. Accordingly, older people experiencing disabilities could purchase transportation and home care services and utilize help from family members or friends and neighbors to continue living independently. We also considered psychological resources including optimism, high self-esteem, and altruistic orientations as contributing to adapting well in the face of normative stressors of aging. Providing older people with access to social resources resonated well with arguments of disability studies scholars that demand resources instead of pity.[61] It also acknowledges that inequality does impact elders' final years as they encounter disabilities.[62]

Our research has found support for elements of the preventive and corrective proactivity theory of successful aging. Health promotion in the form of exercise and healthful diets was found to contribute to maintenance of better physical health, as well as psychological well-being, delaying onset of disability over time.[63] We also found support for the value of volunteering and helping others as contributing to psychological well-being and, in particular, positive affect over time.[64] Furthermore, we found that stressors, including those posed by chronic illness and physical impairments, in the absence of proactive adaptations lead to reduced psychological well-being. However, preventive adaptations (e.g., planning ahead) and corrective adaptations (e.g., marshaling support) serve to mobilize existing social and psychological resources and to ameliorate the negative effects of health-related stressors. This, in turn, results in improved psychological well-being and enhanced social activities that reflect inclusion by disabled elders in the social sphere over time.[65] Recent research by other investigators, who used qualitative methodologies for studying elders living with HIV/AIDS, also found support for our PCP model.[66]

As respondents in our longitudinal study grew to be very old, we became interested in factors that shape quality of life as people live their final years. We recently completed a study funded by the National Institute of Nursing Research (NINR) that illuminates the reluctance of elders to plan for end-of-life care. We discovered that older adults have few conversations with their doctors and even with members of their family about end-of-life care. Nevertheless, elders are concerned about future care planning in the hope that they will receive responsive care from physicians and other health care providers.[67] Our findings also offered us an exciting translational opportunity for providing older adults with resources and skill sets that can activate support and responsive care from health care providers.

As we situate the theory of proactive aging in trends within gerontological scholarship, we appear to be on track. Successful aging has become a key concept highlighted in gerontological analysis with a special issue of *The Gerontologist* dedicated to the subject.[68] The topic of disability has finally made its way into a major handbook on social gerontology.[69] Yet the voices of older adults with disabilities remain curiously absent in the gerontological literature. The American Sociological Association now has a section on Disability and Society (inaugurated in 2011). Until recently, few gerontologists joined this section. I have become an active member, as I bear witness to the graying of disability. How can one explain this divide between gerontology and disability studies? Searching for the answer to this question brings me back to our personal narrative and paves the way for a parallel chapter in our personal and intellectual journey.

Lived Experience as a Roadway to Discovering Links Among Aging, Resilience, and Disability

Soon after joining the Sociology Department at Case Western Reserve University in 1984, I started an interdisciplinary research collaboration with Dr. Kurt Stange, a young MD/PhD in the Department of Family Medicine. Kurt was our new family doctor and, during a medical visit, I asked him to look over a questionnaire we had designed for interviewing physicians. To my surprise he replied that, in exchange for his research feedback, he wanted to learn about the work of the ECRC and attend our weekly conferences. Kurt's visits evolved into a boundary-crossing doctor-patient initiative that offered greater focus on the health care partnerships forged by older adults who are facing disabling health conditions. Kurt also encouraged me to venture into participant observations and narratives that could better describe health care experiences of older people.

I felt empowered by Kurt's encouragement to utilize our own health care experiences as the raw material for building better sociological understandings of disability; health care; health communication; and the interconnectedness of doctors, patients, and family caregivers. One example of my new and more activist orientation to research was based on the changing landscape of health insurance. Boaz and I were notified in the beginning of the 1990s that we were no longer covered to receive health care at the hospital affiliated with our university. I enlisted two graduate students to help design and conduct a study examining the impact of forced discontinuity in health care on patient satisfaction. We found that discontinuity of care undermined patient satisfaction.[70]

Imperceptibly, my willingness to enter into the lifeworld of the older patient brought me closer to the health care activism that had long characterized the disability studies movement.[71] I slowly came to recognize that collecting objective information about characteristics and actions of older persons is insufficient for gaining an in-depth understanding of the nature and meaning of disability.

Dr. Kurt Stange contributed to my insights and to our family's well-being in another important way. He cared for my mother during her eight-year struggle with diabetes that resulted in her becoming an amputee. Sari now lived with us after her initial leg amputation, and we got to learn in much greater depth about both the suffering and the great resilience of older people living with serious disabilities. One unexpected discovery related to the unresponsiveness of the health care system to the very real needs of disabled older adults to maintain independence and live with dignity.

The impetus for my first study that focused on late-life disability came about after I shared our frustrations with professional rehabilitation encountered by Sari as an amputee with her doctor and my colleague, Kurt. I told him about the absence of creative approaches to help disabled elderly persons to remain actively engaged in the outside world and retain their independence. Kurt identified this as a neglected area of research that could be greatly informed by firsthand observations. He encouraged me to apply to the agency that is now the National Institute on Disability, Independent Living, and Rehabilitation Research to study elderly patient-initiated environmental modifications and adaptive device use. I went home and started writing feverishly. I consulted daily with Sari in this process and solicited her ideas and input. I was delighted to learn that my grant application was funded as a Mary Switzer Distinguished Fellowship. In this project, eighty-two-year-old grandma Sari with her many creative ideas, sitting in her wheelchair, became an active (though unofficial) collaborator.[72] Findings of this study are described in detail in Chapter 6.

I also brought these new understandings from my close observations of late life with disabilities to our NIH-funded longitudinal study of adaptation to frailty in late life. We now asked respondents in this larger study who were living with disabilities to describe any environmental or activity modifications initiated by them or by their family caregivers. We learned from open-ended interviews with older adults in our study that environmental modifications offering comfort and independence were most highly valued by patients. This was in marked contrast with both caregiver and professional orientations. The latter were mainly focused on maintaining safety of older adults, often at the expense of comfort and independence.

These discoveries led me to develop an interest in exploring disability from the perspective of the disability studies movement. I discovered that some of the most perceptive portrayals of the full human potential of persons with disabilities are offered by people who can reflect on the lived experience of disability.[73] I recognized that formal studies of disability that use anthropological orientations and qualitative methods can also enrich our understanding of late-life disability. I found such an example in Samantha Solemeo's in-depth interviews with older adults living with Parkinson's disease and with their spouses.[74]

Several further family encounters with the health care system sparked my interest in the challenges faced by older patients with disabilities in communicating with their health care providers in the context of the contemporary health care system.[75] In 2000, my husband, Boaz, encountered a serious illness requiring major surgery. We found limited assistance for finding the surgeons most experienced with the procedure that he needed. It required careful library research to learn about our best options. We recognized that patients and caregivers must engage in assertive advocacy, based on skillful information gathering, to maximize chances for a good medical outcome. We found that the most experienced medical team was in a major city on the East Coast and traveled out of town to obtain the surgery.

After successful surgery, Boaz had to maintain a restricted diet. If his diet included too much fat, he could quickly land in the emergency room. This need brought home the unique challenges of living with invisible disabilities. Traveling and eating out in restaurants now became a major challenge, requiring planning and preparation. Once again, communication and assertiveness became key elements of coping successfully. We had to learn to reject food that appeared unsuitable and make our needs clear to servers. We also needed to master challenges of travel for older adults living with disabilities. Challenges in this area made us appreciate the importance of the ADA and ongoing problems in its full implementation.[76]

We were increasingly motivated and comfortable in translating our lived experiences with illness and disability into our professional work. Our research was now increasingly centered on patient perspectives. We conducted a series of studies to explore illness adaptations considering the patient's vantage point. Some of our conceptual approaches built on notions of health care consumerism, pioneered by medical sociologist Marie Haug.[77] Focusing on elderly cancer patients, we considered determinants of patient well-being, based on patient initiative, assertiveness, and confidence in communication.[78] This research resulted in the formulation of a conceptual framework focused on the active roles in care-getting that patients can and often must assume.[79]

Our research findings have also provided an opportunity for turning to translational research that could make a positive difference in the lives of older adults and particularly in helping the disabled and disadvantaged. Jeffrey's focus on macro issues, including the evolution of social policy to benefit the aged, the disabled, and the poor, has been most influential in this new direction. As Jeffrey became codirector of the Center on Aging and Social Policy at Mount Saint Mary College along with his colleague Lawrence Force, they conducted an NIA-funded study of program initiatives at Area Agencies on Aging (AAAs). This study was instrumental in bringing us closer to intervention research. Our first, still ongoing, National Cancer Institute (NCI) funded intervention study is an educational program to help older adults who attend diverse AAAs senior centers communicate better with their doctors. In a randomized control trial (RCT), we teach older adults to speak up to their doctors to obtain better cancer prevention and screening services.

Intergenerational Connections to Linking Gerontology and Disability Studies

Boaz and I are gratified to see that our professional and personal journeys have converged in ways that offer new insights into late-life disability. My mother died in 1994, but her influence in our lives has continued as we seek honest answers about understanding and bettering the lives of older adults with disabilities. We now have the courage to recognize that gerontologists have not yet aligned their views of late-life disability with insights gained from the disability studies movement. I also realize that the orientations of disability studies are not aligned with self-conceptions of older adults who, after a lifetime of good health, gradually develop disabilities. The encouragement to connect the missing dots, instead of lamenting the lack of common ground between gerontology and disability studies, has come from Jeffrey's insights and urgings. He remained very close to his grandmother, Sari, throughout her battles to retain dignity and seek no pity until the end of her life.[80]

In this chapter, we elaborated on the insights gained by Eva about aging in relation to disability and the growing appreciation of disability studies perspectives in a long career of being a gerontologist. In the next chapter, we turn to the life course perspective as a context for understanding how the disability experience in later life can be shaped by earlier life experiences.

Notes

1. Carolyn Ellis, *Revision: Autoethnographic Reflections on Life and Work* (Routledge, 2009); Shulamit Reinharz, *Observing the Observer: Understanding Our Selves in Field Research* (Oxford University Press, 2010).

2. Elaine Cumming and William Earl Henry, *Growing Old: The Process of Disengagement* (Basic Books, 1961).

3. Ruth Bennett and Lucille Nahemow, "Institutional Totality and Criteria of Social Adjustment in Residences for the Aged," *Journal of Social Issues* 21, no. 4 (1965): 44–78.

4. Diane J. Martin and Laura L. Gillen, "Revisiting Gerontology's Scrapbook: From Metchnikoff to the Spectrum Model of Aging," *The Gerontologist* 54, no. 1 (2014): 51–58.

5. Ethel Shanas, *The Health of Older People: A Social Survey* (Harvard University Press, 1962).

6. Erdman Ballagh Palmore, *Normal Aging,* vol. 2: *Reports from the Duke Longitudinal Studies, 1970–1973* (Duke University Press, 1974).

7. Nathan Wetheril Shock, *Aging: Some Social and Biological Aspects* (Association for the Advancement of Science, 1960); James E. Birren, *Handbook of Aging and the Individual* (University of Chicago Press, 1959).

8. Boaz Kahana and Eva Kahana, "Changes in Mental Status of Elderly Patients in Age-Integrated and Age-Segregated Hospital Milieus," *Journal of Abnormal Psychology* 75, no. 2 (1970): 177; Eva F. Kahana and Boaz Kahana, "Effects of Age Segregation on Affective Expression of Elderly Psychiatric Patients," *American Journal of Orthopsychiatry* 38, no. 2 (1968): 317.

9. Some years later the eminent sociologist Matilda Riley would become an effective and respected champion of the benefits of age integration in the context of community dwelling and presumed healthy older adults.

10. I received my PhD in 1967.

11. Eva Kahana and Rodney M. Coe, "Self and Staff Conceptions of Institutionalized Aged," *The Gerontologist* 9, no. 4, Pt. 1 (1969): 264–267.

12. Eva Kahana, "Emerging Issues in Institutional Services for the Aging," *The Gerontologist* 11, no. 1, Pt. 1 (1971): 51–58; Eva Kahana, "The Humane Treatment of Old People in Institutions," *The Gerontologist* 13, no. 3, Pt. 1 (1973): 282–289.

13. Sidney Katz, Amasa B. Ford, Roland W. Moskowitz, Beverly A. Jackson, and Marjorie W. Jaffe, "Studies of Illness in the Aged: The Index of ADL: A Standardized Measure of Biological and Psychosocial Function," *JAMA* 185, no. 12 (1963): 914–919.

14. Irwin Altman, *The Environment and Social Behavior: Privacy, Personal Space, Territory, and Crowding* (Brooks/Cole, 1975).

15. Sari was a major intellectual influence in shaping my work on the well-being of older adults. She questioned the ultimate value of focusing on generating research publications, and asked me to explain how these ideas could ever be put to use in ways that would concretely benefit older adults.

16. Formulation of this theory was influenced by the work of field theorist Kurt Lewin and was also related to the later work of environmental gerontologist M. Powell Lawton. See Eva Kahana, "Matching Environments to Needs of the Aged: A Conceptual Scheme," in *Late Life: Communities and Environmental Policy,* ed. Jaber F. Gubrium (Thomas, 1974), 201–214.

17. Eva Kahana, Jersey Liang, and Barbara J. Felton, "Alternative Models of Person-Environment Fit: Prediction of Morale in Three Homes for the Aged," *Journal of Gerontology* 35, no. 4 (1980): 584–595.

18. Leon Pastelan and D. Carson, *Spatial Behavior of Older People* (Institute of Gerontology, University of Michigan, 1970).

19. Donald E. Gelfand, *The Aging Network: Programs and Services* (Springer, 2006).

20. Carroll L. Estes, *The Aging Enterprise* (Jossey-Bass, 1979).

21. Toni M. Calasanti, "Bringing in Diversity: Toward an Inclusive Theory of Retirement," *Journal of Aging Studies* 7, no. 2 (1993): 133–150.

22. Peter Messeri, Merril Silverstein, and Eugene Litwak, "Choosing Optimal Support Groups: A Review and Reformulation," *Journal of Health and Social Behavior* 34, no. 2 (1993): 122–137.

23. Ronald J. Berger, *Introducing Disability Studies* (Lynne Rienner, 2013).

24. S. Walter Poulshock and Gary T. Deimling, "Families Caring for Elders in Residence: Issues in the Measurement of Burden," *Journal of Gerontology* 39, no. 2 (1984): 230–239.

25. Joan Ablon, "Stigmatized Health Conditions," *Social Science and Medicine. Part B: Medical Anthropology* 15, no. 1 (1981): 5–9.

26. I conducted some of these projects in collaboration with Rosalie Young, who received her PhD while working with me at Wayne State University.

27. Eva Kahana and Rosalie Young, "Clarifying the Caregiving Paradigm: Challenges for the Future," in *Aging and Caregiving: Theory and Practice,* ed. David E. Biegel and Arthur Blum (Sage, 1990).

28. Ibid.

29. Eva Kahana, David E. Biegel, and May Wykle, *Family Caregiving Across the Lifespan,* vol. 4 (Sage, 1994).

30. Eva Kahana, Boaz Kahana, and May Wykle, "'Care-Getting': A Conceptual Model of Marshalling Support Near the End of Life," *Current Aging Science* 3, no. 1 (2010): 71–78.

31. Jules Henry, "Culture Against Man," *Science and Society* 29, no. 1 (1965): 116–121.

32. Rudolf H. Moos and Jeanne A. Schaefer, "The Crisis of Physical Illness," in *Coping with Physical Illness,* ed. Rudolf Moos (Springer, 1984), 3–25.

33. My new grant was "Adaptation of Older Adults in Institutional Living."

34. Margret M. Baltes, *The Many Faces of Dependency in Old Age* (Cambridge University Press, 1996).

35. Gerda G. Fillenbaum and Michael A. Smyer, "The Development, Validity, and Reliability of the OARS Multidimensional Functional Assessment Questionnaire," *Journal of Gerontology* 36, no. 4 (1981): 428–434.

36. Leonard I. Pearlin, "The Sociological Study of Stress," *Journal of Health and Social Behavior* 30, no. 3 (1989): 241–256.

37. May L. Wykle, Eva Kahana, and Jerome Kowal, *Stress and Health Among the Elderly* (Springer, 1992).

38. Richard Scotch, *From Good Will to Civil Rights: Transforming Federal Disability Policy* (Temple University Press, 2009).

39. Robert H. Binstock and Jeff Kahana, "Setting Limits: Medical Goals in an Aging Society," *The Gerontologist* 25, no. 3 (1988): 424–426.

40. Irving Kenneth Zola, *Missing Pieces: A Chronicle of Living with a Disability* (Temple University Press, 1982); Arthur W. Frank, "Reclaiming an Orphan Genre: The First-Person Narrative of Illness," *Literature and Medicine* 13, no. 1 (1994): 1–21.

41. Eva Kahana and Boaz Kahana, "Conceptual and Empirical Advances in Understanding Aging Well Through Proactive Adaptation" in *Adulthood and Aging: Research on Continuities and Discontinuities,* ed. Vern L. Bengtson (Springer,

1996); Eva Kahana, Boaz Kahana, and Kyle Kercher, "Emerging Lifestyles and Proactive Options for Successful Ageing," *Ageing International* 28, no. 2 (2003): 155–180.

42. Pearlin, "The Sociological Study of Stress."

43. Boaz Kahana, Zev Harel, and Eva Kahana, *Holocaust Survivors and Immigrants: Late Life Adaptations* (Springer Science and Business Media, 2007).

44. Lois M. Verbrugge, Kenzie Latham, and Philippa J. Clarke, "Aging with Disability for Midlife and Older Adults," *Research on Aging*, Special Issue (2017): 1–37.

45. Dale Dannefer, "Cumulative Advantage/Disadvantage and the Life Course: Cross-Fertilizing Age and Social Science Theory," *Journals of Gerontology Series B: Psychological Sciences and Social Sciences* 58, no. 6 (2003): S327–S337.

46. Eva Kahana, Mary Segall, James L. Vosmik, Boaz Kahana, and Kathryn P. Riley, "Motivators, Resources, and Barriers in Voluntary International Migration of the Elderly: The Case of Israel-Bound Aged," *Journal of Cross-Cultural Gerontology* 1, no. 2 (1986): 191–208.

47. Lois M. Verbrugge and Alan M. Jette, "The Disablement Process," *Social Science and Medicine* 38, no. 1 (1994): 1–14.

48. Ibid.

49. Kahana and Kahana, "Conceptual and Empirical Advances in Understanding Aging Well Through Proactive Adaptation."

50. Eva Kahana, Renee H. Lawrence, Boaz Kahana, Kyle Kercher, Amy Wisniewski, Eleanor Stoller, Jordan Tobin, and Kurt Stange, "Long-Term Impact of Preventive Proactivity on Quality of Life of the Old-Old," *Psychosomatic Medicine* 64, no. 3 (2002): 382–394.

51. Elaine A. Borawski, Jennifer M. Kinney, and Eva Kahana, "The Meaning of Older Adults' Health Appraisals: Congruence with Health Status and Determinant of Mortality," *Journals of Gerontology Series B: Psychological Sciences and Social Sciences* 51, no. 3 (1996): S157–S170.

52. Ellen L. Idler and Stanislav V. Kasl, "Self-Ratings of Health: Do They Also Predict Change in Functional Ability?" *Journals of Gerontology Series B: Psychological Sciences and Social Sciences* 50, no. 6 (1995): S344–S353.

53. Valerie Leiter, "Bowling Together: Foundations of Community Among Youth with Disabilities," in *Disability and Community*, ed. Allison C. Carey and Richard K. Scotch, Research in Social Science and Disability Series (Emerald, 2011), 3–25.

54. Eva Kahana, Jessica Kelley-Moore, and Boaz Kahana, "Proactive Aging: A Longitudinal Study of Stress, Resources, Agency, and Well-Being in Late Life," *Aging and Mental Health* 16, no. 4 (2012): 438–451; Jessica A. Kelley-Moore, John G. Schumacher, Eva Kahana, and Boaz Kahana, "When Do Older Adults Become 'Disabled'? Social snd Health Antecedents of Perceived Disability in a Panel Study of the Oldest Old," *Journal of Health and Social Behavior* 47, no. 2 (2006): 126–141.

55. Ibid.

56. Ibid.

57. Kahana and Kahana, "Conceptual and Empirical Advances in Understanding Aging Well Through Proactive Adaptation"; Eva Kahana and Boaz Kahana, "Contextualizing Successful Aging: New Directions in an Age-Old Search," in *Invitation to the Life Course: Toward New Understandings of Later Life* (Baywood, 2003), 225–255; Eva Kahana, Boaz Kahana, and Jeong Eun Lee, "Proactive Approaches to Successful Aging: One Clear Path Through the Forest," *Gerontology* 60, no. 5 (2014): 466–474.

58. Kahana, Kelley-Moore, and Kahana, "Proactive Aging."

59. Baltes and Baltes, "Psychological Perspectives on Successful Aging."

60. Scotch, *From Good Will to Civil Rights.*

61. Joseph P. Shapiro, *No Pity: People with Disabilities Forging a New Civil Rights Movement* (Three Rivers Press, 1994).

62. Corey M. Abramson, *The End Game* (Harvard University Press, 2015).

63. Kahana et al., "Long-Term Impact of Preventive Proactivity on Quality of Life of the Old-Old."

64. Eva Kahana, Tirth Bhatta, Loren D. Lovegreen, and Boaz Kahana, "Altruism, Helping, and Volunteering: Pathways to Well-Being in Late Life," *Journal of Aging and Health* 25, no. 1 (2013): 159–187.

65. Kahana, Kelley-Moore, and Kahana, "Proactive Aging."

66. Charles A. Emlet, Shakima Tozay, and Victoria H. Raveis, "'I'm Not Going to Die from the AIDS': Resilience in Aging with HIV Disease," *The Gerontologist* 51, no. 1 (2010): 101–111.

67. Jeffrey S. Kahana, Loren D. Lovegreen, and Eva Kahana, "Expanding the Time Frame for Advance Care Planning: Policy Considerations and Implications for Research," In *Geriatrics* (InTech, 2012).

68. Successful Aging, *The Gerontologist*, Special Issue, 55, no. 1 (2015), https://academic.oup.com/gerontologist/issue/55/1.

69. Jessica Kelley-Moore, "Disability and Ageing: The Social Construction of Causality," in *The Sage Handbook of Social Gerontology,* ed. Dale Dannefer and Chris Phillipson (Sage, 2010), 96–110.

70. Eva Kahana, Kurt Stange, Rebecca Meehan, and Lauren Raff, "Forced Disruption in Continuity of Primary Care: The Patients' Perspective," *Sociological Focus* 30, no. 2 (1997): 177–187.

71. Tom Shakespeare, "Disability Studies Today and Tomorrow," *Sociology of Health and Illness* 27, no. 1 (2005): 138–148.

72. Eva Kahana, "Dreams of Hot Toast and Smiling Nurses: Toward a Model of Patient-Responsive Care in Nursing Homes," *Research in the Sociology of Health Care* 24 (2006): 109–133.

73. Zola, *Missing Pieces;* Frank, "Reclaiming an Orphan Genre."

74. Samantha Solimeo, *With Shaking Hands: Aging with Parkinson's Disease in America's Heartland* (Rutgers University Press, 2009).

75. Eva Kahana and Boaz Kahana, "On Being a Proactive Health Care Consumer: Making An 'Unresponsive' System Work for You," in *Changing Consumers and Changing Technology in Health Care and Health Care Delivery,* ed. Jennie Jacobs Kronenfeld (Emerald, 2001), 21–44.

76. Peter David Blanck, *Employment, Disability, and the Americans with Disabilities Act: Issues in Law, Public Policy, and Research* (Northwestern University Press, 2000).

77. Marie R. Haug and Bebe Lavin, "Practitioner or Patient—Who's in Charge?" *Journal of Health and Social Behavior* 22 (1981): 212–229.

78. Kahana and Kahana, "Contextualizing Successful Aging."

79. Eva Kahana, Boaz Kahana, May Wykle, and Diana Kulle, "Marshalling Social Support: Active Roles in Care-Getting for Cancer Patients throughout the Life Course," *Journal of Family Social Work* 12, no. 2 (2009): 168–193.

80. Shapiro, *No Pity.*

4

A Life Course Perspective

The relationship between aging and disability over the life course has not been the subject of much research, particularly in the United States. Eva Jeppsson Grassman and her colleagues in Sweden, who have studied this relationship in those who were born disabled or became disabled early in life, report that "little is known about disabled people's lives over time, their experience of ageing with disabilities, and what it means to cope with disabilities over many years."[1]

We know even less about the experiences of those who have become disabled later in life as a result of chronic illness combined with advanced age. That is the focus of this chapter, which highlights the experiential aspects of disability and aging. Disability in later life has practical importance for individuals, their families, and policy systems. The majority of older Americans age in place, within their own communities rather than in an institution.[2] Planning for aging and adjusting to disability both require personal effort, collective support from family and friends, and better public policies. Much has been written about how to age well, without illness or disability. But without minimizing the value of these approaches, it is vital that we set an agenda for aging that normalizes elders who are living with disability—an agenda that encompasses and even embraces the process of aging well with disability.

The Life Course Perspective

A life course perspective sees disability as a contingent condition that has distinct meanings in early, middle, and later life—and for different cohorts.[3] It also addresses how people and families interweave the disability experi-

---

This chapter was coauthored with Alicia Smith-Tran, a Case Western graduate student.

73

ence into their lives and give it meaning. These diverse experiences shape how individuals understand their disability at different ages and moments in time, and how society treats disabled people based on their age.[4]

Disability in youth and disability in old age are marked by variation across two time dimensions. The first dimension is the age at which the person becomes disabled. The second dimension is the way in which that age affects the personal and social meaning of the person's disability. A twenty-year-old and an eighty-year-old who are both living with disability cannot be expected to see themselves—nor will others see them—in a similar light. While the younger person is about to embark on her journey in life, the older person is nearing her journey's completion. The younger person has also grown up during a time of disability rights while the older person's perspective is likely informed by a stigmatized view of disability that was more common in her youth.[5]

Life course research and analysis is concerned with dynamic features in human lives across time. The sociologist Karl Ulrich Mayer observes that there is an "emerging consensus" about the six criteria that distinguish this interdisciplinary perspective:

1. It examines "changes in human lives . . . over a long stretch of lifetime" and assumes that "prior life history has strong impacts on later life outcomes."

2. Compared with other research perspectives, it investigates "a larger series of cohorts rather than a few cohorts or synthetic cohorts based on cross-sectional data."

3. It studies human lives "across life domains, such as work and family," often using "interdisciplinary approaches."

4. It analyzes development over the life course "as the outcome of personal characteristics and individual action as well as of cultural frames and institutional and structural conditions."

5. It views individual lives in "collective contexts" such as couples and families.

6. It considers life course analysis to be "essential for social policies" that seek "preventive intervention."[6]

Jeylan Mortimer and Michael Shanahan's *Handbook of the Life Course* (2003) demonstrates the range of current life course scholarship. It is noteworthy that the handbook emphasizes earlier rather than later periods of life. Old age is, at best, a peripheral topic.[7] Students of aging, however, have adopted varied and broad frameworks to explore old age across the life course, with the aim of answering the question: "How does one correlate individual time and historical time—that is, the synchronization of individual development with historical change?"[8]

Dale Dannefer, in this context, points to "biography and structure" as the "two paradigms of life course scholarship."[9] At its root, this perspective sees a *process* that entails lives intersecting with time and place. According to life course theorist Richard Settersten, this perspective "is about describing individual and collective experiences and statuses over long stretches of time and explaining the short- and long-range causes and consequences of these patterns."[10]

But it was the life cycle approach that was the first framework gerontologists adopted to study old age across the life course. It addressed the question of life stages, was rooted in developmental psychology, and embraced social understandings of the aging process. It viewed aging as developmental (with aspects of growth and decline) and as a social process that empowered (or disempowered) the elderly. The life cycle approach addressed "stages in later life," including middle age, later maturity (ages sixty to seventy), and old age (the final period of life). According to this framework, a person reached the developmental stage of old age "when general decline or debilitating disease . . . resulted in extreme frailty, disablement, or invalidism."[11]

Reflecting the social views of the middle of the twentieth century, the life cycle framework envisioned old age and disability as deeply interconnected. Disability signaled that old age and the end of life had arrived. Old age meant slowing down, engaging in self-contemplation, refocusing on the "meaning of life," and becoming aware of "the approach of death."[12]

During the 1970s, aging research shifted away from psychology toward a wide range of social science disciplines. Aging moved from being seen principally as an individual phenomenon based on life stages (famously articulated by psychologist Erik Erikson in his theory of human development[13]) to a social and historical process. This methodological change was significant because it minimized the experiences of disability, loss, and death in relation to aging. With this expanded social frame of analysis, age mattered less—which meant that old age itself was less connected to disability. In their pathbreaking essay "Age and the Life Course" (1976), gerontologists Bernice L. Neugarten and Gunhild O. Hagestad saw the "age organization of society as a dynamic, socially meaningful and psychologically meaningful system." They argued that a person's biological age has meaning only in relation to a social time frame and that age itself is a social construction. This view that social age rather than biological age "regulates the individual's behavior" drew widespread support among gerontologists.[14]

The path through old age, according to this new view, did not necessarily have to pass through illness, disability, and disengagement. The post–World War II economic expansion meant that many workers could have a secure retirement at a relatively early age. They could begin to think of retirement as a life stage that conferred meaning through leisure activities. This was not idle time, but a period that generated "acceptance and warm response from others." Social activities would provide a welcome structure to lives that had previously been focused on instrumental activities. The person entering into this post–work age would find a stage of life whose social meaning was framed by middle-aged values, by an emphasis on continuity, and with little focus on the "onset of severe illness" or disability that marked the end of life.[15]

By the 1980s, a newly constructed successful aging model portrayed old age as a stage of life defined by autonomy and capability.[16] At least that was the ideal—as expressed by large interest groups such as AARP and by the professional literature on aging that sought to distance the new old age from the decrements of old age past.

Old Age, Disability Identity, and the Life Course

Disability in old age, like disability at any age, is a diverse set of conditions. Disability for the elderly is usually defined in terms of functional limitations that cause a person to require help in performing one or more activities of daily living. Physical and cognitive impairments tend to follow from chronic illness and to increase with very old age. Because the successful aging model has created the expectation that old age—especially in its younger phase—need not be burdened with illness and disability, when these impairments do occur the older person faces a difficult transition into living with disability.[17]

The construction of a disability identity—a view of oneself as disabled—is multifactorial, intersecting with chronological age, the typology of the impairment, and the individual and larger social forces that define the life course trajectory. Illness and the disability process are part of the aging experience,[18] even if we succeed in limiting their reach or compressing them into the very end of life.[19] Old age cannot be stripped of these conditions, and all older adults—including those living with disability—should be included as full members of the community of the aged. This inclusiveness enriches our understanding of the life course since we can learn from the experiences of those whose lives are touched by suffering and pain. The life course perspective as it relates to old age should actively seek to make room for both wellness and illness, both functional ability and disability, in late life.[20]

The idea that it is important for older persons to engage holistically with illness and disability is connected to the subject of meaning in old age. The science of aging has found this concept to be elusive; it is difficult to measure and even harder to define. While meaning is important throughout the life course, it assumes greater significance at the end of life. While much writing on late life, in both scholarly and popular circles, has focused on leisure and retirement, the question of meaning has largely been ignored.[21]

Confronting life's challenges rather than avoiding them is "what really matters," according to Arthur Kleinman who has written a book on this subject: "Dangers and uncertainties are an inescapable dimension of life." In fact, he argues, "they make life matter. They define what it means to be human."[22] Those living with disability know this all too well.[23] Those who are not disabled also need to understand the unique possibilities that exist within themselves to generate meaning and find satisfaction even when they cannot change their life's circumstances. Kleinman emphasizes that "surmounting our own denial" is the first step toward a moral posture that will allow us to start on our journey toward existential meaning.[24]

The way that illness and disability affect daily life is embedded within the life course. In the extended version of Erik Erikson's classic *The Life Cycle Completed* (1997), Joan Erikson's new chapter "The Ninth Stage" provides insight into "old age in one's eighties and nineties." During this last stage of development, when life crises come to define life experiences, "even the best cared-for bodies begin to weaken and do not function as they once did." With the loss of autonomy comes despair: "As independence and control are challenged, self-esteem and confidence weaken." This recognition of the reality of advanced old age led Joan Erikson to reverse the order of presentation for the two opposing categories—the syntonic and the dystonic—that her husband had used to chart the other eight life stages:

> As I review the life cycle, . . . I realize that the eight stages are most often presented with the syntonic quotient mentioned first, followed by the dystonic element second—e.g., trust vs. mistrust; autonomy vs. shame and doubt, etc. The syntonic supports growth and expansion, offers goals, celebrates self-respect and commitment of the very finest. Syntonic qualities sustain us as we are challenged by the more dystonic elements with which life confronts us all. We should recognize the fact that circumstances may place the dystonic in a more dominant position. Old age is inevitably such a circumstance. In writing "The Ninth Stage," I have therefore placed the dystonic element first in order to underscore its prominence and potency.[25]

Reversing the order of categories, Joan Erikson presents this series of paired "elements and tensions" that the "aged individual faces": "*basic mistrust* vs. trust"; "*shame and doubt* vs. autonomy"; "*guilt* vs. initiative";

"inferiority vs. industry"; *"identity confusion* vs. identity"; *"isolation* vs. intimacy"; *"stagnation* vs. generativity"; and, finally, *"despair and disgust* vs. integrity."[26]

In very old age, life ushers in challenges—with or without disability—that impair the individual's abilities. Older persons "are forced to mistrust their own capabilities." They begin to doubt themselves because "they no longer trust in their autonomy over their bodies and life choices" and fear "the shame of lost self-control."[27] The loss of initiative and social role, as well as family connections, can lead to despair. All of this mistrust, doubt, fear, shame, and loss are superimposed on weakening bodies, whose capacity to see and hear, to move about, and to manage the minimum of daily life can require great effort and time.

For older individuals, chronic illness often shapes this stage of the life course. Meaning nevertheless exists in their lives—as they report back to others in the "personal narratives" that they, like all patients, tell "to give coherence" to their "suffering." Kleinman writes that "illness story making and telling are particularly prevalent among the elderly" who "frequently weave illness experience into the apparently seamless plot of their life stories, whose denouement they are constantly revising." By looking backward toward the past—and "constructing a coherent account" of it that they can tell others—the elderly create meaning in the face of the adversity of illness and disability.[28]

Applying a meaning-based model to older persons living with disability, we must ask these questions: How do these individuals manage in their home environments? How are their interactions with others—and especially their family members—affected? How much physical pain, anxiety, or psychological distress do they feel? And as Kleinman emphasizes, the elderly also benefit if we encourage them to report on their lives—and then listen to them when they do. Too often, we see older persons only through the lens of their specific medical complaints and disease categories.[29]

Disability in old age can seem bleak—but this may be because we have yet to articulate a template for finding hope and wisdom in the later stages of life. *Success, continuity, productivity,* and other terms common to the new gerontology create a vocabulary that disables many of the elderly beyond their existing impairments.[30] What we need is a life course language and framework that will validate the person living with illness and disability, both in youth and into old age.

Senescence: A Template

Not all old people are frail, and not all old people can achieve health and high levels of functioning. Even the ideal of continuity in the aging literature is premised on the belief that aging well means carrying midlife functioning and attitudes into late life.[31] Granville Stanley Hall's *Senescence: The Last Half of Life* (1922), considered "the first major work in gerontology by an American social scientist,"[32] is a useful text for determining how older persons can integrate the life they lived in the past without disability with the life they are living in the present with disability.

In his book, Hall tells the story of decline—from the powers and exhilaration of youth to the diminishing capacities and depressing condition of old age. But he insists that because younger people do not see the world from the vantage point of life's final chapter, older persons have a "duty" to share their knowledge with the next generation: "We have a function in the world" to look frankly at old age so that this period can be understood, anticipated, and planned for by those who are not yet old.[33]

According to Hall, passage through life stages happens without any clear signage to indicate which stages a person has left behind and which ones still lie ahead. "Underneath the tenuous memory continuum that is the chief basis of all feeling of identity between our present and former selves . . . are the great changes the years bring. These are, indeed, so great that although they very commonly modulate, each into the next stage of the series by almost imperceptible gradations, we all really live not one but a succession of lives." The passage from one stage of life to the next can be frightening, however, and for that reason "the old cling to" their previous stage of life. Due to the difficulties of embracing this new stage of life, "they refuse to accept old age and to make the most and best of it, to face its tasks and to improve all its opportunities."[34]

To understand the nature of old age as people actually experience it, Hall "selected a few score of mostly eminent and some very distinguished old people . . . and addressed to each a simple questionnaire." Questions included: "How and at what age did you first realize the approach of old age?" "To what do you ascribe your long life?" "How do you keep well?" "Are you troubled with regrets for things done or not done by or for you?" and "What temptations do you feel, old or new?"[35] The responses varied, but throughout his commentary on them, Hall keeps coming back to his impression that "it is very hard for any but the strongest mentalities to realize the changes that age brings, to adjust to, feel at home in, and come to terms consciously with it."[36]

Hall readily understood that acceptance of old age is a "long, complex, and painful experience," and he observes that "each decade the circle of the Great Fatigue narrows around us, restricting the intensity and endurance of our activities."[37] The age of seventy was a particularly sad point since at this age, Hall believed, "society regards us as . . . a class apart."[38] The individual naturally sought to maintain a more youthful appearance and orientation as a reaction against these social currents. But Hall feared that in doing so, older persons diverted time and energy away from cultivating a crucial late-life role for themselves. "Intelligent and well-conserved" old age, he believed, had "very important social and anthropological functions in the modern world," the most important of which was "synthesis" by which Hall meant the experience of bringing past life experiences to bear on the present in an active and pragmatic fashion.[39]

While older persons may lack the energy and specialization of youth, their perspective, Hall thought, "sees through the shams and vanities of life." The imperative is to act, to avoid becoming enmeshed in "amusements, travel, or self-indulgence" and to reach out in service to others. Old age "should not devote itself to rest and rust," but instead should challenge the conventional idea of "old age itself."[40] The larger lesson we can take from Hall's work is that a sober confrontation with the challenges of late life, including life with disability, can propel older persons toward positive actions—and that these actions are different from ones they might have pursued at an earlier stage of life.

What it means to move through life with a disability—and therefore to age with disabilities—is distinct from becoming disabled in old age. Studies have shown that for those who age with disability, age is "of secondary importance next to the long-lived life of disability and impairment."[41] Although the experiences of disability and old age may differ, older persons who become impaired can reorder their priorities to make their lives meaningful, given their new conditions. But they may also face social hurdles along the way—ones they might not expect since disability is a new experience for them.[42]

Commonality and Diversity

Work by disability studies scholars reveals the social basis of disability, the common obstacles faced by people living with disabilities, and the need for a "holistic perspective" when examining the subject of disability.[43] Although differences exist among disabled individuals and groups, the disability perspective emphasizes commonality. One important aspect of that commonality—as Mark Sherry and others have elucidated—is prejudice and discrimination.[44]

A social constructionist approach defines current work in disability studies, replacing the now out-of-date medical model.[45] Questions of perspective and orientation, we now understand, define access issues for the disabled as much as do built environments.[46] The life course perspective adds to our understanding of aging and disability. It helps cast light on the evolving role of the self and its potential for agency.[47]

The life course perspective on aging also finds a diversity of experiences in a heterogeneous older population.[48] A trend in recent research focuses on inequality in health and disability in old age.[49] Too often, researchers make blanket statements about "older adults" and "individuals with a disability" without recognizing the role that one's social location—the intersection of a person's race, class, gender, and other social demographic factors—has on lived experiences and quality of life.

Disability and older adulthood are not homogenous categories, nor are they mutually exclusive experiences. Disparities in disability prevalence exist between older people of color and older whites, and class is also associated with unequal health outcomes. Health and disability disparities are significant, but "much remains unknown about what generates these disparities and how policies can intervene to reduce them."[50] Ongoing longitudinal research shows how "accumulated life experience" impacts "transitions from health to infirmity" and reveals "the institutional and cultural variations" in these and other "life cycle dynamics."[51]

Cumulative advantage/disadvantage theory (CA/DT) is a dominant conceptual approach related to the life course perspective and aging.[52] "CA/DT" has been defined as "the systemic tendency for interindividual divergence in a given characteristic (e.g., money, health, or status) with the passage of time."[53] We know, for example, that blacks are more likely than whites to become more disabled over time, with increasing health disadvantage relative to whites, irrespective of educational attainment.[54]

A disability gap increases over time between blacks and whites, with a disproportionately poor quality of life among blacks through the end of life. Chronic illnesses such as heart disease—one of the leading causes of disability and shortened life expectancy—are more common among older blacks than whites.[55] Structural factors and agency-level decisions are tied to cumulative disadvantage. Challenging living situations and poor lifestyle habits accumulate and manifest themselves in the form of chronic illness and disability.[56] The "long arm" of early life experiences shapes disproportionately high rates of morbidity and disability among blacks. It is rooted in early life and persists throughout the life course.[57]

An alternative to CA/DT is known as the age-as-leveler hypothesis. Research in this vein shows that blacks experience growing disadvantage in functional health until very old age. Black adults who live to around age eighty actually have better physical functioning than their white counterparts—a phenomenon known as the racial crossover.[58]

What do these disparities mean for the ideal of adopting a universal approach to disability? How can we accommodate significant differences among disabled persons if we spread a broad and inclusive canopy over disability? This question specifically relates to disability in old age. The awareness of commonality and diversity should guide us in thinking about how we can accommodate all persons—irrespective of race, class, gender, and age— as we consider "universal policies that recognize that the entire population is 'at risk' for the concomitants of chronic illness and disability."[59]

Life Course Patterns in Disability and Aging

Our special concern is the question of how disability in old age differs from disability at other stages of the life course. How does advanced age intersect with the understanding of self and the meaning that older persons give to their disabilities? Rosalyn Benjamin Darling has identified several life course patterns associated with age and disability. Children with disabilities, she finds, have a positive self-concept, and they engage in acts of "self-presentation" in an effort to "present a normalized self."[60] As they grow older, these individuals continue to maintain "a typicality orientation" if they have the opportunity to engage in work and to participate within society.[61]

The situation differs, however, for elderly persons who become disabled late in life. Because they have spent their formative years without disability, "the acquisition of a disability during adulthood is commonly viewed negatively" and can include the feeling of losing a part of oneself. A large percentage of older individuals who live with functional disability thus resist identifying themselves as being disabled.[62]

In her own empirical research, Darling found that "older people were more likely to espouse a medical model (e.g., desiring a cure, believing that 'doctors know best'), to feel excluded from social participation (e.g., disability keeps them from working and limits their social life), and to reject an identity of disability pride." Darling's research on older adults with disabilities also showed that "life satisfaction decreases with age."[63] Elderly with disabilities have lower rates of social contact and do not engage in social activism. The picture that emerges is that many older adults with serious disabilities are cut off, feeling excluded and marginalized in ways that cannot be accounted for by disability alone.[64]

How older people view their own disability reflects on the meaning of disability for the aging population as a whole. We need further research on the life course if we are to fully understand this attitude—but it does appear that older persons consider disability an unambiguously negative experience. Can such a view be reoriented? Can the elderly learn to think of disability as a form of difference, rather than as a deficiency? A potential path forward entails seeing disability as a process rather than as a condition. Studying older persons with disabilities illuminates the processes of disablement and details how, over time, we all become less able.

Disability as lived experience is more than what a person can or cannot do. It is "a product of attitudes and of the organization of our social world."[65] For many people, disability represents both a transition and a lifelong journey. Closing the book on part of the old "self" makes it possible to venture onto new paths and into new communities that may be particularly welcoming to persons with disabilities. In these physical and social environments that support their current needs, disabled people can learn new ways of doing things.[66] This is true not only for people who were born with disabilities or acquired them early in life, but also for those who develop disabilities in late life. At some point, maintaining life as they have previously lived it may pose a challenge to seniors whose physical condition makes that form of life inaccessible. Finding ways to access environments and people who can make life easier and more meaningful can be important to unleashing the potential of life.

The social and personal meanings of old age and disability can be linked to certain transitions and passages across the life course. Old age and disability are experienced in many different ways by those who fall within these broad categories. Typologies of disability vary based on degree of impairment along with personal and environmental factors. Old age is also beset with variations based on how old a person is and the availability of personal and social resources to cope with age-based challenges. The breadth of both the aging and disability categories—along with the many diverse populations who reside within them—makes it difficult to pinpoint the real differences within the populations that comprise each group as well as the differences between each group's relationship with society at large. Broad commonalities and a desire for inclusivity mask real and important variations.

People who are aging have a tendency to seek a youthful perspective even as they age. According to sociologist Cheryl Laz, age is "something that is accomplished or performed." It is "something we do; it requires action and effort." In her interviews with individuals in their fifties to seventies, she discovered that activity, energy, appearance, and illness were common themes. Her respondents considered themselves in "good health" and felt that they possessed higher energy than their peers. They also avoided talking about ailments and illnesses, preferring to focus on what they *can* do.[67] This idea that older people expend effort in avoiding a label of illness and disability has considerable support in the aging literature.[68] As we get older—and specifically, when we must confront a serious illness and its disabling effects—this youthful orientation is eroded and the passage of time marks a transition into illness.[69]

The social and personal processes that lead a person away from being able to manage illness and disability mark a significant turning point in someone's life. When this change occurs, individuals and their families are profoundly affected. It happens not only to the elderly, but to younger persons who experience a loss in capability as a result of disease progression. In *The Body Silent* (1987), Robert Murphy explains that "this assault on the self" can create bitterness and anger, and that the intensity of these feelings is tied to "the depth and type of disability."[70] When the losses continue—and Murphy painfully recounts how much greater each additional loss of capability is to the functioning of the body and the constitution of the self—the person ultimately falls into a state of dependency.[71]

Disruption and Reconciliation in Old Age

Disability is a disruptive event—for the young and for the old. Those who experience it understand how it relocates us into a new physical and phenomenological space.[72] The process entails elements of tragedy, suffering, and loss as well as hope and the capacity for reconciliation. Through the disability experience, lives are also transformed. Before disability, most people sought validation from others based on dominant social norms. After disability, they become less concerned with such approval since, for many people, it is not a possibility. They are different, and they realize that the world sees them differently too. Most importantly, a life they formerly would have imagined as impossible becomes not only possible but valuable and cherished.

Chronic illness is central to the disability experience for many older people. In *Good Days, Bad Days: The Self in Chronic Illness and Time* (1991), Kathy Charmaz shows the "private face of a public problem," illuminating how "living with serious illness and disability can catapult people into a separate reality," where "a once calm day with a smooth schedule or a taken-for-granted routine now teeters with ups and downs."[73] The most destabilizing aspects of chronic illness and disability, says Charmaz, are the ways they affect a person's experience with time. She describes three degrees of illness and disability across a spectrum, with each making increasingly greater demands on a person's time and resources: illness as "interruption," as "intrusion," and as "immersion."[74]

The life course relevance of Charmaz's work lies in her observation that "the structure of elderly people's lives usually differed from younger respondents," as did their "expectations." These differences, along with fewer "time pressures," had the effect of muting symptoms of illness. "If I wake up stiff and tired, I just stay in bed longer where it's warm and comfortable," stated one respondent. A ninety-one-year-old living with chronic illness insisted, "I'm not ill; I'm just *old*."[75] Older people are also more likely to consider their illness as a "condition"—which is another way to distance themselves from an association with illness.[76] The consequences of being older—and often less engaged in matters of work and family—can thus provide the elderly with a buffer against the disrupting effects of illness and disability.[77]

Charmaz's good days, bad days conceptualization helps us appreciate how older persons can alternate between states of hope and joy (on good days) to fear and sadness (on bad days). In the process of navigating these emotional states, they become "innovators" in planning and organizing their illnesses to account for their changing needs. This "handling" of illness can take the form of a "one day at a time" outlook. Paradoxically, by keeping their focus set on the present (the daily aspects of illness and disability), the elderly can avoid defining themselves by the present—and when a crisis passes or an improvement in their health occurs, they can envision (and maintain hope in) a better future.[78]

Although disability in old age is a subjective experience, social scientists and physicians have nevertheless tried to come up with a broad definition. In the most recent *Handbook of Aging and Social Sciences* (2016), Douglas Wolf defines *late-life disability* "as difficulties in carrying out everyday tasks or participating in social activities" as the result of a poor fit between the individual and his or her environment.[79] For gerontologists, conceptualizing disability as both "complex and multidimensional" leads to "a great deal of heterogeneity within any group of individuals classified as having disability."[80] The common approach of measuring disability based largely on subjective "self- or proxy-reported responses to survey questions" adds to the variability of findings regarding disability prevalence.[81]

Noted difficulties in the domains of conceptualization, measurement, and evidence stand out in gerontologists' efforts to quantify disability prevalence and trends for older persons. For example, Wolf notes the challenges in attempting to identify and explain "*between*-group differences in disability trends" and suggests that better data might "reveal still more *within*-group differences." He concludes that "no single set of allegedly causal factors can explain the full spectrum of late-life disability trends."[82] Yet despite the complexity of late-life disability patterns, "the most consistent finding" is that "people become more likely to have a disability as they age."[83]

Age itself is thus a key aspect to late-life disability. We cannot forget that living into old age and experiencing disability is a part of the human condition. So, too, is the human suffering that accompanies the usual combination of illness and disability. In one of the few studies on this topic, Helen Black and Robert Rubinstein report that the elderly "revealed that they had not shared their experiences with health professionals or clergypersons" because they viewed their suffering "as more than mental, physical, or spiritual pain, as having an existential quality that is rooted in being human, and because they were not asked."[84]

A definition that emerges from Black and Rubinstein's study is that suffering is "a visceral awareness of the self's vulnerability to be broken or diminished at any time and in many ways."[85] The life course shapes the elderly's understanding of suffering because older persons "interpreted suffering as alien in light of how they viewed and defined themselves before suffering began." Their suffering "heralded a need to reevaluate the self but also to find a way to reintegrate the self."[86] This reevaluation and reintegration of the self are the tasks confronting older persons living with severe impairments and facing disability.

Black and Rubinstein identify three ways in which the elders in their study accomplished these difficult tasks: "by maintaining . . . the roles that gave meaning to identity, by assuming a new identity . . . and breathing life into it, and by telling a story about it."[87] Noting that no matter which approach an older person took, "the suffering story generally reflected the life story as a whole," these authors draw the following conclusion:

> Suffering in older age is distinct in quality and meaning. This distinctiveness resides in elders' perceptions that their unique voices will soon be silent, their place in this world will soon be vacant, and their individual and cohort history is coming to an end. As elders perceive a diminishment of strength, cognition, and usefulness, there is constant awareness that time is running out; finding meaning in suffering, and in life, has a particular urgency.[88]

The journey from disruption to reconciliation and reintegration involves a personal striving that can be transformative. But for this reconciliation to occur, we must find a way to give old age its own special meaning. Some have argued that gerontologists avoid or only gingerly use labels such as "old person" or "old age" because these terms have negative connotations. The result, as Settersten points out, "is an ideology of 'agelessness' . . . in which old age is viewed as something that can be transcended."[89] By giving old age relevance as part of the life course—as a time when people pursue specific goals that are often different in nature from those they previously pursued—we can diminish the fear that currently surrounds late-life disability.

Staring directly at the most difficult parts of aging—disability and the end of life—lets us put into action Alexander Pope's dictum: "The proper study of mankind is man." The struggles in the last period of life allow the elderly to forge interpersonal and intergenerational connections that are different in nature from the ones they developed earlier in life. While the time ahead may be limited, the capacity to infuse social meaning into the time that still remains can empower older persons. How they choose to handle time—and other resources—may also change. By giving old age its due, we enable the elderly to separate the essential from the nonessential and to assert priorities they may have overlooked or even rejected at earlier stages of their lives.

Disability in the Context of the Life Course

Our aim in this chapter has been to offer some thoughts on bridging disability studies and aging research, using the framework of a life course perspective. Both disciplines have developed valuable formulas, and the two fields can learn from each other. For gerontology, the key questions are: What are the trends of disability in late life, and what causes them? These questions are important for the larger issues of divergence and commonality in the aging experience. This orientation tends toward macro-level research, with gerontologists examining large datasets and evidence presented in the form of survey responses.

The life course perspective is well suited to the study of disability in old age. The theory of cumulative advantage/disadvantage and the paradigm of successful aging consider early, middle, and later life as linked together. But disability, like aging and the life course, is not a static concept but a process.[90] Only by situating disability in the context of a person's life—by understanding when and how someone encountered disability—can we appreciate the social barriers and personal adaptations that are part of the disability process.

For disability studies, with its connection to a social interactionist tradition, disability is less a thing that is measurable and more a perspective that is informed by life experience. As a concept, disability links many different lives and typologies of impairment. The locus of disability studies is both social and political because so much of the disability experience relates to social barriers and discrimination. But the physical embodiment of disability and how it affects a person's day-to-day life are also central concerns. Different bodies and minds interact differently with time and their environments.

One concept that deserves further study is the continuity principle in gerontology and what it means for disability. According to the health, stress, and well-being models of aging, continuity in life represents the ideal. If people aim to maximize continuity, then how do they adjust to and make sense of disability as a disruptive force in their lives? This ideal of continuity, like the ideal of successful aging, also privileges those who age without disability and leaves little room to address old age holistically. Gerontology must find a way to incorporate an approach that accepts the contingent nature of late life, including the disruptions and discontinuities that are part and parcel of this period.

Notes

1. Eva Jeppsson Grassman, Lotta Holme, Annika Taghizadeh Larsson, and Anna Whitaker, "A Long Life with a Particular Signature: Life Course and Aging for People with Disabilities," *Journal of Gerontological Social Work* 55, no. 2 (2012): 95–111.

2. Janine L. Wiles, Annette Leibing, Nancy Guberman, Jeanne Reeve, and Ruth E. S. Allen, "The Meaning of 'Ageing in Place' to Older People," *The Gerontologist* 52, no. 3 (2011): 357–366.

3. "The life course may be defined as an age-graded sequence of socially defined roles and events that individuals enact over time." Ron Berger, *Introducing Disability Studies* (Lynne Rienner, 2013), 79.

4. Vern L. Bengtson, Glenn H. Elder Jr., and Norella M. Putney, "The Lifecourse Perspective on Ageing: Linked Lives, Timing and History," in *The Cambridge*

Handbook of Age and Ageing, ed. Malcolm L. Johnson (Cambridge University Press, 2005), 493–494.

5. Rosalyn Benjamin Darling, "Toward a Model of Changing Disability Identities: A Proposed Typology and Research Agenda," *Disability and Society* 18, no. 7 (2003): 881–895.

6. Karl Ulrich Mayer, "New Directions in Life Course Research," *Annual Review of Sociology* 35 (2009): 414. See also the much-cited chapter by Glen H. Elder Jr., Monica Kirkpatrick Johnson, and Robert Crosnoe, "The Emergence and Development of Life Course Theory," in *Handbook of the Life Course*, ed. Jeylan T. Mortimer and Michael J. Shanahan (Springer, 2003), 3–19.

7. Jeylan T. Mortimer and Michael J. Shanahan, *Handbook of the Life Course* (Springer, 2003), 103–329. A leading review noted that "aging is hardly touched on, although the subject is at the forefront of future policy concerns." See Karl Ulrich Mayer, review of *Handbook of the Life Course*, ed. Jeylan T. Mortimer and Michael J. Shanahan, *Social Forces* 84, no. 4 (2006): 2364.

8. Tamara K. Hareven, "The Last Stage: Historical Adulthood and Old Age," *Daedalus* 105, no. 1 (1976): 13.

9. Dale Dannefer, "Age, the Life Course, and the Sociological Imagination: Prospects for Theory," in *Handbook of Aging and the Social Sciences*, 7th ed., ed. Robert H. Binstock and Linda K. George (Academic Press, 2011), 3–5. "The *biographical* perspective is focused on depicting the trajectories and transitions that characterize individual lives" (with sufficient room to include collective analysis), while "the *institutional* perspective focuses on the life course as a component of social structure and culture." Dannefer sees a broad distinction in analysis between a North American emphasis on "biographical life course outcomes" and a European focus on "the life course as a structural feature of society." Ibid., 5.

10. Richard A. Settersten Jr., "Aging and the Life Course," in *Handbook of Aging and the Social Sciences*, 6th ed., ed. Robert H. Binstock and Linda K. George (Academic Press, 2006), 4. See also the essays in Richard A. Settersten, *Invitation to the Life Course: Toward New Understandings of Later Life* (Baywood, 2003); Bengsten, Elder, and Putney, "The Lifecourse Perspective on Ageing," 494–495, highlight the five principles of: linked lives, historical time and place, life transitions, agency, and lifelong processes.

11. Clark Tibbitts, *Handbook of Social Gerontology: Societal Aspects of Aging* (University of Chicago Press, 1960), 9–10. The life cycle approach also held that the individual changes that occurred with aging were tied into social and psychological experiences: "One's self-concept is conditioned by what his group thinks of him." Although this self-concept was influenced by the physiological effects of aging, the person was seen as "a responsive and responding nexus for social and sociological judgments." Leonard Z. Breen, "The Aging Individual," in *Handbook of Social Gerontology: Societal Aspects of Aging*, ed. Clark Tibbitts (University of Chicago Press, 1960), 160. It is noteworthy that the life cycle approach did not make room for variability in the aging experience. As Tamara K. Hareven points out, "definitions of aging . . . have not only changed significantly over time but have also varied among cultures." Hareven, "The Last Stage," 14.

12. Tibbitts, *Handbook of Social Gerontology*.

13. See Erik H. Erikson, *Childhood and Society* (Norton, 1950); Erik H. Erikson and Joan M. Erikson, *The Life Cycle Completed*, extended version (Norton, 1997).

14. Bernice L. Neugarten and Gunhild O. Hagestad, "Age and the Life Course," in *Handbook of Aging and the Social Sciences*, ed. Robert H. Binstock and Ethel Shanas (Von Nostrand Reinhold, 1976), 35–55. Neugarten and Hagestad also

observe that "social age regulates the individual's behavior. Individuals develop a mental map of the life cycle; they anticipate that certain events will occur at certain times; and they internalize a social clock that tells them whether they are on time or off time. They also internalize other social norms that tell them if their behavior in various areas of life is age-appropriate." Ibid., 35.

15. Chad Gordon, Charles M. Gaitz, and Judith Scott, "Leisure and Lives: Personal Expressivity across the Life Span," in Robert H. Binstock and Ethel Shanas, *Handbook of Aging and the Social Sciences* (Van Nostrand Reinhold, 1976), 322–323. On the social meaning of "retirement," see Joel S. Savishinsky, *Breaking the Watch: The Meanings of Retirement in America* (Cornell University Press, 2000).

16. John W. Rowe and Robert L. Kahn, "Human Aging: Usual and Successful," *Science* 237, no. 4811 (1987): 143–149; John W. Rowe and Robert L. Kahn, "Successful Aging," *Gerontologist* 37 (1997): 433–440; John W. Rowe and Robert L. Kahn, *Successful Aging* (Random House, 1998).

17. A person's reactions to illness are a component of "health and illness behavior." Aging influences "symptom interpretation," patterns of "help-seeking," and "medical care use." See Kenneth F. Ferraro, "Health and Aging," in *Handbook of Aging and the Social Sciences,* 6th ed., ed. Robert H. Binstock and Linda K. George (Academic Press, 2006), 245–247.

18. According to Arthur Kleinman, "illness" is distinct from "disease," as the former "refers to how the sick person and the members of the family or wider social network perceive, live with, and respond to symptoms and disability." Arthur Kleinman, *The Illness Narratives: Suffering, Healing, and the Human Condition* (Basic Books, 1988), 3.

19. The classic studies advancing the process components of disability in old age and the compression of disability into later life are Lois M. Verbrugge, "Survival Curves, Prevalence Rates, and Dark Matters Therein," *Journal of Aging and Health* 3, no. 2 (1991): 217–236; and Lois M. Verbrugge and Alan M. Jette, "The Disablement Process," *Social Science and Medicine* 38, no. 1 (1994): 1–14. See also Renée H. Lawrence and Alan M. Jette, "Disentangling the Disablement Process," *Journals of Gerontology Series B: Psychological Sciences and Social Sciences* 51, no. 4 (1996): S173–S182.

20. Older individuals maintain high ratings of life satisfaction despite substantial losses in health, resources, and relationships. The reason for this paradox is not fully understood and runs counter to theories of subjective well-being, "which posit that life satisfaction is high when objective life conditions are favorable and lower when they are unfavorable." See Linda K. George and Frank J. Whittington, "Understanding Well-Being in the Oldest Old," *The Gerontologist* 52, no. 6 (2012): 873.

21. Freya Dittmann-Kohli. "The Construction of Meaning in Old Age: Possibilities and Constraints," *Ageing and Society* 10, no. 3 (1990): 279–294.

22. Arthur Kleinman, *What Really Matters: Living a Moral Life Amidst Uncertainty and Danger* (Oxford University Press, 2006), 1.

23. Nick Watson, "Well, I Know This Is Going to Sound Very Strange to You, but I Don't See Myself as a Disabled Person: Identity and Disability," *Disability and Society* 17, no. 5 (2002): 509–527.

24. Kleinman, *What Really Matters,* 514–519. A common theme in the self-narratives of those living with disability is that they do not seek pity and find *disability* to be a term that is not sufficiently descriptive of who they are. Nancy Mairs writes, "One of the underlying problems with a comprehensive term like 'disability' . . . is that there has never been any universal agreement about who belongs in the

company and who does not, or even what to call the presumed members." In a frequently noted passage, she then says, "As one of my idiosyncrasies, I prefer to call myself a cripple." Nancy Mairs, *Waist-High in the World: A Life Among the Nondisabled* (Beacon Press, 1996), 12.

25. Erikson and Erikson, *The Life Cycle Completed,* 105–106. Joan Erikson notes that despite the dominance of the dystonic element during the ninth stage, "it is important to remember that conflict and tension are sources of growth, strength, and commitment." Ibid., 106.

26. Ibid., 107–108 (emphasis added to highlight the dystonic aspect of each pair).

27. Ibid.

28. Kleinman, *The Illness Narratives,* 49–50. Kleinman sees a linkage between biographical past and present through this illness storytelling ("the tale of the aged"), and through this narration, a linkage between older and younger generations: "Few of the tragedies at life's end are as rending to the clinician as that of the frail elderly patient who has no one to tell the life story to. Indeed, becoming a surrogate for those who should be present to listen may be one of the practitioner's finest roles in the care of the aged." Ibid., 50.

29. The older person gains satisfaction simply from being heard and cared for, even in the absence of intervention. Kleinman has developed a "practical clinical method" based on the ideal of "humane care." It offers an "alternative therapeutic approach" that reconceptualizes "medical care as (1) empathetic witnessing of the existential experience of suffering and (2) practical coping with the major psychosocial crises that constitute the menacing chronicity of that experience." Ibid., 9–10, 227–251.

30. Martha B. Holstein and Meredith Minkler, "Self, Society, and the 'New Gerontology,'" *The Gerontologist* 43, no. 6 (2003): 787–796.

31. Heather E. Dillaway and Mary Byrnes, "Reconsidering Successful Aging: A Call for Renewed and Expanded Academic Critiques and Conceptualizaitons," *Journal of Applied Gerontology* 28, no. 6: 706.

32. Thomas R. Cole, "The Prophecy of *Senescence:* G. Stanley Hall and the Reconstruction of Old Age in America," *The Gerontologist* 24, no. 4 (1984): 360.

33. Granville Stanley Hall, *Senescence: The Last Half of Life* (Appleton, 1922), ix.

34. Ibid., 319–320. Hall classifies the five stages into: (1) childhood; (2) adolescence; (3) middle age; (4) senescence ("which begins in the early forties, or before in woman"); and (5) senectitude ("old age proper").

35. Ibid., 321–330.

36. Ibid., 332.

37. Ibid., 366.

38. Ibid., 368.

39. Ibid., 405–408.

40. Ibid., 408–411.

41. Grassman, Holme, Larsson, and Whitaker, "A Long Life with a Particular Signature," 102. See also Gerry Zarb and Mike Oliver, *Ageing with a Disability: What Do They Expect After All These Years?* (University of Greenwich London, 1993).

42. Philippa Clarke and Sandra E. Black, "Quality of Life Following Stroke: Negotiating Disability, Identity, and Resources," *Journal of Applied Gerontology* 24, no. 4 (2005): 319–336. Clarke and Black note that "some survivors [of stroke] used various adaptive strategies to return to self-defining life activities, even in a modified or reduced way, to restore their sense of identity and bring renewed meaning to their lives." Ibid., 333. See also Wendy Seymour, "Time and the Body: Re-embodying Time in Disability," *Journal of Occupational Science* 9, no. 3 (2002): 135–142.

43. Harlan Hahn, "Introduction: 'Disability Policy and the Problem of Discrimination,'" *American Behavioral Scientist* 28, no. 3 (1985): 293–318.

44. Mark Sherry, *Disability Hate Crimes: Does Anyone Really Hate Disabled People?* (Ashgate, 2010); Mark Sherry, "Overlaps and Contradictions Between Queer Theory and Disability Studies," *Disability and Society* 19, no. 7 (2004): 769–783. See also Berger, *Introducing Disability Studies.* The long history of discrimination against people with disabilities is documented in Kim E. Nielsen, *A Disability History of the United States* (Beacon Press, 2012).

45. See Rosemarie Garland-Thomson, "Disability Studies: A Field Emerged," *American Quarterly* 65, no. 4 (2013): 915–926. In reviewing a group of five books within the genre of "critical disability studies," Garland-Thomson notes that they all "highlight disability's generative force, what disability *makes* in the world, as opposed to the more standard descriptions of disability as an occasion for oppression and discrimination." Ibid., 918.

46. See Tanya Titchkosky, *The Question of Access: Disability, Space, and Meaning* (University of Toronto Press, 2011); Rosalyn B. Darling and D. Alex Heckert, "Orientations Toward Disability: Differences over the Lifecourse," *International Journal of Disability, Development and Education* 57, no. 2 (2010): 131–143. Darling and Heckert's orientation toward disability is conceptualized to include: "disability identity, adherence to either a medical or social model of disability, and level of disability rights activism. Thus, disability orientation includes both cognitive/evaluative (self/identity) and behavioral (role-playing) variables, along with beliefs about whether disability is a personal or a social problem."

47. Elder, Johnson, and Crosnoe, "The Emergence and Development of Life Course Theory," 11–12.

48. Angela M. O'Rand, "The Precious and Precocious: Understanding Cumulative Disadvantage and Cumulative Advantage over the Life Course," *The Gerontologist* 36, no. 2 (1996): 230–238; Angela M. O'Rand, "Stratification and the Life Course: Life Course Capital, Life Course Risks, and Social Inequality," in *Handbook of Aging and the Social Sciences,* 6th ed., ed. Robert H. Binstock and Linda K. George (Academic Press, 2006), 145–162.

49. See Vicki A. Freedman, Linda G. Martin, Robert F. Schoeni, and Jennifer C. Cornman, "Declines in Late-Life Disability: The Role of Early- and Mid-Life Factors," *Social Science and Medicine* 66, no. 7 (2008): 1588–1602; Renato Maia Guimarães, "Health Capital, Life Course and Ageing," *Gerontology* 53, no. 2 (2007): 96–101; Yoav Ben-Shlomo and Diana Kuh, "A Life Course Approach to Chronic Disease Epidemiology: Conceptual Models, Empirical Challenges and Interdisciplinary Perspectives," *International Journal of Epidemiology* 31, no. 2 (2002): 285–293.

50. See Pamela Herd, Stephanie A. Robert, and James S. House, "Health Disparities Among Older Adults: Life Course Influences and Policy Solutions," in *Handbook of Aging and the Social Sciences,* 7th ed., Robert H. Binstock and Linda K. George (Academic Press, 2011), 129.

51. William P. Butz and Barbara Boyle Torrey, "Some Frontiers in Social Science," *Science* 312, no. 5782 (2006): 1898.

52. Dale Dannefer, "Cumulative Advantage/Disadvantage and the Life Course: Cross-Fertilizing Age and Social Science Theory," *Journals of Gerontology Series B: Psychological Sciences and Social Sciences* 58, no. 6 (2003): S327.

53. Ibid.

54. Kenneth F. Ferraro and Melissa M. Farmer. "Double Jeopardy, Aging as Leveler, or Persistent Health Inequality? A Longitudinal Analysis of White and

Black Americans," *Journals of Gerontology Series B: Psychological Sciences and Social Sciences* 51, no. 2 (1996): S319–S328; Kim M. Shuey and Andrea E. Willson, "Cumulative Disadvantage and Black-White Disparities in Life-Course Health Trajectories," *Research on Aging* 30, no. 2 (2008): 200–225.

55. David R. Williams and Pamela Braboy Jackson, "Social Sources of Racial Disparities in Health," *Health Affairs* 24, no. 2 (2005): 325–334; Youlian Liao, Daniel L. McGee, Guichan Cao, and Richard Cooper, "Black-White Differences in Disability and Morbidity in the Last Years of Life," *American Journal of Epidemiology* 149, no. 12 (1999): 1097–1103.

56. See James J. Dowd and Vern L. Bengtson, "Aging in Minority Populations: An Examination of the Double Jeopardy Hypothesis," *Journal of Gerontology* 33, no. 3 (1978): 427–436. The double jeopardy hypothesis contends that elderly African Americans grapple with a double-edged sword of disadvantage—being both black and older. This concept also highlights intersectionality—the inextricably linked nature of aspects of social identity such as race, age, and social class. See Kimberlé Crenshaw, "Demarginalizing the Intersection of Race and Sex: A Black Feminist Critique of Antidiscrimination Doctrine, Feminist Theory and Antiracist Politics," *University of Chicago Legal Forum* 140 (1989): 139–167.

57. Jessica A. Kelley-Moore and Kenneth F. Ferraro, "The Black/White Disability Gap: Persistent Inequality in Later Life?" *Journals of Gerontology Series B: Psychological Sciences and Social Sciences* 59, no. 1 (2004): S34–S43; Mark D. Hayward and Bridget K. Gorman, "The Long Arm of Childhood: The Influence of Early-Life Social Conditions on Men's Mortality," *Demography* 41, no. 1 (2004): 87–107.

58. Jinyoung Kim and Richard Miech, "The Black-White Difference in Age Trajectories of Functional Health over the Life Course," *Social Science and Medicine* 68, no. 4 (2009): 717–725; Nan E. Johnson, "The Racial Crossover in Comorbidity, Disability, and Mortality," *Demography* 37, no. 3 (2000): 267–283.

59. Irving Kenneth Zola, "Toward the Necessary Universalizing of a Disability Policy," *The Milbank Quarterly* 67, Suppl. 2, Pt. 2 (1989): 401.

60. Rosalyn Benjamin Darling, *Disability and Identity: Negotiating Self in a Changing Society* (Lynne Rienner, 2013), 123–125.

61. Ibid., 128–129.

62. Ibid., 129–131.

63. Ibid., 132.

64. Ibid., 132–136.

65. Jessica A. Kelley-Moore, John G. Schumacher, Eva Kahana, and Boaz Kahana, "When Do Older Adults Become 'Disabled'? Social and Health Antecedents of Perceived Disability in a Panel Study of the Oldest Old," *Journal of Health and Social Behavior* 47, no. 2 (2006): 135. In this study, factors other than physical health—especially degree of social connectedness and networks—shaped self-perceptions of disability. Ibid., 136–137.

66. Irving Kenneth Zola, *Missing Pieces: A Chronicle of Living with a Disability* (Temple University Press, 1982), 233–234.

67. Cheryl Laz, "Age Embodied," *Journal of Aging Studies* 17, no. 4 (2003): 503–519. On the utility of "narrative analysis" as a research tool to better understand similarities and differences in aging from a life course perspective, see Cassandra Phoenix, Brett Smith, and Andrew C. Sparkes, "Narrative Analysis in Aging Studies: A Typology for Consideration," *Journal of Aging Studies* 24, no. 1 (2010): 1–11.

68. Jean A. Langlois, Stefania Maggi, Tamara Harris, Eleanor M. Simonsick, Luigi Ferrucci, Mara Pavan, Leonardo Sartori, and Giuliano Enzi, "Self-Report of Difficulty in Performing Functional Activities Identifies a Broad Range of Disability

in Old Age," *Journal of the American Geriatrics Society* 44, no. 12 (1996): 1421–1428; Cecil Helman, *Culture, Health and Illness* (CRC Press, 2007).

69. For a general overview of work on the aging body, embodiment, and body image, see Laura Hurd Clarke and Alexandra Korotchenko, "Aging and the Body: A Review," *Canadian Journal of Aging/La Revue Canadienne Du Vieillissement* 30, no. 3 (2011): 495–510.

70. Robert F. Murphy, *The Body Silent* (Henry Holt, 1987), 106–107. For a discussion of the connection between the stress process and age identity, see Markus H. Schafer and Tetyana Pylypiv Shippee, "Age Identity in Context: Stress and the Subjective Side of Aging," *Social Psychology Quarterly* 73, no. 3 (2010): 245–264.

71. Murphy, *The Body Silent,* 195–220.

72. See Wendy Seymour, *Remaking the Body: Rehabilitation and Change* (Routledge, 1998), 36–50.

73. Kathy Charmaz, *Good Days, Bad Days: The Self in Chronic Illness and Time* (Rutgers University Press, 1991), 4–5.

74. Illness and disability create "meanings" that "are imbedded in experiences of time." Ibid., 4. The first degree in the spectrum is illness as "interruption," when people treat illness as "a separate event, distinct from other events." The second degree is illness as "intrusion," when it "demands continued attention, allotted time, and forced accommodation." Finally, the third degree is illness as "immersion," which "recasts" people's "self-concepts as well as their bodies and lives." As they "become immersed in illness, the structure of their lives changes and immediate concerns inundate them." Ibid., 23, 42, 79.

75. Ibid., 58–61.

76. Ibid., 67–68. Charmaz describes the use of "condition" (not only by the elderly, but also by "family, friends, and professionals") as "conceptual camouflaging." Samantha Solimeo reports that elderly Parkinson's respondents also used "condition" rather than "illness." Samantha Solimeo, *With Shaking Hands: Aging with Parkinson's Disease in America's Heartland* (Rutgers University Press, 2009), 14–17, 81–83, 157–159.

77. Although older people may be less engaged with work and family, social contact is still important to them. This need for sociability is especially great in the case of the elderly who are ill. "Sociability affirms that the self remains, that illness has not claimed all of one's being." Charmaz, *Good Days, Bad Days,* 97–98.

78. Ibid., 135, 178–185, 190–191.

79. Douglas Wolf, "Late-Life Disability Trends and Trajectories," in *Handbook of Aging and the Social Sciences,* 8th ed., ed. Linda George and Kenneth Ferraro (Academic Press, 2016), 77. In the second part of his definition, Wolf quotes Lisa I. Iezzoni and Vicki A. Freedman, "Turning the Disability Tide: The Importance of Definitions," *JAMA* 299, no. 3 (2008): 332–334.

80. Wolf, "Late-Life Disability Trends and Trajectories," 81.

81. Ibid., 82–84.

82. Ibid., 88–89.

83. Ibid., 95.

84. Helen K. Black and Robert L. Rubinstein, "Themes of Suffering in Later Life," *Journal of Gerontology Series B: Psychological Sciences and Social Sciences* 59, no. 1 (2004): S22.

85. Ibid., 22–23.

86. Ibid., 23.

87. Ibid.

88. Ibid.

89. Richard A. Settersten Jr., "Linking the Two Ends of Life: What Gerontology Can Learn from Childhood Studies," *Journal of Gerontology Series B: Psychological Sciences and Social Sciences* 60, no. 4 (2005): S174.

90. Richard A. Settersten Jr., "Aging and the Life Course," in *Handbook of Aging and Social Sciences,* 6th ed., ed. Robert H. Binstock and Linda K. George (Academic Press, 2006), 3–19.

5

Adventurous Aging Through International Travel

Part of the desire of older adults to maintain their long-standing identity is expressed in efforts to engage in leisure activities that offer an expanded, rather than shrinking, life space.[1] Travel is considered to be a highly desirable leisure activity that is a cherished goal of many retirees.[2] The challenges and triumphs of traveling with disabilities offer an ideal case study of the experiences of older adults who want to retain highly engaged lifestyles even in the face of increasing frailties of late life. Older adults who undertake travel are likely to seek accommodations and often operate within a social model of disability.[3]

In this chapter, we offer another personal narrative account by coauthor Eva about international travel she undertook with her husband, Boaz, at a time that both were in their seventies and living with physical limitations. We aim here to illustrate the capacity of many older adults living with disabilities to retain expectations about vital involvement in life.[4]

It is recognized that prospects for long-distance travel may be available only to older adults who are well educated, who have financial means, and whose disabilities are not overwhelming. Nevertheless, this is an important group to consider. These elders link to gerontological ideas about successful and proactive aging and aspirations for living a full and autonomous life even in the face of increasing frailty. On the surface, this might appear to be inconsistent with positions of disability studies that seek structural accommodations. Indeed, a policy equivalent of the ADA has not been implemented in Europe, and many old buildings are ill-suited to the needs of travelers with disabilities. Yet the assertiveness inherent in undertaking international travel by older adults with disabilities embodies orientations of the disability rights movement to actively resist social exclusion.[5]

This chapter was coauthored with Boaz Kahana, professor of psychology at Cleveland State University.

Much has been said about the new cohorts of older adults since 1964 when Robert Kastenbaum wrote his almost forgotten classic *New Thoughts on Old Age.*[6] Older adults today are, on the whole, more educated, technology savvy, and assertive, and they loathe sitting in the armchair that has long symbolized this phase of life.[7] As part of a more risk-taking and adventurous orientation to late life, older adults are moving to the Sunbelt, starting new jobs after retirement, taking out-of-town trips to new destinations, and generally are on the move. The great success of Elderhostel and the growing investment of retired older adults in civic engagement initiatives attest to this trend.[8]

Yet accompanying this new image of late-life activity is a misconception that healthier lifestyles and youthful attitudes can insulate against frailty of old age. "Disability-free life expectancy" is a favorite term used by demographers to describe a life that is worth living.[9] However, the lived experience of those who cross into the territory of old age offers a more complex picture. As noted in prior chapters, older people typically suffer from multiple chronic illnesses and are likely to have attendant physical impairments and functional limitations.[10] Those limitations are not always visible. They may also differ from traditional descriptions of disabilities in their unpredictable manifestations. Common chronic illnesses such as heart disease, diabetes, asthma, and arthritis often have flare-ups, particularly when travel disrupts typical routines. Sensory impairments reflected in hearing loss, along with poor vision, may add to vulnerabilities in coping with new and demanding environments for elderly travelers. For ease of communication and convenience, in this chapter we refer to older adults with disabilities as "frail travelers" or "senior travelers." Additionally, we note that in the context of travel, the term *handicapped* is typically applied to persons with disabilities. We use this term as it reflects common usage, but recognize that scholars in the field of disability studies do not favor this term.[11]

One way of ensuring that travel does not turn into travail is by joining organized groups that cater to the needs of slower-paced travel by senior travelers. However, participation in such groups is generally costly and assumes a willingness to give up individual initiative and flexibility in trip planning. Such arrangements appeal most to travelers who are willing to accept or who enjoy age-segregated and group-based travel. Furthermore, older adults who live with disabilities that have unpredictable or fluctuating symptoms may find it difficult to conform to prearranged schedules. Thus, many older adults may pursue independent travel alone, with friends, or as an older couple.

Long-distance travel by older adults need not be restricted to tourism. Many older adults embark on travel to visit friends, family, or colleagues in distant lands, or to attend conferences or cultural events. Prior studies of disabled travelers have covered sports and medical travel and focused on needs of younger travelers suffering from specific illnesses acquired during travel.[12] Some studies have considered travel with specific disabilities, often involving mobility limitations, and focused on wheelchair-bound travelers.[13]

The opportunity for independent international travel allows for maintaining personal growth and innovation as older travelers visit new places, meet new people, and encounter new experiences that can enrich their lives.[14] The tourist industry is slowly recognizing the growing market share and revenues generated by older and disabled travelers, particularly as the baby boomer generation is entering old age.[15]

An interesting trend in research on disabled travelers relates to consideration of information resources accessed by members of this group. Indeed, changing cultural patterns for sharing travel tips relate to user-generated content (UGC), which is viewed as increasingly replacing word-of-mouth travel information.[16] However, there has been little attention directed at understanding environmental demands and barriers posed by international travel for older tourists.

There is some recognition in the literature that access may be limited and that insufficient organized efforts exist for enhancing access for elderly tourists.[17] Yet the individual older traveler must deal with realities of existing environmental demands and barriers. To pursue rewarding travel experiences, older travelers must engage in proactive adaptations such as careful planning and marshaling social support when needed.[18] Such adaptations can prevent environmental stressors and demands from diminishing positive experiences in travel.

In this chapter, we seek to unpack the challenges faced by moderately disabled older travelers who venture outside the familiarity of language, customs, and facilities of their homeland. These circumstances are of theoretical interest to social scientists and health care professionals as they challenge stereotypes of aging and of coping in late life.[19] They also help expand our understanding of resourcefulness of older adults who are living with disabilities.[20]

Experiential Perspectives

In discussing experiences of older adults traveling in distant lands, we use an autoethnographic approach. The chapter is organized around adaptive tasks and recommended coping strategies that are based on the personal narratives of Eva and Boaz's travel experiences while taking two four-week summer trips in 2010 and one in 2011. Eva was seventy years old on our first trip and Boaz was seventy-seven. Our trips involved air transportation and travel by train. We were traveling with moderate health challenges that were not plainly visible to observers. Nevertheless, we required accommodations in diet and levels of physical activity. Specifically, our health challenges required that we avoid fried or oily food. Furthermore, we had mobility limitations in walking long distances and climbing stairs, resulting in requests for wheelchair assistance during train and air travel and help with luggage for train transfers. Such needs and limitations are common to many senior travelers. Nevertheless, we acknowledge that the specific examples we provide were unique to our experiences, needs, and preferences.

We fit the typical picture of a dual-career academic couple that is well educated and middle class. We also note that more limited financial resources can constrain options available to frail older travelers. We aimed to economize where possible and lacked the means for luxury travel. Thus, we traveled tourist class rather than business class. This mode of travel is quite challenging for frail older adults because cramped seating arrangements make it difficult to sleep or even rest. Of course, there are many older adults for whom travel abroad is totally out of reach. And there are others who can make travel much more comfortable with the use of business-class amenities and private guided tours. While financial resources, education, and access to the Internet can better enable frail older adults to be adventurous and engage in long-distance travel, they cannot ensure that all obstacles will be removed.

During our trips, we each kept detailed notes that we wrote up by hand each evening, regarding stressors or challenges encountered, coping efforts, and the success of these efforts in meeting the challenges of the day. Our methodology thus fits qualitative research guidelines of autoethnography.[21] Our trips took us to twelve airports (eight outside the United States) and ten European countries, and involved eight segments of train travel in five countries. The countries visited included the United States, the United Kingdom, Austria, Hungary, Germany, France, the Netherlands, Denmark, Sweden, and Norway. All of the countries we visited are developed, relatively affluent countries.

We observed that privatization and outsourcing of services for the handicapped have resulted in more limited, cumbersome, and inflexible services that close doors to assistance for older travelers. We thus found much unexpected variability among the countries we traveled to regarding obtaining travel accommodations. Thus, while advance reservations or notice were encouraged in England, services could also be obtained on the spot at railroad stations when necessary. In Germany, extensive paperwork was typically required in arranging for assistance for travel by rail, yet completion of forms did not ensure that the requested service would be present at the assigned time. In Denmark, where services are offered more informally, wheelchairs could materialize on short notice. However, this happens only if travelers succeed in locating the separate office in the station for handicapped travelers and if the office is open for business. In Sweden, there were no services for frail travelers at the railroad stations, but a private service may be contacted with a minimum four-day prior notice. This time frame made marshaling assistance impractical for international travelers. In the next sections of this chapter, we highlight unique stressors of international travel for older travelers who have some disabilities.

Stressors of Traveling

Person-Based Health-Related Stressors and Challenges

A major complicating factor in international travel for older adults can be due to multiple comorbidities that afflict many older persons. Elderly travelers have to deal with the management of these chronic illnesses while en route. Furthermore, exacerbation of health conditions may occur due to travel-related stressors and environmental demands. Chronic illnesses are also likely to be associated with attendant physical impairments and functional limitations.[22] Such manifestations of disability are likely to limit the amount of standing, walking, carrying bags, and other strenuous activities that long-distance travel often demands. Disabling health conditions also result in becoming more vulnerable to environmental demands, such as exposure to heat, cold, sleeplessness, thirst, or hunger, that can arise in problematic travel situations.[23]

Environment-Based Stressors and Challenges

Physical demands. Travel involves demands that defy the environmental expectations and routines of all travelers; yet for those with functional limitations, these demands are especially taxing. For example, a promising and leisurely sightseeing tour on the hop-on/hop-off bus can turn into a hot and bumpy obstacle course if frail travelers board an older model bus without air-conditioning. Additionally, long cab rides in non-air-conditioned taxis and those with poor suspensions can contribute to car sickness for anyone, but are particularly risky for older and frail travelers. Airports may require carrying luggage up steps when escalators are out of order, and hotels that advertise air-conditioning often limit air-conditioning to public areas. Poor air quality can also precipitate breathing problems for frail older travelers.

Environmental legibility. Linguistic and cultural barriers often converge to make environments more difficult to navigate. Such lack of legibility can be problematic for all travelers, but it compounds challenges for the frail older traveler—particularly because they are more likely to require interaction with locals when seeking assistance. Simple differences in symbols can make washrooms for the handicapped difficult to operate. Similarly, symbols on many computers differ, creating communication challenges for senior travelers who want to stay connected through the Internet. We purchased cell phones in the United States for use in Europe and found it easy to call home, but we experienced great difficulty in making local calls. In case of an emergency where an ambulance had to be called, we lacked information about emergency access codes in different countries. Travelogues and tales of journeying to faraway lands usually abound with accounts of surprises and cultural differences in understanding of everyday life experiences. These very attractions of travel depart from the routine and familiar. They often involve physical and psychological challenges for older travelers based on illegibility of novel environments.[24]

Language barriers. Inability to speak and understand the language of the country visited can pose special stressors as well as barriers to successful adaptation for travelers with disabilities. In our case, Boaz requested a wheelchair for transfer at the train station and was happy with the papers handed to him confirming the arrangements. However, he found out, to his dismay, that the letter written in German indicated "wheelchair supplied by traveler" rather than "wheelchair requested." This misunderstanding created a long delay for obtaining a wheelchair and resulted in our missing the train.

Ageism. Older travelers in general, and frail older adults in particular, encounter special challenges based on societal attitudes that devalue old age and tend to be dismissive of opinions, requests, and preferences of older adults.[25] Such ageism may be manifested in lack of special consideration, even for visibly frail travelers. We often experienced a lack of patience by younger people who showed no inclination to allow us access in crowded elevators or trains.

At times, we experienced disregard for our requests to accommodate our needs. We were labeled "fussy complainers" whose wishes may be reasonably ignored. This type of response was exemplified by the conductor of a train we took from Berlin to Copenhagen. Since we had a Eurail Pass prepurchased travel plan, we traveled in first class. However, the air-conditioning stopped working in all of the first-class cars. To my surprise, I discovered that there was air-conditioning in some of the second-class cars. I explained to the conductor about our distress due to the heat and requested to be reseated in second class where the air-conditioning was working and there were empty seats. He had little sympathy and indicated that everyone must remain where their original reservations were made. He turned to another staff member, noting, "Old people are fussy."

Coping with Challenges:
Managing Environmental Demands

Obtaining Comfortable Lodging

Older travelers with physical frailty, are especially vulnerable to environmental discomforts. Accordingly, hotels without temperature control for heat and air-conditioning can result in sleepless nights, or exacerbation of medical conditions such as asthma or heart problems. Well-designed toilet and bathing facilities are also essential for the safety and comfort of travelers with disabilities. A common problem we experienced relates to lack of safety rails in bathtubs and difficulty in regulating hot and cold water. In quaint local hotels, we also faced challenges in finding comfortable mattresses to avoid low-back pain. While back pain from a bad mattress can inconvenience any traveler, for older travelers with back issues it can be particularly debilitating. This challenge is exacerbated by carrying luggage and by extended periods of sitting during long-distance travel. Older travelers must also ensure that there is no need to climb steps to reach their room or toilet facilities.

Hotels in Europe do not routinely provide in-room refrigerators. Having access to a refrigerator in our room was needed to ensure availability of healthy and readily digestible food. We found that the location of the hotel was also important to make sure that railroad stations, buses, or taxis could be reached without too much walking. Having a nice hotel in an isolated or difficult-to-reach locale poses unique challenges. Facilities, common in US hotels such as affordable laundering services are not readily found abroad. We found it preferable to exchange charm and architectural beauty offered by local hostels for predictable comforts provided by larger hotel chains. This was a major change in orientation from travel in our younger days when we much preferred local color to familiar comfort.

Many major US hotel chains offer special discounts for senior travelers from the United States. One challenge we faced on arrival in Europe was the ability to check in early at our hotel after an overnight transatlantic flight. While check-in times at hotels are typically in the afternoon, most flights from the United States arrive in Europe early in the morning. It was important to arrange for morning check-ins on arrival in Europe since it was difficult to sleep on tourist-class flights between the United States and Europe.

In the Internet era of today, private apartment rentals are aggressively advertised online. Thus, frail elder travelers may be tempted to rent private apartments in lieu of traditional hotel rooms. We were among those so tempted, especially when younger colleagues recommended such spacious and economical arrangements. Yet we found out the hard way that private arrangements may present unique problems for travelers with disabilities. In one case, we needed urgent medical care at night. We did not know how to call an ambulance. We failed to realize the benefits of hotels in helping travelers obtain medical care should an emergency arise.

At times, we had to request intervention by a manager to obtain special accommodations due to our health problems and age. This was to avoid lengthy and tiring waits for a room to be made ready after our arrival. We found that pointing to our references to disability generally helped us in US-based chain hotels. European hotels appeared to respond better to age- and health-related concerns, but often seemed unfamiliar with the concept of accommodations for disabilities. In terms of planning ahead for residential comfort, older travelers may benefit from checking their prospective accommodations on Trip Advisor (www.tripadvisor.com) where comments are available based on experiences of other travelers categorized by age.[26]

Obtaining Accommodations During Train Travel

Seeking accommodations may be best exemplified by needs of frail older travelers for special assistance on trains. Even for older adults who do not have major mobility limitations, distances involved in transfer from one train to the next may be great, and getting luggage on and off trains poses physical challenges. Services for handicapped travelers are available in most European countries, but means of obtaining such services vary from place to place. We found that ingenuity and assertiveness were needed to marshal existing support services. For travel outside of Britain, requests for assistance must be made three days in advance by phone, but last-minute assistance can be made available at the station. For international travel on the Eurostar train from London to Brussels or Paris, assistance was readily available by simply reporting our needs on arrival at the station. However, such efficient service at our starting point did not ensure adequate help at our next destination. Thus, on arriving in Brussels, the assistance was not present. Thankfully, Eurostar personnel called the stationmaster, and help did arrive to assist with transfer to a local train to Cologne. Tipping is expected for such extra help. We found that having a stack of $5 and $10 bills was a great asset. US currency was accepted for tips in all of the countries in Western Europe where we traveled.

The availability of assistance was much diminished in Cologne. Here, we were on our own, as we were informed that there is no assistance for travelers with disabilities at the station. We managed to get a cab driver to come into the station to pick up our luggage. The next day, we returned to the station to make sure that we locate help for our next train trip. Neither the information kiosk attendants nor the ticket agents were aware of options to help frail travelers. At this point, we contacted the special assistant for first-class travel. She provided us with a phone number to use to marshal assistance and provide a wheelchair for our next trip. We elicited support from the hotel concierge to arrange for help at the station for departure from Cologne and arrival in Berlin. Boaz and I were instructed to obtain seat reservations and personnel would meet us at the train station entrance a half-hour before departure of our train.

There were no seats at the main entrance of the train station and cabs could only stop at the side door. Boaz was seated with the suitcases at the side entrance while I proceeded to summon the assistant from the main entrance. We arrived at the train platform where we heard an announcement regarding our train, which we only partially understood. Instead of the direct train, a local train was substituted that required a change of trains to get to Berlin. Luckily, our assistant was still with us and was able to make alternative arrangements, so we could depart on a later direct train. Awaiting the next direct train required sitting in a hot station. We found that initiative and persistence in marshaling assistance were essential to making travel possible. We also had to be ready to change plans rapidly to overcome unforeseen obstacles.

Getting Adequate Rest

A major attraction of travel is the opportunity to experience novel situations, and be stimulated by change rather than sameness in one's environment. During brief trips, there is pressure to compress many experiences into short time frames. When we were younger, it was not uncommon to take several demanding sightseeing tours, involving much walking, with little time allocated for rest and relaxation. Such itineraries often followed soon after long distance travel from city to city or country to country. As frail older travelers, such schedules result in exhaustion and can readily provoke health-related crises. We experienced this firsthand when we tried to take advantage of discounts offered for taking both morning and afternoon tours. We were so exhausted after returning from our afternoon excursion that we fell asleep and missed dinner.

Older travelers must learn to regulate demands on their body by learning to pace themselves. Getting adequate sleep and rest during the day and at night are important goals in this regard. We found traveling light (i.e., carrying little baggage) to be useful protection against demands for lifting heavy objects. Avoiding outdoor activities in the heat can also protect older travelers from heat-related health problems. One should also avoid taking walks in cold or rainy weather, or taking an evening sightseeing tour after a full day's program. We found that, in joining organized sightseeing tours, we must avoid the temptation to follow others in climbing up to lookout points.

In the beginning, we found it difficult to pace ourselves and needed to learn to recognize that at times we must be content with watching the world go by from the coffee shop in our hotel. We learned to savor small pleasures, as we would alternate morning or afternoon sightseeing with resting at the hotel and sitting at an outdoor cafe. To maintain comfort and health when environmental demands are high, we found it useful to utilize cabs liberally.

While public transportation is economical and generally recommended in tourist guidebooks, as older travelers we encountered unexpected challenges. These included the need for climbing stairs at metro stations, long waits for trains and buses with no place to sit while waiting, and lack of seats in crowded streetcars or buses. Thus, we learned to balance the expenditure of energy involved in getting to our destination with the energy expenditure needed for seeing and enjoying that destination (e.g., a museum). We found it helpful to take self-guided walks with headphones in museums. This allowed for frequent rest stops that are not possible on group walking tours, which usually call for a great deal of standing and walking. We often visited smaller or less popular attractions that offered a good substitute for the demands of popular and busy attractions. For example, we resisted the temptation to visit the Oslo Opera House, as it was described as having many levels. Hop-on/hop-off sightseeing bus tours are generally user friendly for older travelers since they can get off when it is too hot, raining, or when they need a rest.

Of course, watching the colorful street life of European cities can be a special treat for many travelers from the United States and being a spectator in interesting surroundings can be a fulfilling pursuit. When one of us was feeling exhausted, we were often tempted to follow our companion's desire for being more active. During our travels, we learned that it is okay to part ways when one of us felt energetic and wanted to go for a walk while the other was content reading a book in the hotel coffee shop or in our room. Given that we enjoy staying up later to attend plays and concerts or sit at a café, we needed to make sure that we avoided early morning activities, and we even selected hotels that served breakfast at a later hour. We also made an effort to get rooms in the back of the building where nighttime noise and lights from the street would be minimized.

Managing Illness and Maintaining Health

Environmental demands of travel can often interfere with routines for health maintenance and chronic illness management. Travel schedules are likely to disrupt routines of taking medications, managing sleep and wakefulness, getting sufficient rest, and getting enough exercise. Long flights lead to jet lag, limit passengers' ability to move around for healthy circulation, and typically offer rich and hard-to-digest foods. Bus trips, even on sightseeing tours, also limit elders' ability to walk around. Bathroom breaks might be too hard to come by due to infrequent stops or inaccessible locations, and passengers might arrive exhausted at their destination.

To maintain good health and achieve adequate chronic illness management, we found it useful to engage in health monitoring and self-care; limit strenuous activity; get sufficient rest and sleep; eat a proper diet; and, when needed, access competent medical care.

Self-Monitoring and Self-Care

Older travelers often take medications for multiple chronic conditions. We found it important to take along both our prescription medicines and sufficient amounts of routine medication for the duration of the trip. These included Tylenol for pain relief or fever reduction, cortisone cream for skin irritations, Imodium for diarrhea, and antacids for indigestion due to reactions to unfamiliar foods. A list of medications providing dosages and generic, rather than brand names, may be helpful should medications be lost or require refills. Monitoring devices, ranging from compact blood pressure monitors to thermometers, are useful to stay on top of potential exacerbations of chronic health problems. For the frail older traveler, these precautions assume special importance as these travelers are likely to need to manage multiple chronic health conditions.

Eating a Proper Diet

Obtaining a healthy diet can be challenging, especially for older travelers with unique dietary needs. Thus, although brewed decaf coffee is widely served in the United States as a healthful option compared with caffeinated beverages, it is unavailable in most European countries, even in high-quality hotels and restaurants. Similarly, lactose-reduced products are difficult to obtain abroad. Coping with these general challenges may require information seeking to make sure that one is aware of the product being consumed and, in some cases, just changing expectations and making do with less desirable substitutes, such as instant decaf.

In our case, eating a largely fat-free diet was a critical health need for Boaz, who has serious adverse reactions to fried food or even a rich meal. This posed major challenges while traveling since baked potatoes and broiled fish, staples in US hotels and restaurants, are not readily available outside the United States. Eating at buffet restaurants was sometimes helpful, as we could observe and inspect the food. We found it useful to try to avoid surprises that are common due to language barriers to understanding menus and in communicating with waiters. For example, asking for a salad without dressing may result in getting a salad that has "only" oil and vinegar dressing. The widespread market penetration of Subway restaurants was of some help, as were breakfast buffets that included soft- or hard-boiled eggs as a choice. Dietary restrictions can also pose a problem to older travelers in social settings where a festive meal is being shared with others. We found this to be a problem at shared meals or banquets offered at conferences.

Accessing Competent Medical Care

In spite of precautions, older travelers will occasionally encounter unexpected medical emergencies. It is judicious to purchase travel insurance for senior travelers and to pay additional insurance charges that cover medical evacuation to a hospital of one's choice. Some plans offer evacuation to a hospital in the United States after a patient is stabilized at a local hospital. If outpatient or emergency room care is needed, the toll-free numbers available from insurance providers will direct the frail older traveler to competent care. We had occasion to call such a number on a trip to Paris when I fell at a conference, spraining a knee that became swollen. We were directed to the "American" hospital in Paris. This was a high-quality English-speaking hospital, and we were reimbursed for the efficient care that I received there by the travel health insurance we purchased.

We also had an encounter with emergency care on another trip. We landed at the Birmingham, UK, airport and literally started off our trip with a crisis. After a sleepless night on our flight and a breakfast served only two hours after a rich dinner, we encountered an extremely bumpy taxi ride to our hotel. My husband got carsick and we had to direct the cab to head to the nearest emergency room. Fortunately, we were in an English-speaking country and had brought along our medical records. We found the National Health Service to be efficient and competent, and the nurses to be kind and sympathetic. We were discharged after the hospital was satisfied that no heart problems were involved.

Maintaining a Positive Self-Concept While Needing Assistance

One of the key requisites for being able to enjoy travel in spite of physical limitations is the ability to maintain a positive self-concept, even while grappling with insecurities about one's health and one's ability to deal with constantly changing environmental demands. Maintenance of a positive self-concept can also help older travelers against excess disability. We found three mechanisms to be helpful for maintaining a positive self-concept. These include: (1) minimizing stigma; (2) maintaining grooming and appearance; and (3) staying connected to significant others.

Avoiding stigma becomes particularly important as one seeks accommodations for disability.[27] Spencer E. Cahill and Robin Eggleston documented the negative responses that accrue to wheelchair users who ask for assistance.[28] To minimize stigma dealing with our dietary limitations, we had to develop explanations for our inability to patronize restaurants that did not fit our dietary needs and for selecting restricted menu items that preclude sharing meals with friends. In regard to needing assistance with luggage or needing to call a taxi, we made reference to a tiring day of travel and how books were weighing down our luggage.

While travel is often a time to dress casually and pay less attention to one's appearance, we found that wearing neat clothing helped get better service in hotels and restaurants. We felt that it minimized stigma, particularly when we attended conferences and sought to avoid a "spoiled identity."[29] Maintaining good grooming was both more important and more challenging during long-distance travel than in normal life at home. We planned carefully to have versatile lightweight clothing that we handwashed on the first day of reaching a new destination.

We felt a particular assault on our self-concept as we were unable to join colleagues for a meal or an outing by boat. In such situations, we found that our self-concept was enhanced after calling or e-mailing friends and family back home and being reassured about our social connectedness. Staying connected to significant others back home and at the conferences we attended also helped maintain our positive self-image. Familiar individuals interacted with us based on long-term family or professional relationships and social roles. Our travel-related physical limitations did not impact their interactions with us.

Regulating Expectations and Attitudes

Attaining positive outcomes also involves changing attitudes and expectations. Goals had to be restructured to appreciate the rewards of tourism, even when activities had to be curtailed to conserve energy and spend more time resting. The cognitive maneuvers needed include: (1) accepting limitations; (2) maintaining good humor in the face of frustrating situations; (3) savoring small pleasures; and (4) enjoying spectator activities.

Recognizing and accepting our limitations was facilitated by changing expectations regarding the scope of activities on a trip or on a given day. Taking frustrations of travel due to frailty in stride can be well served by maintaining a sense of humor. On our most recent trip, we planned to take an evening sightseeing excursion that we had paid for in advance. The bus was supposed to arrive sometime after 7 P.M. after picking up tourists from other hotels. We waited for about twenty minutes at the designated hotel entrance on a cool drizzly evening. There was no place to sit down and we got tired. We agreed that one of us would sit in the lobby while the other would wait for the bus. Five minutes after this arrangement, the bus sped by the door, not slowing down long enough to notice one person waiting. The plans for the evening were ruined. We felt frustrated by the fact that our caution regarding exposure to inclement weather resulted in missing the tour. We also felt upset with the bus driver. However, we soon realized that we were vacationing in an attractive city and decided to see the humor in our missed venture. We also concluded that we were better off resting in the evening after a full day of activities.

This was one example of the many times we had to come to terms with our limitations. After an episode of car sickness at the start of our trip, we chose to avoid boat rides, including sightseeing by boat at Oslo Fjord. We also limited visits to museums, as they involved too much standing and walking. We recognized that we had to save our physical resources for city-to-city train trips and be content with sightseeing by bus, walking around in city centers, and sitting in coffee shops and quaint restaurants to soak up the ambience of each city. Our diminished expectations for adventure went a long way toward making our trip enjoyable.

Planning Ahead, but Adjusting to the Unexpected

An important resource for making travel successful was planning ahead. The importance of planning ahead for air or train travel, itineraries, and hotel reservations cannot be overemphasized. Planning for seat reservations on trains (even for travelers with a Eurail Pass) is a critical prerequisite for obtaining handicapped assistance. For such assistance both the train and seat number must be specified in advance. As we noted earlier, it is wise to purchase high-quality travel insurance that can facilitate receiving good medical care should problems arise. Proper planning also calls for taking along medical records that can provide valuable data to treating physicians.

Even as we focus on the virtues of planning, our experiences confirmed that even the best-laid plans can cover only a relatively small fraction of the challenging situations that older travelers will likely encounter. Thus, successful adaptation also requires the ability to change plans and demonstrate flexibility when personal needs or situational options change. Thus, for example, well-laid plans for getting assistance with luggage upon disembarking from a train did not materialize on several occasions. In these situations we had to be willing to impose on fellow travelers and ask for assistance, which was typically provided.

Information Seeking

Active information seeking is an important resource during long-distance travel. For frail older travelers, being well informed can make the difference between health maintenance and exacerbation of health problems. Having access to train schedules, to functional cell phones for the region, and to the Internet greatly facilitated our ability to gain needed information. International travel poses challenges to reliance on traditional information resources offered by print media, such as train schedules, which may be outdated. Double-checking departures on the Internet or with train stations is extremely helpful. Organization and resourcefulness are needed for information seeking, marshaling support, and engaging in advocacy when problems arise.

Circumstances are constantly changing and thus information must be updated throughout travel. We found it helpful to seek advice of other experienced travelers or local citizens. Ability to use international cell phones and have Web access can prove highly beneficial. Since frail travelers must limit the weight of their luggage, it is not always feasible to take along computers. Nevertheless, by selecting hotels with business centers, it was possible to connect to the Web using hotel computers. In some cases, we found it useful to phone the United States and to have friends or family assist in obtaining needed information or rescheduling travel.

Paying for Services and Conveniences

An old adage proclaims that "sometimes a penny is like a dollar and sometimes a dollar is like a penny." This statement is most apt for facilitating travel in late life. Many older travelers were socialized to economize and become concerned when unfavorable exchange rates of the US dollar against foreign currencies make costs seem particularly high. Unique foreign customs can result in expenditures that are typically avoided in the United States. One case in point is the need to purchase bottled water. Free tap water, which is generally good in Europe, is seldom made available. Yet at times it is well worth shelling out $3 for a bottle of water to avoid dehydration. Buying a costly cup of coffee or tea or a soft drink at a nice coffee house is also a good investment for finding a place to rest and for locating clean toilet facilities. Taxis can be exorbitantly expensive in Europe too. Yet the frail older traveler may well find that after a strenuous day of sightseeing, when buses do not drop travelers off at their hotel, it is well worth the convenience to take an overpriced taxi. As growing numbers of travelers now wheel their own luggage to their rooms, bellhops have become increasingly rare. Offering a tip to staff at the front desk can lead to greater willingness to assist an older traveler to their room with their luggage. Considering more major expenditures, the extra cost of staying at a better hotel or even flying business class, if an older traveler is at risk for phlebitis, are also worth consideration.

It should be recognized that what may be a luxury or splurge to the healthy adult traveler often becomes an essential expenditure for the physically challenged older traveler. Traveling business class to avoid edema or an embolism, liberal use of cabs and individual guided tours, and meeting of specific accommodation needs can add substantially to travel costs. Yet they open horizons of full participation in life for older adults with disabilities. This is consistent with goals of full inclusion articulated by the disability rights movement.[30]

Self-Advocacy

Standing up for our needs or for those of our travel companion were important skills for resource mobilization. We often found it surprising how rigidly rules were applied outside the United States. When a rule makes no sense or jeopardizes your health and welfare, older adults must be brave and advocate for getting an exception made or getting more immediate attention. One important area of advocacy that we encountered related to having restaurants disregard our dietary requests. If the "boiled" fish is clearly fried or the "baked" potato is smothered in butter, there is no substitute for sending the offending food back to the kitchen even if the server is unhappy. Where special accommodations such as wheelchairs were promised but did not show up, there was a need to appeal to a person with greater authority.

Advocacy was also often required to avoid delays in checking into hotels. It was useful to go to a manager and note that housekeeping simply needs to reprioritize cleaning of rooms to accommodate the health needs of older travelers. In some cases, assertiveness was needed to ask a teenager or young person to give up a seat on a bench to an older person waiting for a bus or train. We found it easier to advocate for one another than to do so for our individual benefit.

Achieving Positive Outcomes

Based on our experiences, enjoyment of travel consists of many small victories and pleasant experiences that in aggregate make the trip worthwhile and result in the traveler seeking future international travel. These positive outcomes are largely a function of successful and competent behavioral management of person and environment–based challenges and of successful regulation of attitudes and expectations. Satisfaction with a trip and satisfaction with one's own mastery of travel challenges each shape the overall evaluation of the travel experience. If these evaluations are favorable, it is likely that the frail older traveler will consider taking future trips.

A trip may be deemed to have been successfully executed even if there are minor health crises or symptoms necessitating physician visits. Planning for good travel insurance and medical care abroad can facilitate this positive outcome. Since many frail elders travel in twosomes (either as an older couple or two older friends traveling together), an important positive outcome relates to maintenance of well-being by the travel companion.

Often the companion may have fewer or less disabling health problems, but experiences greater stress and demands in the caregiving role. Caregiver or companion satisfaction with travel is likely to influence decisions about undertaking future trips. As frail elders venture on trips involving international travel, one of the most basic goals and hopes is that the trip itself materializes with minimal health-related glitches between the time of planning the trip and the date of departure. Having achieved the goal of going on the trip, older adults can look forward to enjoying long distance travel even if they encounter delay or interruption.

Conclusion

Our discussion has described stressors that can act as barriers as well as adaptations that can facilitate long-distance international travel by disabled older adults. Good outcomes depend on interactions between social and environmental structures and personal agency. We sought to identify discrete elements of environment and person that shape successful adaptations.[31] It is important to emphasize that the older adults who we designated as frail travelers may or may not accept a disability identity.[32]

In this chapter, we offered some insights about challenges faced by elderly persons who desire to live adventurous lives that include international travel even in the face of disabilities. We focused on the ways that proactive adaptations on the one hand and skillful search for accommodations on the other can bring goals within reach. In the next chapter, we consider more limited goals of aging in place, in one's familiar environment, as more serious disabilities are encountered by older adults. We do so in the context of a more formal community survey that we conducted to understand attitudes of community-dwelling older adults toward living with disabilities and the environmental and activity modifications that they undertook to help them age in place. In the chapter, personal narrative illuminates the experience of dealing with physical environments while aging in place with disabilities.

Notes

1. Taina Rantanen, Erja Portegijs, Anne Viljanen, Johanna Eronen, Milla Saajanaho, Li-Tang Tsai, Markku Kauppinen, et al., "Individual and Environmental Factors Underlying Life Space of Older People—Study Protocol and Design of a Cohort Study on Life-Space Mobility in Old Age (LISPE)," *BMC Public Health* 12, no. 1 (2012): 1.

2. Galit Nimrod, "In Support of Innovation Theory: Innovation in Activity Patterns and Life Satisfaction Among Recently Retired Individuals," *Ageing and Society* 28, no. 6 (2008): 831–846.

3. Tom Shakespeare, *Disability Rights and Wrongs Revisited* (Routledge, 2013).

4. Erik H. Erikson, Joan M. Erikson, and Helen Q. Kivnick, *Vital Involvement in Old Age* (Norton, 1994).

5. Tom Shakespeare, "Disability Studies Today and Tomorrow," *Sociology of Health and Illness* 27, no. 1 (2005): 138–148.

6. Robert Kastenbaum, *New Thoughts on Old Age* (Springer, 1964).

7. Ann Bowling, "Enhancing Later Life: How Older People Perceive Active Ageing?" *Aging and Mental Health* 12, no. 3 (2008): 293–301.

8. Lawrence Force, Jeffrey S. Kahana, and Valerie Capalbo, "The Role of AAAs in Promoting Health for Seniors: A Preliminary Research Report," *Open Longevity Science* 4 (2010): 30–35.

9. Kenneth G. Manton, XiLiang Gu, and Gene R. Lowrimore, "Cohort Changes in Active Life Expectancy in the US Elderly Population: Experience from the 1982–2004 National Long-Term Care Survey," *Journals of Gerontology Series B: Psychological Sciences and Social Sciences* 63, no. 5 (2008): S269–S281.

10. Lois M. Verbrugge and Alan M. Jette, "The Disablement Process," *Social Science and Medicine* 38, no. 1 (1994): 1–14.

11. Ronald J. Berger, *Introducing Disability Studies* (Lynne Rienner, 2013).

12. Christie M. Reed, "Travel Recommendations for Older Adults," *Clinics in Geriatric Medicine* 23, no. 3 (2007): 687–713.

13. John J. Burnett and Heather Bender Baker, "Assessing the Travel-Related Behaviors of the Mobility-Disabled Consumer," *Journal of Travel Research* 40, no. 1 (2001): 4–11.

14. Galit Nimrod and Arie Rotem, "Between Relaxation and Excitement: Activities and Benefits Gained in Retirees' Tourism," *International Journal of Tourism Research* 12, no. 1 (2010): 65–78.

15. Burnett and Baker, "Assessing the Travel-Related Behaviors of the Mobility-Disabled Consumer."

16. Wolfgang Drews and Christiane Schemer, "eTourism for All? Online Travel Planning of Disabled People," in *Information and Communication Technologies in Tourism 2010*, Proceedings of the International Conference in Lugano, Switzerland, February 10–12, 2010, ed. Ulrike Gretzal and Rob Law (Springer, 2010), 507–518.

17. Tanya L. Packer, Bob McKercher, and Matthew K. Yau, "Understanding the Complex Interplay Between Tourism, Disability and Environmental Contexts," *Disability and Rehabilitation* 29, no. 4 (2007): 281–292.

18. Eva Kahana and Boaz Kahana, "Contextualizing Successful Aging: New Directions in an Age-Old Search," in *Invitation to the Life Course: Toward New Understandings of Later Life*, ed. Richard A. Settersten, Jr. and Jon Hendricks (Baywood, 2003), 225–255.

19. Theodore Roszak, *The Making of an Elder Culture: Reflections on the Future of America's Most Audacious Generation* (New Society, 2009).

20. Nimrod, "In Support of Innovation Theory"; Kahana and Kahana, "Contextualizing Successful Aging."

21. Carolyn S. Ellis and Arthur Bochner, "Autoethnography, Personal Narrative, Reflexivity: Researcher as Subject," in *Handbook of Qualitative Research*, ed. Norman K Denzin and Yvonne S. Lincoln (Sage, 2000).

22. Verbrugge and Jette, "The Disablement Process."

23. M. Powell Lawton, "Aging and Performance of Home Tasks," *Human Factors* 32, no. 5 (1990): 527–536.

24. Terry Hartig, Florian G. Kaiser, and Peter A. Bowler, *Further Development of a Measure of Perceived Environmental Restorativeness* (Institutet för bostadsforskning, 1997).

25. Richard W. Butler, "The Concept of a Tourist Area Cycle of Evolution: Implications for Management of Resources," *The Canadian Geographer/Le Géographe Canadien* 24, no. 1 (1980): 5–12.

26. Ulrike Gretzel and Kyung Hyan Yoo, "Use and Impact of Online Travel Reviews," in *Information and Communication Technologies in Tourism 2008*, ed. Peter O'Connor, Wolfram Hopken, and Ulrike Gretzel (Springer, 2008), 35–46.

27. Erving Goffman, *Behavior in Public Places* (Free Press, 1963).

28. Spencer E. Cahill and Robin Eggleston, "Reconsidering the Stigma of Physical Disability," *Sociological Quarterly* 36, no. 4 (1995): 681–698.

29. Goffman, *Behavior in Public Place.*

30. Berger, *Introducing Disability Studies.*

31. Eva Kahana, Boaz Kahana, "Stress and Agentic Aging: A Targeted Cancer Adaptation Model," in *The Sage Handbook of Social Gerontology*, ed. Dale Dannefer, and Chris Phillipson (Sage, 2010), 280–293.

32. Jessica A. Kelley-Moore, John G. Schumacher, Eva Kahana, and Boaz Kahana, "When Do Older Adults Become 'Disabled'? Social and Health Antecedents of Perceived Disability in a Panel Study of the Oldest Old," *Journal of Health and Social Behavior* 47, no. 2 (2006): 126–141.

6

Managing the
Physical Environment

The focus of this chapter is on environmental and activity modifications implemented by older adults who are living with significant disabilities. Unlike the adventurous travelers discussed in Chapter 5, here we turn to those older adults who desire to "age in place."[1] Environmental gerontological research demonstrates that home modifications are central to this effort.[2] However, older adults who seek to make their home environment more manageable and user-friendly also share much in common with the adventurous travelers. Both groups engage in proactive adaptations, including planning ahead and marshaling supports to achieve their goals for maintaining independence.

Most older adults, including those living with disabilities, desire to remain in their homes, even as they face physical impairments and environmental risks.[3] There are risks inherent in resolving to stay in one's home when a combination of physical disabilities and lack of social resources contribute to making the home an inhospitable environment. Such was the case for many poor and frail elders who perished in the Chicago heat wave of 1995.[4]

While social research in the field of gerontology has directed little attention to place-based challenges of frail elders, environmental gerontologists have long been fascinated by the links between home and identity in late life.[5] Given the strong attachment to their homes by most older people, creating environmental modifications and using assistive devices to compensate for functional limitations offers a desirable option. Home modifications are generally conceived of by experts who make changes in housing design so as to be more fitting to needs of older adults with disabilities. While many developed countries, particularly in Europe, have long offered systematic programs for remodeling housing to better fit the needs of frail elders, such programs are recent innovations in the United States.[6] To the extent that environmental modifications can facilitate continued independent living, such changes are desirable.

Home environments have been associated with both positive and negative disability-related outcomes in late life.[7] The landmark report of the Institute of Medicine's Committee on a National Agenda for the Prevention of Disabilities, *Disability in America,* argues for research on factors that delay the onset of disability among the elderly and minimize the severity of its consequences.[8] Yet efforts to enhance opportunities and quality of life for persons with disabilities often lack an understanding of the special needs and preferences of older adults.[9] They also lack an appreciation of the inventiveness and creative potential of older adults and their families to implement solutions that enhance autonomy and functioning in the face of disability. Therefore, a contradiction exists between the universalizing design efforts of experts on one hand, and the unique preferences and resources of seniors.

Older adults' desire to continue living independently, even with disabling functional limitations,[10] is consistent with goals articulated by advocates for the disabled who propose "independent living" as a legitimate social movement with a distinct ideology.[11] Independent living as a social movement also reflects increasing efforts to demedicalize assistance for those confronting chronic illness.[12] These recent social trends share the assumption that all individuals, including the elderly and the disabled, can and should play key decisionmaking roles in maintaining their own health and quality of life. Thus, management of medically stabilized disabilities may benefit from self-care and active initiatives of individual patients, rather than being solely the domain of the formal health care system.[13]

The traditional rehabilitation paradigm focuses on interventions such as medical care or physical and occupational therapy, which can assist individuals to improve their capabilities for self-care in the face of illness-related impairments. In contrast, the independent living paradigm focuses on removing environmental barriers. It calls for altering inaccessible buildings, providing accessible transportation, and involving the person with disability as an active consumer or advocate in affecting such change.[14] Approaches in the field of lifespan design are consistent with this orientation for enhancing independence of elders with disabilities. In the latter approach, intervention efforts are not aimed at reducing the older person's disabilities, but instead aim to diminish disabling features of the home environment by appropriate modifications. Environmental modifications can include anything from better lighting to aid activities of those with vision loss to more accessible kitchen environments that can support food preparation. Environmental facilitation of social participation by disabled elders is highly compatible with approach of disability studies.[15]

Goals of lifespan design have been formulated to improve safety, reduce barriers to mobility, and enhance seniors' ability to carry out ADL and instrumental activities of daily living (IADL) functions.[16] Paralleling the shift in the rehabilitation paradigm from medical care to independent living, an interesting paradigm shift has also occurred in the field of gerontology regarding our understanding of person-environment transactions in late life.[17] There has been a growing recognition that even frail elders can play an important role in shaping their environments. M. Powell Lawton has termed this recognition the "environmental proactivity hypothesis."[18]

Lawton recognized that even as life space of impaired elderly persons may shrink, increasingly confining elders to their homes, there may be a surge in their control of the remaining space in the home environment. Older adults thus engage in "highly goal directed behavior designed to shape their environment for personally congruent need satisfaction."[19] This view departs from traditional approaches to illness adaptation, which describe older adults as passive victims of illness and impairment. Instead, it considers elders as proactive agents who engage in preventive and ameliorative adaptations to maximize functioning in spite of chronic illness and impairment.[20]

In the section below, we consider proactive adaptations by older adults who implement creative environmental modifications. We focus on accommodations to disability that have been initiated by older persons by considering spontaneous activity and environmental modifications implemented by and for frail elders. This can offer guidelines for developing better tools for living and tips for aging in place for elderly persons with disabilities.[21]

A major goal of the research we report here was to consider ameliorative adaptations of older adults who face varied physical impairments. We used a comprehensive ecological framework to consider the full spectrum of potential and actual adaptations among older adults living with physical impairments. The level of proactivity reflected in their adaptations was also of interest. We undertook a multimethod project, which resulted in the development of a refined taxonomy of ameliorative adaptations that can be initiated by disabled elders or by their family caregivers.

Designing Our Study

In our research, self report as well as observational data was obtained about the full range of environmental and behavioral modifications utilized by older adults who lived with disabilities in the community. We conducted in-depth interviews with sixty-four older adults who were living with significant physical impairments. When available, interviews were also conducted with spouses ($N = 18$). Environmental observations of each household were conducted to provide multiple sources of data. Demographic predictors of different types of ameliorative adaptations and unmet needs were also considered. Interviews and environmental observations were conducted with community-dwelling older adults in two locations: Cleveland, Ohio, and Clearwater, Florida.

Our study included participants who had significant functional limitations and impairments, defined by at least two limitations in activities of daily living. This allowed for observing varied adaptations to impairments. A total of thirty-two respondents comprised the Cleveland sample, with the remaining forty-eight respondents in the Clearwater sample. Persons who had been hospitalized in the past month were excluded from the study so that respondents were medically stable. Respondents had a sufficiently long-term disability to allow for environmental and activity modifications to occur. Inclusion of elderly respondents from both an urban community (Cleveland) and a retirement community (Clearwater) ensured that a broad spectrum of environmental modifications, as well as activity modifications, could be noted. Clients served by the Cleveland Visiting Nurses Association were referred by health care professionals who were aware of environmental modifications implemented by these elders and their spouses to deal with impairments. The Clearwater participants were selected from among the panel of participants in our longitudinal Florida Retirement study.[22]

In this study of environmental modifications we included respondents who were age sixty-five or older and who were referred for home health care within one month prior to the interview. Eighty-five percent of the study respondents were white and 15 percent were black. The study included fifty-one women (64 percent) and twenty-nine men (36 percent). The mean age of respondents was seventy-eight years, with age ranging from sixty-six to ninety-five years. Forty-five percent of respondents were married, 43 percent were widowed, 5 percent separated or divorced, and 8 percent never married.

We asked each older adult questions about their physical impairments and their functional (ADL and IADL) limitations. We also inquired about their goals of adaptations and the location within the home where modifications were made. Respondents were also asked to show the interviewer how they had modified their home environment. This allowed for extending the researchers' view of adaptations made beyond self-reports to actual observations.

Our multimethod data collection strategy proved useful. Our interviews revealed considerable concordance between patients' reports, spouses' reports, and researchers' observations of environmental modifications. They also suggested that elderly persons who suffer from impairments are in the best position to provide information about the full range of their environmental adaptations. We organized information obtained about adaptations made to cope with physical frailty in a three-dimensional matrix: (1) the *problem* requiring adaptation; (2) the type of *adaptation* made in response to the problem; and (3) the *level of proactivity* in initiating the action.

The response categories that emerged from our data encompass adaptations ranging from those that aim to alter characteristics of the environment to those that aim to enhance capacities of the person. This continuum also includes interventions at varying levels of person-environment interactions. The five broad categories include the following: (1) environmental modifications; (2) use of assistive devices; (3) use of social assistance; (4) activity modifications; and (5) therapeutic measures. These adaptations represent a continuum that reflects interaction between the person and his or her social and physical environment; as such, they may best be understood in the framework of ecological models of human behavior. Descriptions of each category are as follows:

1. *Environmental modifications* are adaptations of the environment designed to reduce task demand or burden on the impaired older person by diminishing barriers in the home.[23] A person who is environmentally proactive alters the current environment or chooses a new environment that is more likely to provide resources necessary to satisfy the person's needs and preferences and reduce undue environmental demands.[24] Such changes may include: structural modifications (e.g., ramps, extrawide doors, handrails, trapezes); functional modifications (e.g., create command center, move objects to lower shelves); and relocation (e.g., move to assisted living or move in with adult children).

2. *Assistive device use* involves objects that help to compensate for functional deficiencies. This category may include prosthetic devices (e.g., brace, hearing aid, walker); common devices (e.g., cordless phone, brighter lights); and custom-made devices (e.g., basket for walker). Along the person-environment adaptation continuum, device use is primarily focused on the environment with moderate change in the person as they modify themselves or their activities to use the device.

3. *Social assistance use* refers to assistance that may be utilized to lessen the impact of impairment either through helping the person perform a task or eliminating the person's need to perform that task. This category includes the source, amount, and type of assistance, from formal and informal support sources. Utilizing Lawton's definition of environment, which includes physical, interpersonal, and social factors, social assistance may be viewed as a part of the environment.[25]

4. *Activity modifications* involve reduction in demand through altering customary ways of performing functions. For example, persons with cardiac impairments may develop strategies for maintaining involvement in social activities in ways that involve less exertion.[26] Modification of an activity may include changing the amount of time, method, or frequency of performing a task. Activity modification falls closer to the person end

of the person-environment adaptation continuum since it requires greater modification of behaviors by the person than of the environment.

5. *Therapeutic measures* involve efforts to reduce to impairment aimed at enhancing function.[27] Such measures may include health-promoting self-care through exercise, diet, and rest. They can also involve medical intervention or rehabilitation, including physical and occupational therapy.[28]

Descriptive Data on Adaptations to Impairment

We now present results about types of adaptations that were undertaken by disabled elderly persons who participated in our study.

Type and Severity of Impairment

The decision to make environmental or activity modifications hinges on a number of determinants, including the perceived severity of the impairment by the older adult. Respondents reported having the most trouble with impairments that were classified as sensory, mobility, and physical indicators of frailty. Within the category of sensory impairments, 32.1 percent reported "very much" trouble with vision, but only 14.1 percent reported "much trouble" with hearing. Under mobility problems, both impairments of legs and balance had high percentages of respondents reporting very much trouble (37.2 percent and 24.7 percent, respectively). This finding is consistent with the documented prevalence and burden of mobility impairments in late life.[29]

Regarding cognitive or memory impairments only a very small percentage (2.6 percent) reported having "much" or "very much" trouble. Notably, 26.9 percent reported experiencing a little or some trouble with memory, reflecting mild memory loss. Range of motion or reaching did not appear to be major problems among respondents, nor did breathing problems or chest pain. However, weakness and fatigue were reported by almost one-third (29.5 percent) of respondents as posing "very much" trouble to them. Furthermore, over one third (37.2 percent) of respondents reported trouble with incontinence.

Types of Adaptations

Almost all of the respondents (99 percent) had made at least one environmental modification. The mean number of environmental modifications was 4.55 modifications (*SD* = 3.65), with a range of 0 to 18 modifications. Of all adaptations reported, device use was the most prevalent (47 percent).

Therapeutic measures, assistance from others, and activity modifications were reported infrequently (under 10 percent).

Of those environmental modifications that had been reported in previous research, extrawide doors, handrails, and raised toilet seats were the most common modifications reported. Assistive device use was most frequently related to mobility problems. Canes and walkers were shown to be the most frequent assistive devices used by individuals with impairments of legs, mobility, and balance. The largest percentage (76 percent) of modifications were undertaken to deal with impairment of mobility and balance. Respondents with lower limb impairment reported raised toilets and handrails as the most common environmental modifications. Furniture rearrangement and adaptive door handles were reported as the most common environmental modifications for respondents with upper limb impairment.

These responses demonstrate that mobility limitations generally elicit the most extensive adaptive responses. Respondents noted modifications primary to physical impairments and sensory limitations rather than to chronic illnesses.

Focus on Sensory Impairments

Problems in vision and hearing represent frequent and potentially disruptive impairments for older adults. Impairments in these areas affect almost every aspect of functioning, and older adults may not be fully aware of potential hazards, such as falls, which may result from limitations. It is particularly useful to examine adaptive initiatives in these areas as guidelines by human factors experts have been formulated.[30] For vision, these include the following: (1) increased levels of illumination; (2) control of glare; (3) increased stimulus contrast; (4) reduction of visual complexity or clutter.

It is interesting to review interventions mentioned by our sample of older adults against this background to determine which areas are most likely to be explicitly addressed in adaptations that they select. Only six respondents reported interventions in these categories and all of these related to increasing the level of illumination. Although the above noted categories have strong face validity, they are not readily recognized by older adults or they cannot be directly addressed through personal adaptations. Vision and hearing decrements occur over time, so adaptations and accommodation may be second nature and therefore underreported.

Unmet Needs

In addition to focusing on ameliorative adaptations undertaken by disabled elderly, our study also afforded an opportunity for exploring unmet needs for adaptive devices and environmental modifications. Unmet needs were reported primarily in the area of major structural modifications such as installation of railings, lowering of counters, widening of doors, or installation of new baths. Technologically sophisticated devices such as motorized scooters, lifters, heart monitors, or vans were also needed. Relatively few respondents reported needs for less costly devices, but those noting such needs often referred to devices requiring installation such as grab bars or storm windows. Assistance from caregivers represented another noteworthy area of unmet need.[31]

Spontaneous mention of technological devices among unmet needs of our respondents supports the notion that technological solutions are desirable and would find acceptance among older adults who seek to remain independent in the face of impairments.[32] It is notable that more young-old respondents (age sixty-five to seventy-five) reported having needs for environmental modifications than older-old (age seventy-six and older). Forty-seven respondents over age seventy-six reported having no unmet needs while only sixteen respondents under the age of seventy-five had no unmet needs. This unanticipated difference may be attributable to the fact that the young-old are less willing to accept impairments and are more likely to report need and seek modifications. After the age of seventy-five, older adults may be more willing to accept limitations in lifestyle posed by impairments and therefore may not identify needs for modifications. To the extent that older adults may feel stigmatized by an admission of unmet needs and disability, such needs may go underreported.

Demographic Antecedents of Adaptations

Although gender was not significantly related to modification behavior, women were more likely than men to report making three or more activity modifications. Unmarried respondents tended to make fewer activity modifications than married ones. Accordingly, more married respondents (86 percent) than unmarried respondents (58 percent) reported making three or more environmental modifications. The data also reveal that living with a spouse or with others makes it more feasible to undertake environmental modifications relative to living alone.

Proactivity Versus Compliance
in Different Types of Adaptations

After describing environmental and activity modifications, respondents were queried as to who initiated or provided the ideas for the modifications. Results were categorized as self, caregiver, or professionally initiated. We considered self-initiated modifications as reflections of proactivity. Other initiated modifications were viewed as more likely to be reflections of compliance.

Generally, respondents credited themselves for initiating modifications. Few respondents referred to recommendations by physicians about activity or environmental modifications or social assistance use. Professional input was most frequently reported in areas of improving health or functioning and ways to increase personal comfort in terms of simple prosthetic device use. Caregivers were least influential as information sources for modification, except in areas that would benefit them directly by making caregiving tasks easier. The majority (62 percent) of modifications to increase personal home comfort were self-initiated. Answers to problems with environmental accessibility came predominantly from the individual while recommendations to improve health and functioning were largely made by professionals. Adaptations associated with specific functional limitations were distributed rather evenly in terms of being initiated by self, caregiver, or professionals. The only area that deviated from this pattern was food preparation, where 71.4 percent of ideas were generated by the respondent and the remaining 28.6 percent came from professionals. Overall our findings point to limited proactivity within constraints among older adults with disabilities in modifying their environment and activities and in utilizing assistive devices in the face of health-related challenges.[33]

Case Studies

We now turn to the presentation of three case studies that illustrate the multi-faceted nature of adaptations to disability among older adults. We consider the role of individuals and of families in initiating creative environmental and activity modifications. We also illustrate the role of social supports, help-seeking, and planning ahead in the process of coping with disabilities.[34] These case studies reveal the exceptional roles played by some families in caregiving. They also illustrate strong preferences by older adults to remain in familiar home environments and pursue adaptations with the aid of their families.

Case Study 1: Mr. Barnes

Mr. Barnes, an eighty-six-year-old retired shopkeeper, suffered a stroke that resulted in paralysis of his left side. Following this health event, Mr. Barnes was in the hospital and then in a nursing home for a brief time. Unhappy with living in a congregate setting, Mr. Barnes returned home, hoping to live independently again with his wife acting as caregiver. However, shortly after his return home, Mrs. Barnes fell and broke her hip, requiring a hip replacement. No longer able to care for her husband, she needed to rely on her son and daughter-in-law, with additional help from a teenage grandson.

Respectful of their parents' desire for independence, the couple's son and daughter-in-law moved Mr. and Mrs. Barnes into a condominium in their building and provided care to both of them. Their grandson moved to Florida to help his parents in caring for his grandparents. The Barnes family seemed close and supportive. Their teamwork provided compassionate care to Mr. and Mrs. Barnes, enabling them to remain at home, rather than moving into a nursing home. Their daughter-in-law was a certified home health aide. She used her skills to care for her mother-in-law and father-in-law. She also attended seminars related to issues of caring for elders.

Two assistive aids were devised for Mr. Barnes. His daughter-in-law designed a clear plastic bib that attaches at the neck and falls to the lap. This was beneficial because it caught spills and kept Mr. Barnes's clothes clean. Since it was made of clear plastic, it was less conspicuous than the childlike bib that he previously used. The second device was constructed by a family friend. It was a finished plywood utility tray that rested on the arms of Mr. Barnes's wheelchair. It was kept in place by a cord that extended around the back of the chair attaching at the sides. A pillow beneath the tray provided further stability. The tray was used when Mr. Barnes ate and when he worked at hobbies. This functional handmade device was less expensive and more user friendly than those available at medical supply stores.

Mr. Barnes also used devices and aids for rehabilitation of his left side. At the advice of the physical therapist, long elastic surgical tubing was tied to the bedpost. This was used by Mr. Barnes in the morning and evening to stretch his legs and increase his range of motion. This material came in different colors, each indicating a different degree of resistance. Mr. Barnes also worked with a small squeezable ball and a pliable putty-like substance to strengthen and improve the dexterity of his hands. For mobility of his left arm, he used a small skateboard-like device. His arm rested on this device and could be moved about on a flat surface. At night, Mr. Barnes wore a cushioned hand and arm brace to reduce the curve of his wrist resulting from his stroke. He used a triangle trapeze above his bed for exercise. This device also enabled him to pull himself up to a sitting position at the side of the bed. Both Mr. and Mrs. Barnes used motorized chairs in the living room that brought them up to a standing position.

The bathroom was adapted to Mr. Barnes's needs. Handrails were installed in the shower and a hose with showerhead was added to allow Mr. Barnes to wash while seated on the shower seat. The seat extended out toward the toilet seat for ease of transfer. Additionally, there was a free-standing commode that could be moved if needed. It was adapted to fit over the installed toilet in the bathroom, acting as a raised toilet seat with armrests. Two additional changes that the family wanted to make in the bathroom were the removal of the door and the installation of handrails for the toilet. These changes would have enabled Mr. Barnes to be more independent in his access and use of the bathroom.

Several devices were used to ensure safety and easily accessible communication in the Barnes's home. All throw rugs were removed. A safety belt was employed when Mr. Barnes used his walker. A clever communication device was utilized in the form of a cordless door chime with a remote control button. The cordless chime was placed wherever it was needed, usually in their son and daughter-in-law's bedroom. Mr. Barnes kept the remote. Whenever he needed assistance during the day or night, he pushed the button to sound the chimes. He and his wife also had a cordless landline phone that was easily moved about where needed.

The Barnes family has been successful in providing care for both Mr. and Mrs. Barnes, benefiting from good communication and teamwork within the caregiving process. This family represents a rare example of devotion to caregiving in order to allow their parents to age in place.

Case Study 2: Mr. King

Mr. King had three distinct health problems that impaired his functioning. At age seventy-five, Mr. King suffered from peripheral neuropathy, knee pain, and general arthritis. The peripheral neuropathy was first diagnosed nine years ago and Mr. King's condition slowly deteriorated since. His balance was greatly affected, and difficulties with his knees and arthritis contributed to experiencing major problems with ambulation. He walked with a slow unsteady gait, using a cane to steady himself. His reliance on environmental modifications and devices was limited as he preferred to focus on overcoming his difficulties through willpower and health promotion efforts. He owned a walker, but was reluctant to use it. Mr. King preferred to restrict his life space and activities to avoid extensive reliance on prosthetic devices. Through daily use of a bidet, he reduced the number of showers he took to twice weekly. He felt that this limitation of exposure reduced his chances of falling in the shower. He preferred to sit on a firm wingback chair with arms. This chair provided sufficient height and support for Mr. King to sit and stand without assistance.

Mr. King was able to adapt to his environment rather than change his environment to fit his needs. He accomplished this through two main strategies. The first was to remain in the best physical condition possible through rigorous structured exercise. He was active in the hospital wellness center exercise facility, which was stringently monitored by medical personnel. Second, he approached every movement with careful planning, thinking through each task to eliminate risk and to maximize safety. Mr. King was determined to remain independent as long as possible. Additionally, Mr.

King's wife encouraged his independence. When Mr. King fell, which occurred at least once a month, his wife allowed him to get up by himself, so long as he was not hurt. This was no small feat. To pull himself up off the floor took planning, willpower, concentration, and time. Mr. and Mrs. King amiably agreed to this arrangement.

Mr. King's case illustrates the reluctance of some older adults who experience late-life disabilities to modify their environments. This may be based on the fear of being labeled as dependent or with the shame associated with reliance on prosthetic aids. Such older adults may find it more socially acceptable and desirable to rely on activity modifications. Mr. King accepted greater risks in exchange for managing his self identity.

Case Study 3: Mr. Greene

Mr. Greene suffered a stroke and was also diagnosed with Alzheimer's disease. His wife was his primary caregiver until his condition worsened to the point that she had to place him in a nursing home. While Mr. Greene was at home, his condition and responses to his environment were constantly changing. For a short time, he used a walker, a cane, and a wheelchair. He also ate with a special fork. Before retirement, Mrs. Greene had been a teacher of children with special needs. She employed some of the techniques from her work with children to the care of her husband. For example, she placed labels on his underwear and other items of clothing to designate the front and back of each garment. Mrs. Greene also labeled much of the furniture, and this helped to reduce confusion for Mr. Greene for a short time. But soon he could no longer understand the labels. For safety, Mrs. Greene installed a deadbolt lock with a key on the front door to reduce the risk of Mr. Greene's wandering from the apartment. She used nightlights in wall sockets to reduce his anxiety and uncertainty at night. There was slip-resistant flooring in the kitchen, and handrails were placed in the bathroom. Mrs. Greene also restricted Mr. Greene to furniture from which she could more readily lift him. This eliminated the use of certain low chairs and couches. All breakable items were cleared from surfaces in the home. Mrs. Greene helped her husband with all of the activities of daily living. She took him into the bathroom and went into the shower with him. A raised toilet seat was also installed to assist him.

When it became too difficult for Mrs. Greene to care for her husband at home, she placed him in a nursing home. He was there for nine and a half months until he died. Mrs. Greene now does extensive volunteer work. She works with children at a local elementary school and also assists with activities at the local nursing home. She founded a support group in a nursing home for spouses of residents who are living with Alzheimer's disease.

The case of Mr. Greene illustrates the changing needs of older adults as their frailty increases and the differential efficacy of specific modifications during different stages of disability progression. The case of this patient with Alzheimer's disease also underscores the all-important role of caregiver-initiated and -implemented modifications for older adults who are suffering from dementing illness. It provides an example of the creative use of adaptations that may arise from life histories characterized by flexibility, adaptability, and creativity. Older adults or their caregivers who were engaged in professions involving creative problem solving earlier in their lives were particularly inclined to employ creative adaptations as they confronted disabling health conditions. Mrs. Greene also exemplified extreme devotion of some spouses in willingly undertaking demanding caregiving tasks.

Lessons Learned from Older Adults Coping with Late Onset Disability

The cases we described illustrate creative adaptations undertaken by older adults and by their families to ensure meaningful living in the face of disability in late life. Most older adults confronting disabilities maintain a positive attitude and cope by acceptance of their shrinking life space and increasingly difficult life situations. The latter orientation is exemplified by the phrase "I do the best I can," which was a frequently noted theme. This was complemented by focusing on the limited time frame, exemplified by comments of "take things one day at a time" or "live day by day." This temporal aspect of adaptation is seldom discussed in the literature dealing with disability. A focus on the present may be seen as a temporal counterpart of the spatial adaptation of constructing a command post, which has been identified by Lawton.[35] Just as concentrating important objects close within one's reach adds to controllability of the environment, defining time in smaller units provides an important element of cognitive or secondary control for disabled older adults. Focusing on smaller segments of time is also useful in achieving another frequent adaptation of pacing oneself. This helps those who are frail and suffer from fatigue to maintain an acceptable level of activity. Thus, it is useful to consider cognitive maneuvers as additional forms of adaptation that round out the spectrum of person-environment transactions.

Such cognitive restructuring introduces secondary control when the primary control of the environment is no longer possible.[36] Accordingly, modifications of one's outlook and attitudes in response to disability may also be viewed as a useful adaptation.

Conclusion

Research centered on older adults living with disabilities has generally focused on decrements, needs, and vulnerabilities.[37] Thus, it is not surprising that a cadre of gerontological experts have researched topics ranging from chronic illness, health care use, elder abuse, stress, coping, and institutionalization.[38] Such studies have identified needs for service supports ranging from assisted living to case management, mental health services, and institutional programs. To generate funds for such programs and services, compassionate stereotypes about isolated, sick, poor, and dependent aged have to be promulgated.[39] Once legislation was created to provide funding, an extensive aging service establishment had to be created.

However, an important dynamic disregarded by policy planners is that acceptance of services is difficult for a cohort that values self-sufficiency, independence, and not being a burden on others.[40] In an incisive analysis of the "aging enterprise," Carroll L. Estes calls attention to the long-overlooked conflict of interest between the needs of aged consumers and the often self-serving professional bureaucracy interested more in finding clients for its programs than in meeting the real needs of older adults.[41]

Part of the reason for the underutilization of formal services by older adults may be the lack of input by clients about their values and preferences regarding programs and services directed at them. In his classic article "Client Control and Medical Practice," Eliot Freidson posits that clients' "ideas about what they want differ markedly from those supposedly held by [the] professionals."[42] Thus, it may be difficult, if not misleading, to develop practice guidelines that are largely based on practitioners' definitions of patient needs and appropriate interventions. Indeed, our consideration of environmental adaptations undertaken by older adults and by family members to aid elders in living independently with disabilities underscored this point. Older adults generally sought and appreciated self-initiated ways of dealing with their disability.

In recent years, there has been a shift from the dependency model of aging and greater focus on social problems of late life. This shift also parallels a movement toward the demedicalization of social problems propelled largely by the disability rights movement.[43] Disillusioned by an expensive and unwieldy health care system, older adults are seeking empowerment, consumerism, and rights for self-determination, even in the face of frailty.[44] They have been described as moving from self-perception as clients and patients to being members of an interest group demanding equal rights. Our study highlighted clients' perspectives on useful interventions and considered solutions by disabled and elderly persons and their family members for adapting to living in the community with disabilities.

Incorporating self-reported successful adaptations by this group into programs and services for the disabled aged reflects respect for them as partners in health care and enhances the likelihood that they will accept and utilize services. This is related to the recognition that the environment must be linked to agency and belonging among frail older adults.[45] Data from our study underscores the complex nature of adaptations involving person-environment transactions. We find that older adults prefer self-initiated and family-initiated solutions and are reluctant to accept expert-initiated solutions in addressing challenges of disability in late life. It also confirms a position articulated by scholars in disability studies that social support systems, especially based on informal caregivers, can represent an important bridge between individuals and environments.[46] Our findings also point to the need for developing help-seeking and care-getting skills to address late-life disability.

Building on this understanding of the desire by older adults for self-determination and by their families for advocacy, in the following chapter we will share personal experiences with a family member to illuminate how the family can enhance the experience of living in a nursing home.

Notes

1. Graham D. Rowles, "Evolving Images of Place in Aging and 'Aging in Place,'" *Generations* 17, no. 2 (1993): 65–70.
2. Laura N. Gitlin, "Conducting Research on Home Environments: Lessons Learned and New Directions," *The Gerontologist* 43, no. 5 (2003): 628–637.
3. Ibid.
4. Eric Klinenberg, *Heat Wave: A Social Autopsy of Disaster in Chicago* (University of Chicago Press, 2015).
5. Graham D. Rowles and Habib Chaudhury, *Home and Identity in Late Life: International Perspectives* (Springer, 2005).
6. Laura N. Gitlin, Laraine Winter, Marie P. Dennis, Mary Corcoran, Sandy Schinfeld, and Walter W. Hauck, "A Randomized Trial of a Multicomponent Home Intervention to Reduce Functional Difficulties in Older Adults," *Journal of the American Geriatrics Society* 54, no. 5 (2006): 809–816.
7. Hans-Werner Wahl, Agneta Fänge, Frank Oswald, Laura N. Gitlin, and Susanne Iwarsson, "The Home Environment and Disability-Related Outcomes in Aging Individuals: What is the Empirical Evidence?" *The Gerontologist* 49, no. 3 (2009): 355–367.
8. Saad Z. Nagi, "Disability Concepts Revisited: Implications for Prevention," in *Disability in America: Toward a National Agenda for Prevention,* ed. Andrew M. Pope and Alvin R. Tarlov (National Academy Press, 1991), 309–372.
9. Hans-Werner Wahl, Susanne Iwarsson, and Frank Oswald, "Aging Well and the Environment: Toward an Integrative Model and Research Agenda for the Future," *The Gerontologist* 52, no. 3 (2012): 306–316.

10. Marianne Granbom, Ines Himmelsbach, Maria Haak, Charlotte Löfqvist, Frank Oswald, and Susanne Iwarsson, "Residential Normalcy and Environmental Experiences of Very Old People: Changes in Residential Reasoning over Time," *Journal of Aging Studies* 29 (2014): 9–19.

11. Jenny Morris, "Community Care or Independent Living?" in *Independent Lives?* ed. Jenny Morris (Macmillan Education, 1993), 147–172.

12. Fredric D. Wolinsky, *Health and Health Behavior Among Elderly Americans: An Age-Stratification Perspective* (Springer, 1990).

13. Gordon H. DeFriese and Marcia G. Ory, *Self Care in Later Life: Research, Program, and Policy Issues* (Springer, 1998).

14. Morris, "Community Care or Independent Living?"

15. Ronald J. Berger, *Introducing Disability Studies* (Lynne Rienner, 2013).

16. Robert Crosnoe and Glen H. Elder, "Successful Adaptation in the Later Years: A Life Course Approach to Aging," *Social Psychology Quarterly* 65, no. 4 (2002): 309–328.

17. Eva Kahana, Boaz Kahana, and Jennifer Kinney, "Coping Among Vulnerable Elders," in *The Vulnerable Aged: People, Services and Policies,* ed. Zev Harel, Phyllis Ehrlich, and Richard Hubbard (Springer, 1990), 64–85.

18. M. Powell Lawton, "Residential Environment and Self-Directedness Among Older People," *American Psychologist* 45, no. 5 (1990): 638.

19. Ibid.

20. Eva Kahana, Boaz Kahana, and Jeong Eun Lee, "Proactive Approaches to Successful Aging: One Clear Path Through the Forest," *Gerontology* 60, no. 5 (2014): 466–474.

21. Cara Bailey Fausset, Andrew J. Kelly, Wendy A. Rogers, and Arthur D. Fiske, "Challenges to Aging in Place: Understanding Home Maintenance Difficulties," *Journal of Housing for the Elderly* 25, no. 2 (2011): 125–141; Christopher L. Seplaki, Emily M. Agee, Carlos O. Weiss, Sarah L. Szanton, Karen Bandeen-Roche, and Linda P. Fried, "Assistive Devices in Context: Cross-Sectional Association Between Challenges in the Home Environment and Use of Assistive Devices for Mobility," *The Gerontologist* 54, no. 4 (2013): 651–660.

22. Eva Kahana, Jessica Kelley-Moore, and Boaz Kahana, "Proactive Aging: A Longitudinal Study of Stress, Resources, Agency, and Well-Being in Late Life," *Aging and Mental Health* 16, no. 4 (2012): 438–451.

23. Seplaki et al., "Assistive Devices in Context."

24. M. Powell Lawton, "Environmental Proactivity and Affect in Older People," in *The Social Psychology of Aging,* ed. Shirlynn Spacapan and Stuart Oskamp (Sage, 1989), 135–163.

25. M. Powell Lawton, Paul G. Windley and Thomas O. Byerts, *Competence, Environmental Press, and the Adaptations of Older People* (Springer, 1982).

26. Monique A. M. Gignac, Cheryl Cott, and Elizabeth M. Badley, "Adaptation to Chronic Illness and Disability and its Relationship to Perceptions of Independence and Dependence," *Journals of Gerontology Series B: Psychological Sciences and Social Sciences* 55, no. 6 (2000): P362–P372.

27. David E. Krebs, Donna Moxley Scarborough, and Chris A. McGibbon, "Functional vs. Strength Training in Disabled Elderly Outpatients," *American Journal of Physical Medicine and Rehabilitation* 86, no. 2 (2007): 93–103.

28. George E. Ruff, *Aging and Rehabilitation: Advances in the State of the Art, Vol. 1* (Springer, 1986).

29. Anne Shumway-Cook, Marcia A. Ciol, Kathryn M. Yorkston, Jeanne M. Hoffman, and Leighton Chan, "Mobility Limitations in the Medicare Population:

Prevalence and Sociodemographic and Clinical Correlates," *Journal of the American Geriatrics Society* 53, no. 7 (2005): 1217–1221.

30. Arthur D. Fisk, Wendy A. Rogers, Neil Charness, Sara J. Czaja, and Joseph Sharit, *Designing for Older Adults: Principles and Creative Human Factors Approaches* (CRC Press, 2009).

31. Laura N. Gitlin, Laraine Winter, Mary Corcoran, Marie P. Dennis, Sandy Schinfeld, and Walter W. Hauck, "Effects of the Home Environmental Skill-Building Program on the Caregiver–Care Recipient Dyad: 6-Month Outcomes from the Philadelphia REACH Initiative," *The Gerontologist* 43, no. 4 (2003): 532–546.

32. Claudine McCreadie and Anthea Tinker, "The Acceptability of Assistive Technology to Older People," *Ageing and Society* 25, no. 1 (2005): 91–110.

33. Kahana, Kahana, and Lee, "Proactive Approaches to Successful Aging."

34. Kahana, Kelley-Moore, and Kahana, "Proactive Aging."

35. Lawton, "Residential Environment and Self-Directedness Among Older People."

36. Jutta Heckhausen and Richard Schulz, "A Life-Span Theory of Control," *Psychological Review* 102, no. 2 (1995): 284.

37. Lois M. Verbrugge and Alan M. Jette, "The Disablement Process," *Social Science and Medicine* 38, no. 1 (1994): 1–14.

38. George Demiris, Marilyn J. Rantz, Myra A. Aud, Karen D. Marek, Harry W. Tyrer, Marjorie Skubic, and Ali A. Hussam, "Older Adults' Attitudes Towards and Perceptions of 'Smart Home' Technologies: A Pilot Study," *Medical Informatics and the Internet in Medicine* 29, no. 2 (2004): 87–94.

39. Robert Binstock, "Old-Age Policies, Politics, and Ageism," *Generations* 29, no. 3 (2005): 73–78.

40. Jeffrey S. Kahana, Eva Kahana, and Loren D. Lovegreen, *Expanding the Time Frame for Advance Care Planning: Policy Considerations and Implications for Research* (InTech Open Access, 2012).

41. Carroll L. Estes, *The Aging Enterprise* (Jossey-Bass, 1979).

42. Eliot Freidson, "Client Control and Medical Practice," *American Journal of Sociology* 65, no. 4 (1960): 374–382.

43. Renee C. Fox, "The Medicalization and Demedicalization of American Society," *Daedalus* 106, no. 1 (1977): 9–22; Michael Oliver, "The Social Model in Action: If I Had a Hammer," in *Implementing the Social Model of Disability: Theory and Research,* ed. Colin Barnes and G. Mercer (Disability Press, 2004), 18–31.

44. Carroll L. Estes and James H. Swan, *The Long Term Care Crisis: Elders Trapped in the No-Care Zone* (Sage, 1993).

45. Wahl, Iwarsson, and Oswald, "Aging Well and the Environment."

46. Simi Litvak and Alexandra Enders, "Support Systems: The Interface Between Individuals and Environments," in *Handbook of Disability Studies,* ed. Gary L. Albrecht, Katherine Delores Seelman, and Michael Bury (Sage, 2001), 711–733.

7

Enhancing Care in the
Nursing Home Environment

In this chapter, we consider the values of family caring and advocacy for severely disabled older adults living in nursing homes. When older adults no longer find it possible to maintain their autonomy and engage in self-advocacy due to disabling health conditions, family caregivers can assume important roles in facilitating connectedness and patient-centered care.[1] Most older people consider life in a nursing home as only a last resort. Accounts of residents, close family members, and qualitative researchers have documented feelings of desperation, anomie, and hopelessness, which accompany the last years, months, and days of those elders who reluctantly find themselves in institutional facilities at the end of their days.[2] The perspectives of elderly residents in such facilities are generally discordant from those of staff who care for them.[3]

Irving Zola, in his classic work *Missing Pieces: A Chronicle of Living with a Disability,* articulated the importance of giving authenticity to the lived experiences of disabled people in our social world. Following in Zola's footsteps, in this chapter we offer a glimpse into the lived experience of nursing home residents and family advocates by providing personal narratives based on two years of observations during daily visits to a high-quality nursing facility to see our mother and grandmother, Sari Frost, who was a resident. Our hope is that by sharing the experience of advocating for one disabled elderly person, some of the backstage interactions of nursing home life can be illuminated and some explanations may emerge about the disconnect between specific interventions offered by nursing homes and adverse experiences of disabled elderly residents and their families.[4] It is our hope that the articulation of a resident-centered view of the existing disconnect and the potential partnership between residents, staff, and family will spur on further research in this area.

We begin this chapter with a brief review of literature about the role of family advocacy in facilitating patient-responsive care in nursing homes. We conclude the chapter with recommendations about ways of enhancing patient responsiveness of care in nursing homes through participation of family members.

Elderly residents of nursing homes typically suffer from multiple chronic illnesses, disability, and cognitive impairment.[5] However, institutional placement also involves major social components and generally comes about after families are no longer able to care for elders in the community.[6] Families, as well as the disabled older adults, attempt to delay institutional placement as long as possible.[7] Once the move to a nursing home becomes inevitable, families can make a difference in the life of a relative living with disabilities in the nursing home.

Sociologists have been at the forefront of offering an understanding of the social isolation of institutionalized persons. Erving Goffman's classical work on asylums has expounded on the barriers between the outside social world and the inside world of the total institution.[8] In nursing homes, these are manifest in limited involvement by representatives of the outside world: the family members, friends and neighbors, volunteers, and physicians who had previously provided emotional support and instrumental care to the resident.[9] The social organization of care in nursing homes has also been explored within sociological frameworks, elucidating the meaning of institutional life for both staff and "clientele." It has been documented that direct care staff in nursing homes earn low wages, receive minimal training, and work in highly stressful conditions.[10] Researchers have paid relatively little attention to the actual and potential roles of families in breaking through the barriers of institutional life and in enhancing the responsiveness of care in nursing homes. Some families may bring with them the skills and the burdens that can arise from convergent caregiving to both elders and children coping with disabilities.[11]

After numerous exposés of depersonalization and humiliation experienced by nursing home residents, there has been growing research interest in efforts to improve quality of care in nursing homes through regulation and the introduction of therapeutic programs.[12] Such programs range from specific efforts at reduction of restraints, incontinence, and falls.[13] Yet there remains a fundamental disconnect between achievements in care provision and the lived experience of those living and dying in nursing homes.[14] As we recognize the structural barriers that prevent residents from accessing the outside world, we must also turn our attention to opportunities presented by family members who can serve as a readily accessible link to the outside world. Proactive efforts of family members can penetrate the walls of the institution and can subsequently change the lived experience of residents. This is an area that has not been emphasized in the disability studies literature where focus on caring relationships has not been a central area of inquiry.[15]

Research on family involvement in the care of institutionalized older adults has advanced in prevalence and sophistication in recent gerontological research. Studies have documented greater psychological well-being among institutionalized aged who receive more visits from families.[16] Continued family involvement in hands-on caregiving has also been found to benefit family members who can sustain intimacy in their relationships with their loved one.[17] However, there is also some evidence of negative associations between family involvement in care and satisfaction with institutional services.[18] This may be due to less than welcoming attitudes expressed by direct care staff as well as administrators toward family involvement.[19] Highly involved caregivers may also be dissatisfied because they obtain a close-up view of problems in nursing home care and, yet, feel excluded by staff from an active caregiving role.[20]

The family advocate for a disabled older person can contribute to enhancing care of the resident through multiple pathways. These transcend the value of visitation or involvement in helping with care related to activities of daily living.[21] Advocacy by family caregivers may provide special benefits based on the family member's special knowledge of the patient's values, preferences, and health care history and the strong emotional bonds that exist among kin.[22] Such family advocacy shares much in common with roles of family members in offering support to children and grandchildren living with disabilities.[23]

In their early treatise on nursing homes, Linda K. George and George L. Maddox point out that little is known about the day-to-day life experiences of nursing home residents.[24] Just how much of the residents' day is spent participating in the innovative programs described in the literature? In what way does nursing home life support identity maintenance of residents? How can family advocacy help in humanizing the social environment of residents and support resident autonomy and dignity? In the next section of this chapter, we attempt to breathe life into our understandings of the potentials and limitations of personal and family advocacy to enhance lives of severely disabled older adults who are cared for in nursing homes. We provide some insight into the ways that residents and their family members size up life and respond to programs in a nursing home. This account is based on notes taken by Eva Kahana during participant observation throughout a two-year period while her mother, Sari, was a nursing home resident.

Glimpses of Nursing Home Life:
Perspectives of Disabled Residents and Advocates

The description of watching the life of a loved one with severe disabilities on a day-to-day basis in a nursing home offers valuable insights in light of prior research findings. Quantitative studies may lack passion and humanity when they are based only on surveys or objective test data.[25] This observation echoes orientations of disability studies that discount meaningfulness of data that excludes the perspectives of those living with disabilities.[26]

Sari was both exceptional and ordinary. She was a self-educated survivor of the Nazi Holocaust. With eight grades of formal education, she
learned English by reading the *New York Times* with a dictionary and later
became a hospital bookkeeper. She retired early to help raise her grandchildren. Sari was well liked because of her caring attitude toward people. She
sometimes embarrassed us with her uncanny propensity to tell it like it is.

On a cold February evening a number of years ago, Sari died at the age
of eighty-five from complications due to diabetes. After her first leg amputation, she lived for several years with our family (including me, my husband,
and our two college-age sons). She continued to manage our household from
her wheelchair. During the last two years of her life, after the amputation of
her second leg, she lived in a nursing home. Like the vast majority of older
adults entering nursing homes, Sari dreaded the idea of residing in one. In
fact, she made us promise that we would let her die if she ever needed more
care than our family could provide. She would never say that she was living
in a nursing home. Sometimes she referred to the facility as a department
store, sometimes as a railroad station, and most of the time as "this place."
This was attributed to her declining memory, but we believed that she was
unable or unwilling to acknowledge her unwelcome habitat.

Like many old-old disabled adults currently living in nursing homes,
Sari was both physically and mentally frail. By the time she entered the
nursing home, she had suffered multiple ministrokes and was unable to
respond correctly to most of the questions in the Folstein Mini-Mental
Status Examination (MMSE). Nevertheless, essential aspects of her personhood remained intact until the day she died. She continued to recognize and
value her physician, and enjoy members of her family. She responded with
a big grin whenever her grandsons called long-distance. She cried or
screamed when attendants approached her without being gentle, particularly
as she was transferred on a Hoyer lift. Although she did not seem to know
that she lived in a nursing home, when she was transferred to a hospital for
a brief stay she told visitors and health care staff that she was pleased to be
treated at this specific hospital, clearly enunciating the hospital's name.

Sari was admitted to a not-for-profit nursing home, which met high
standards for patient care in a state-of-the-art physical facility. This home
boasts a broad array of programs and interventions, ranging from regular
visits by community volunteers (including a visiting pet program) to a
miniature zoo and intergenerational activities. Yet the day-to-day experience of spending the last phase of her life in this institution was a traumatic
experience for Sari. Her customary optimism and vigilance were dulled by
physical pain. Her ability to communicate was compromised by ministrokes. During her nursing home stay, she often reverted to speaking in her
native Hungarian. Nevertheless, she retained her will to live, stubborn personality, and radiant grin to the very end.

Sari remained secure and happy that her regular physician continued seeing her in the nursing home. In his trusted presence, she was still able to express herself. She regularly chided him on his visits for taking too much time out of his busy schedule to see her. She also enjoyed my daily visits and admonished me in the morning not to stay too long lest I be late for work or get the nurses mad at us. She particularly liked being wheeled to the volunteer-run visitors' coffee shop to have toast and coffee and look out of the window. Sometimes during these outings, sitting near me in the coffee shop and eating a crunchy piece of toast, she thought she was home. She was still able to draw on her prior social skills to smile at the volunteers at the coffee shop and say, "Sir, please make sure the toast is hot." She liked the volunteers and could make a human connection with them. They helped add normalcy to her life.

For the most part, Sari was nervous when nursing staff approached, and was often agitated when given her medications. She always wanted to know what pills she was taking and I found it hard to explain to busy staff why a woman, who doesn't seem to know who the president of the United States is, needs to know the dosage of her medications. Her inquiries ran the risk of agitating the nurses and staff. However, by complimenting nurses regularly about their care, I was able to generate sufficient goodwill to get them to let Sari know the dosage of medication prior to taking her pills.

Sari became incontinent while in the nursing home. Toileting a double amputee is a real challenge to staff. Aides did not take too kindly to false alarms after using a Hoyer lift to toilet her. After a while, her pleadings to be toileted fell on deaf ears. After spending over a year in the nursing home, classified as an incontinent patient, Sari was transferred to an acute care hospital due to a bladder infection. There, it was determined that she was not incontinent at all, as long as her yells for a nurse were heeded and she was taken to the toilet.

I always made sure to provide positive feedback to staff who acted kindly to Sari or other residents around her. Sari never directly complained about care. However, there were times when she was frightened and agitated and, on those occasions, she worried that my presence or loud voice would upset the nurse's aides. She wanted to protect me from harm should I provoke the staff or administration. Her fears were also evoked by animals. Like many immigrant city dwellers, she had not had much experience with pets. She insisted that I not wheel her near the petting zoo area, which was a program highlight for the nursing home. As we would approach the zoo area en route to the coffee shop, she would get agitated and tell me, "Go fast, the animals can hurt us."

She did not like attending the arts and crafts program and, after some initial attempts to involve her, staff concluded that she was not high functioning enough for these activities. Nevertheless, I vividly remember my own embarrassing role in ending her sporadic participation in the activity program. On a wintry morning prior to going to work, I wheeled Sari into the room housing the activities program. There, she was handed two sheets of paper and some crayons and told: "Sari, you need to choose the one you would like to color." She appeared uninterested and did not respond. She turned to me, "Eva, tell the lady which one I will color and then you can go to work." Following her request, I reached for the picture depicting two boys on a sled and handed it to the therapist. I heard an icy but professional command, "May I speak to you outside?" The therapist turned to me as we left the room, "We are making a real effort to include your mother in a new program to help residents make choices, and you took that opportunity away from her." When we reentered the room, Sari announced that she wanted to go back to her room and go to sleep.

One of the hardest challenges for Sari as an amputee was sitting all day in her wheelchair without the ability to change her position or lie down when she got uncomfortable. One of our great victories came when, on my behest, our family doctor wrote an order for Sari to be lifted into bed after lunch or when she got tired. After three unsuccessful attempts to involve Sari in organized activities that had little meaning for her, I was able to enlist the help of sympathetic nursing staff in getting Sari small towels from the laundry to fold. Given her work-oriented values, she found this tedious task to be a meaningful activity. She happily noted, "I like being busy."

Two attempted interventions created major crises for Sari during her nursing home stay. Extricating her from those interventions took patience, skill, and advocacy. Her quality of life was enhanced when she escaped these interventions. After initial placement in an observation ward, she appeared to be doing well. However, after a periodic reassessment of patient functioning, I was told that she was being relocated to a unit for severely demented Alzheimer's patients because of her low Folstein memory test scores. Staff suggested that she would benefit from the relocation, as she would be "well matched to programs we offer there." A quick visit to the dementia care unit convinced me that Sari would not benefit from encountering combative residents who may frighten a double amputee in a wheelchair.

I was told by a social worker that my mother's friendly demeanor masked serious cognitive impairment. Her test scores proved this point and they were planning to relocate her to the ward where she belonged. Fortunately, after my request for a meeting with the director of social work, I succeeded in arguing that overt behavior is a more valid indicator of functioning than are brief screening measures. Sari was placed in a unit of physically frail, but relatively cognitively intact, residents. This unit provided a safe and comfortable setting for her. In spite of her poor test scores, Sari presented few management problems and remained in the unit for physically frail residents for the remainder of her nursing home stay.

A second adverse intervention occurred after Sari temporarily became unable to feed herself after a new medication caused the side effect of hand tremors. In the course of being fed by an aide she choked, requiring a Heimlich maneuver, which fortunately was delivered by a vigilant staff member. Subsequent to the episode, Sari was evaluated by a speech therapist. Although no identifiable pathology was noted, she was placed on a liquid diet as a preventive measure. She reacted poorly to this intervention. She stopped eating, lost weight, became morose, and appeared to be losing her will to live. Antidepressant medication was considered. Nevertheless, whenever I took her to the volunteer-run coffee shop, Sari would become animated and asked for coffee and hot toast. When served her favorite breakfast, she ate with enjoyment and little difficulty. I started to advocate to have her put back on a soft diet, but to little avail. At this time Sari stopped eating.

Sari's condition deteriorated to the point that tube feeding was mentioned as a prospect. This led me to reappraise the administration of liquid food. After some consideration, I suddenly had an insight. The liquid food was an intervention—and we had the right to refuse it. With trepidation, I went to see the director of nursing. When I presented my request to stop the intervention of liquid food she responded, "Yes, if you are willing to take the risk of her choking, she may be put back on a soft regular diet." After obtaining legal advice and having me sign forms stating that I was willing to assume responsibility for the decision, the nursing home reluctantly went along with my request. When I visited Sari the next day, she was eating and her big grin was back. "I have good news for you," she told me, "They hired a much better cook."

As mandated by the Federal Nursing Home Reform Act of 1987, Sari was asked to specify her wishes regarding life-sustaining treatment. When I visited her the evening after the document was handed out, she appeared concerned and excited. She took a crumpled paper that she was holding and handed it to me. "You must get a lawyer," she noted, "to advise us what to do about these papers. They are too hard for us to figure out." I took a closer look at the papers and then I knew what she meant. The document about advance directives was written in legal jargon. So much for yet another well-intentioned and mandated intervention, which had little meaning to the frail residents that it most impacted.

Sari died untouched or bypassed by most of the innovative nursing home–based interventions. The morning she died, she was not hungry but she let me wheel her to the volunteer-run coffee shop, which was her favorite spot in the nursing home. Her last words to me were: "I can't eat today, but you have a cup of coffee and some toast and I will sit with you." She retained significant remnants of her personhood even in the face of memory impairments and extreme physical disabilities. She did so feeling loved and cared about by close family and representatives of the outside world, including her doctor. She died peacefully later that evening.[27]

Family Advocacy and Developing Patient-Responsive Nursing Home Care

Based on the case study of Sari, several principles of nursing home advocacy can be noted. Institutionalized residents—particularly disabled residents—experience two distinct sources of stress. The first set of stressors relate to the physical illnesses and cognitive impairments that contributed to their institutional placement.[28] These stressors are likely to threaten the psychological well-being and social functioning of the older patient.

The second major source of stressors is based on constraints of institutional living. There have been diverse conceptualizations of the stressful features of institutional environments.[29] These problems relate to the physical environment and the policy structure of institutional care as well as the social milieu defined by interactions with staff members and with other impaired residents. Perhaps the most astute summary of problems posed by institutional living has been articulated in the early work of Robert W. Kleemeier.[30] His formulations refer to the congregate, segregate, and institutional control dimensions of the social environment of nursing homes. These characterizations define environments where all activities are conducted in the company of other residents (congregate), the residents are kept apart from the outside world (segregate), and rules and regulations of the institution must be followed (institutional control). These qualities of the social environment reflect aspects of a total institution that have an adverse effect on patient well-being and maintenance of identity.[31]

Family members who can visit often and remain involved in the patient's life can help diminish isolation and ameliorate adverse effects of institutional stressors on residents. Family involvement can contribute to greater patient-centeredness of care, even in the face of resistance by some health care providers.[32] Family members can have a direct effect on patient well-being by the social supports that they provide through visitation. The very presence of family members can yield substantial benefits based on both physical care and emotional supports they offer.

Another important influence of family involvement is through advocacy for the patient. This includes providing information to staff about a patient's needs, values, and preferences, which is a key element of building partnerships with staff through communication. The value of effective communication among health care partners (providers, family members, and patients) has been articulated in our prior work.[33]

Family members can also achieve more patient-responsive care by establishing alliances with staff through expressing appreciation.[34] Staff members are more likely to provide responsive care to those residents whose family advocates establish a positive relationship reflected in a respect for and recognition of the efforts of the staff member.[35] Information sharing and expressions of esteem or positive affect toward staff members may be viewed as engaging in preventive aspects of patient advocacy. The family member who is able to work with staff by alerting them to the needs of the resident and enlists the goodwill of staff members is likely to minimize problems in delivery of care. Highly committed families may find it easier to interact with professional staff and articulate their appreciation. At the same time families can also forge ties with direct service staff focusing on shared cultural backgrounds.[36]

As depicted in Sari's case, there are many instances where preventive advocacy is insufficient to deal with lack of responsiveness by nursing home administrators and staff. These are the times when family members must summon the courage to stand up for the needs of the disabled resident, even at the cost of confrontation with staff or administration.[37] Responsiveness of care is reflected in greater staff involvement in the care of the patient, better communication, greater instrumental and affective support, and greater cultural sensitivity. Although we focus on family advocacy in this discussion we acknowledge that, in the absence of successful family advocacy, more formal advocacy by nursing home ombudsmen can benefit residents of nursing homes.[38] Such advocacy is consistent with demands for accommodations by the disability rights movement.[39]

The experiences of overcoming structural barriers to family advocacy reported here reflect on a major paradox experienced in institutional living. Even as family members seek to penetrate the barriers of institutional life to maintain meaningful relationships with their loved ones, institutional policies and practices converge to limit family involvement in care.[40] This is an area where gerontologists could greatly benefit from adopting some of the more assertive advocacy strategies of the disability studies movement.[41]

Considering Patient-Responsive Intervention and Care

The relative irrelevance of many existing programs to the daily life of a nursing home resident should not be taken to imply a cynical view—that is, that programs are useless or unnecessary. Rather, they point to a need to focus on daily life in the nursing home and to consider special interventions as only a small part of the whole of residents' daily lives. Interventions have the promise of high impact and must enhance overall care rather than reflect a brief departure from ongoing routinized care practices. Most importantly, they must be responsive to individual patient or resident needs.[42] Additionally, bringing representatives of the outside community into the institution or taking residents back into the community would break down the barriers between the institution and the outside world and diminish "totalistic features of institutions."[43]

Exemplifying such approaches, aides who care for disabled elderly patients must be trained to redefine their jobs from custodial care to provision of therapeutic measures.[44] For example, it is typical for frail elders in a nursing home to receive occupational and physical therapy to enhance their ability to perform activities of daily living such as dressing or eating independently.[45] At the same time, little is done to reinforce or encourage such independence outside the therapy program. Daily meals provide tremendous opportunities for socialization as well as a motivating context to improve self-care, nutrition, and morale. Family visits as well as programmatic attention to residents during meals could go a long way toward achieving improvements in physical function as well as psychosocial well-being. Personnel delivering meals should be trained to engage in conversation with residents during meals, explaining what the resident is eating and contributing to the enjoyment of the meal. Meaningful choices can also be provided by allowing residents some choice in their meals.

In terms of diminishing barriers to the outside world, church groups and community or neighborhood groups may be used as a framework for arranging for resident visits back into the community. Encouraging families to take residents out for meals or to special events by assisting with transportation also holds great promise for patient-responsive care. Such trips can provide residents with a window to their past. Sharing information with patients and family about treatment regimens and medications can enhance a sense of involvement and allay anxieties. Organizationally, an important requisite for implementing such gestalt approaches is establishing direct and open communication between families and staff.[46]

In a study considering markers of excellence in nursing home care, SaraJane Brittis found that the major unifying thread among nursing homes that were judged by both residents and staff as excellent was not related to programs or resources. Rather, it was based on a fundamental human connection between family, residents and staff. Brittis terms this unique humanistic ingredient "sharing destinies."[47]

Most nursing homes are characterized by an absence of this emotional connection. This could be changed if visiting family members and nursing home staff would routinely express affection, affirmation, and communication in dealing with residents.[48] Volunteers and family members are major sources of connectedness for residents, and encouraging their active involvement in residents' lives can facilitate patient-responsive care.[49]

In evaluating existing interventions through a review of the literature, we located relatively few examples of patient-responsive interventions.[50] However, many helpful and high-impact programs implemented by nursing home staff who are sensitive to resident needs and perspectives never find their way into the literature. It is important to acknowledge that there are fundamental separations between clinical, practice, and research domains, which serve as barriers to disseminating clinical programs to the scientific community. The very professionals most deeply committed to developing practice innovations may lack the training and the time to design program evaluations and write them up for publication in scientific journals. Conversely, the scientists best equipped to design, implement, and get funding for scientifically sound innovative programs tend to work in academic settings. Often they design intervention programs for nursing homes without familiarity with the day-to-day living situations or perspectives of residents or staff.

Patient-responsive care demands staff involvement, communication, and support. Staff members could benefit from better training programs that emphasize "caring" attitudes. We have long advocated such approaches following up on seminal work of social scientists such as Erving Goffman and Jules Henry.[51] The challenge still stands, as growing numbers of older adults will live the final chapter of their lives within the confines of nursing homes. In this chapter we focused on family advocacy as an important and, thus far, largely overlooked opportunity for linking patients to the outside world and for enhancing patient-responsive care.

Promoting Patient-Responsive Care
Based on Hierarchy of Patient Needs

Development of practices and programs that are responsive to patients must move beyond medical models to allow for an appreciation of resident needs and preferences.[52] Family members can serve a useful function in articulating such needs where residents' ability to communicate is limited. Systematically considering the residents' perspectives on daily life in nursing homes can help in making programs salient to the experience of the individual resident. Abraham Maslow's hierarchy of needs provides a useful context for classifying the full array of resident needs and organizing them in a hierarchical fashion.[53] As we noted previously, programs targeting residents' social function may hold little interest for older adults whose most basic physical needs have not been met.[54] Residents may thus express disinterest in attending a carefully planned community birthday party or an activity session simply because they fear that there will be no one there to take them to the toilet when needed. Consequently, priority must be placed on meeting more immediate needs first, and then move toward creating programs that address higher-order needs. The family advocate can help communicate to staff about patient values and preferences. Some of these documents may be modeled after birth preferences documents that are increasingly used with expectant mothers.[55]

Four major areas of need are to be met by nursing home administrators and staff: reducing physical distress, meeting basic physiological needs, meeting emotional needs, and meeting social needs. It is important to acknowledge that psychosocial needs are often neglected in the context of a medical model of care and that staff who are focused on meeting basic biologically anchored needs may overlook patients' desires to retain their dignity and humanity. The needs we outline here are broadly related to Maslow's hierarchy of needs and are adapted from a framework we used to consider patient-responsive care for elderly in acute care hospital settings.[56]

We recognize that cognitively impaired and frail elders may be limited in their ability to articulate and communicate their needs, and therefore a major challenge of patient-responsive care is to elicit expression of needs and preferences. It is important to go beyond traditional need assessments, that are based on objective test data. Such assessments have limited value for understanding patients' perspectives. Instead, we advocate for empathetic listening to the patient's lived experience as a basis for developing patient-responsive care.[57] Such listening involves creation of a staff environment where residents do not fear sanctions if they express needs or place demands on staff. It also involves active efforts on the part of the staff to solicit expressions of resident need, as articulated by both family members and by residents. The framework that we offer below helps organize family-staff and patient-staff communication about areas of need.

Alleviating Discomfort

Discomforts, such as pain, dizziness, or nausea are experienced by many nursing home residents due to physical frailty and multiple chronic illnesses. Medical regimens or the nursing home environment can also contribute to physical discomfort. Pain may be due to poor circulation or arthritis. Discomforts may be caused by dressings or by a catheter. Residents may also suffer from backache or soreness due to a lumpy or soft mattress. Diminishing physical discomforts represents the first challenge to be met in providing patient-responsive care. This is an area where family communication with physicians and skilled nurses becomes particularly important. Side effects of medications need to be dealt with and attention needs to be directed to proper nutrition and exercise. In our case study about Sari, being confined all day to a wheelchair without being able to rest in bed during the day caused great discomfort. It is not uncommon for staff to position wheelchair-bound residents in their chairs early in the morning so that they spend a very long day confined to the chair. Only when physical discomfort is minimized can interventions to meet higher-order needs become effective.

Meeting Physical Needs

The second major area of needs involves basic physiological needs of hunger, thirst, toileting, sleep, temperature regulation, and breathing. These are needs that healthy people living in the community can routinely meet without difficulty. However, for the frail nursing home resident, each of these needs can pose major challenges. Nursing home residents are likely to have difficulty in meeting their basic physiological needs, in part due to illness and physical limitations and in part due to environmental barriers posed by the nursing home.[58] To the extent that environments and care are not individualized, frail residents will find problems in meeting their physical needs even in situations where healthy persons might be comfortable.

In describing issues related to physiological needs of residents, we provided some examples where environmental barriers may present problems. In terms of hunger, problems arise when residents are given diets to which they are not accustomed or where trays are placed out of reach of a bedridden resident. In regard to temperature regulation, many nursing homes do not offer temperature controls for individual residents. Since the majority of residents prefer extreme warmth during the winter, the temperature may be set too high for meeting needs of those elderly who are uncomfortable in excessive heat.

Restful sleep is important for maintenance of physical and psychological well-being, yet Sari often complained that her sleep was disrupted in the nursing home to implement toileting programs. Another frustration that made life difficult for Sari was related to lack of fresh air in rooms where windows were not designed to open. In my daily visits, I also noted the problems of frail residents in wheelchairs who asked to be assisted to use the toilet after meals. The typical wait for a response by an aide to these requests appeared to be staggeringly long. Inattention to toileting needs and problems with heat regulation presented a major area of unmet needs in the case study of Sari. Advocacy by family members can be particularly useful in alerting staff to unique physical needs of a resident such as feeling overly warm when the majority of residents tend to feel cold. Lack of patient-responsive care in meeting these most basic of human needs may result in psychological problems and unmet psychological needs to which we next turn.[59]

Meeting Emotional Needs

Four areas of emotional need may be identified as particularly salient to elderly nursing home residents: harm avoidance, personhood, dependency, and autonomy. Here, we illustrate approaches of patient-responsive care by focusing on harm avoidance and personhood. Extensive discussions of issues of autonomy and dependency have already been presented in the literature.[60]

Disabled nursing home residents need to feel secure and unharmed in the face of frailty. The extreme vulnerability experienced by old-old persons with physical, sensory, and cognitive limitations calls for constant reassurance that those caring for them will not hurt or neglect them. Patient-responsive care in this area demands that there be reassuring touching and verbal communication whenever personal care is provided. Patients must be actively queried about their concerns and specific reassurance provided in areas of fear. Typical concerns may involve fears of falling out of bed or having a medical emergency with no one noticing. During my visits to Sari, I noticed that she was fearful of being raised on a Hoyer lift or bathed in tubs where she was suspended while bathing. In Sari's case, I was not permitted to be in Sari's room while staff transferred her using a Hoyer lift. This practice was presumably undertaken to protect her privacy. But my presence was actually reassuring to Sari. Establishing positive and appreciative ties with staff members helped in this situation, as some staff members were willing to bend this rule and allow me to stay in Sari's room.

A second area of unique emotional concern for nursing home residents involves the need to maintain a sense of personhood and respect in the face of losses and institutionalization. Examples of concerns in this area include fears that requests, wishes, and opinions of the resident will be disregarded. This emotional need is exacerbated in nursing home settings where there is little individualization of care. Patient-responsive care must seize opportunities to acknowledge resident opinions. The challenge is to do so in ways that are meaningful to residents. Patient-responsive care is not about offering choices about pictures to color, but about actions that show that the resident truly matters. One example of such a gesture may be a staff member spontaneously asking advice from a resident. Spiritual needs of residents and their concerns about having a good death also need to be acknowledged through empathetic listening and sensitively responsive comments. The family advocate can make important contributions by sharing personal stories with staff about the resident, and keeping staff motivated to relate to the resident as a unique person rather than just a case to manage.

Meeting Social Needs

Social needs of residents include maintaining meaningful social ties with family and attachments with those in their immediate social environment, including staff and other residents. Recognition of the cultural and religious background of the resident also represents an important contribution to identity maintenance.[61]

A major social need concerns the fear of abandonment by family and the outside world.[62] Residents may make frantic and seemingly unnecessary demands for staff to contact members of their family. In Sari's case, she frequently beseeched staff to contact us to check on her pending doctor's appointments. Even when staff indicated that they had the information, she insisted that I be called. Such actions were likely to mask emotional needs for close human contact and attachments. Patient-responsive care calls for active listening by staff for these signals. Instead of vacuous reminders (e.g., "your children were here just a few hours ago"), residents' concerns should be heard and empathetically acknowledged. Active efforts by staff to create meaningful bonds with residents reflect examples of patient-responsive care. The involvement by family caregivers in meeting social needs is key, through visitation, phone calls, and, where possible, taking the resident out of the nursing home for community visitation.

Conclusion

In this chapter, we dealt primarily with nursing home care of elders living with disabilities. A second and equally important focus was on the role of family advocacy in humanizing care of frail older adults. Positive relationships with caregivers represent an important component of the aspirations of older adults with disabilities that require high support needs.[63]

How can these different approaches of scholarship be harnessed to ultimately improve quality of care in nursing homes? To transfer the everyday experience of residents in the nursing home into policy change and better practices, research strategies must better capture the richness of the lived experience of institutionalized older adults. Life in a nursing home can further accentuate the marginalization of frail and disabled elders by cutting them off from the protective features of social integration.[64] Recognizing the value of family advocacy in the context of frailty and long-term care can contribute to better quality of care and quality of life for residents with late onset disabilities. Specification of mechanisms by which family advocacy can contribute to better quality of life for disabled older adults should facilitate development of practice guidelines for diminishing barriers between the outside world and life in institutions.

Notes

1. Marie-Luise Friedemann, Rhonda J. Montgomery, Bedonna Maiberger, and A. Ann Smith, "Family Involvement in the Nursing Home: Family-Oriented Practices and Staff-Family Relationships," *Research in Nursing and Health* 20, no. 6 (1997): 527–537.

2. Timothy Diamond, *Making Gray Gold: Narratives of Nursing Home Care* (University of Chicago Press, 2009); Barbara K. Haight, Yvonne Michel, and Shirley Hendrix, "The Extended Effects of the Life Review in Nursing Home Residents," *International Journal of Aging and Human Development* 50, no. 2 (2000): 151–168.

3. Joyce Parr and Sara Green, "Systemic Characteristics of Long-Term Care in Residential Environments: Clinical Importance of Differences in Staff and Resident Perceptions," *Clinical Gerontologist* 25, nos. 1–2 (2003): 149–171.

4. Erving Goffman, *The Presentation of Self in Everyday Life* (Anchor, 1959).

5. Rosalie A. Kane, Robert L. Kane, and Richard C. Ladd, *The Heart of Long Term Care* (Oxford University Press, 1998).

6. Eva Kahana, David E. Biegel, and May Wykle, *Family Caregiving Across the Lifespan,* vol. 4 (Sage, 1994).

7. Robyn I. Stone and Pamela Farley Short, "The Competing Demands of Employment and Informal Caregiving to Disabled Elders," *Medical Care* 28, no. 6 (1990): 513–526.

8. Erving Goffman, *Asylums: Essays on the Social Situations of Mental Patients and Other Inmates* (Anchor, 1961).

9. Bruce C. Vladeck, *Unloving Care: The Nursing Home Tragedy* (Basic, 1980).

10. George J. Agich, *Autonomy and Long-Term Care* (Oxford University Press, 1993).

11. Sara E. Green, "Convergent Caregiving: Exploring Eldercare in Families of Children with Disabilities," *Journal of Loss and Trauma* 18, no. 4 (2013): 289–305.

12. Diamond, *Making Gray Gold*; Arif Nazir, Kathleen Unroe, Monica Tegeler, Babar Khan, Jose Azar, and Malaz Boustani, "Systematic Review of Interdisciplinary Interventions in Nursing Homes," *Journal of the American Medical Directors Association* 14, no. 7 (2013): 471–478; Audrey S. Weiner and Judah L. Ronch, *Culture Change in Long-Term Care* (Routledge, 2003).

13. Eva Kahana, Boaz Kahana, H. Chirayath, D. Biegel, and A. Blum, "Innovations in Institutional Care from a Patient-Responsive Perspective," in *Innovations in Practice and Service Delivery Across the Lifespan,* ed. David E. Biegel and Arthur Blum (Oxford University Press, 1999), 249–275.

14. Jaber F. Gubrium, *Living and Dying at Murray Manor* (University of Virginia Press, 2012).

15. Tom Shakespeare, *Disability Rights and Wrongs Revisited* (Routledge, 2013).

16. Friedemann et al., "Family Involvement in the Nursing Home."

17. Joseph E. Gaugler, K. A. Anderson, Steven H. Zarit, and Leonard I. Pearlin, "Family Involvement in Nursing Homes: Effects on Stress and Well-Being," *Aging and Mental Health* 8, no. 1 (2004): 65–75.

18. Jane B. Tornatore and Leslie A. Grant, "Family Caregiver Satisfaction with the Nursing Home after Placement of a Relative with Dementia," *Journals of Gerontology Series B: Psychological Sciences and Social Sciences* 59, no. 2 (2004): S80–S88.

19. Heather Russell and Peter E. Foreman, "Maintaining a Relationship with a Family Member in a Nursing Home: The Role of Visitor," *Journal of Family Studies* 8, no. 2 (2002): 147–164.

20. Lené Levy-Storms and Dana Miller-Martinez, "Family Caregiver Involvement and Satisfaction with Institutional Care During the 1st Year After Admission," *Journal of Applied Gerontology* 24, no. 2 (2005): 160–174.

21. U. M. Kellett, "Searching for New Possibilities to Care: A Qualitative Analysis of Family Caring Involvement in Nursing Homes," *Nursing Inquiry* 6, no. 1 (1999): 9–16.

22. Neal Krause, "Social Relationships in Late Life," in *Handbook of Aging and the Social Sciences*, 6th ed., ed. Robert H. Binstock, Linda K. George, Stephen J. Cutler, Jon Hendricks, and James H. Schulz (Elsevier, 2006), 181–200.

23. Eva Kahana, Jeong Eun Lee, Jeffrey Kahana, Timothy Goler, Boaz Kahana, Sarah Shick, Erin Burk, and Kaitlyn Barnes, "Childhood Autism and Proactive Family Coping: International Perspectives," *Journal of Intergenerational Relationships* 13, no. 2 (2015): 150–166.

24. Linda K. George and George L. Maddox, "Social and Behavioral Aspects of Institutional Care," in *Ageing and Health Care: Social and Policy Perspectives*, ed. Marcia G. Ory and Kathleen Bond (Routledge, 1989).

25. Bruce A. Ferrell, Betty R. Ferrell, and Lynne Rivera, "Pain in Cognitively Impaired Nursing Home Patients," *Journal of Pain and Symptom Management* 10, no. 8 (1995): 591–598.

26. Joseph P. Shapiro, *No Pity: People with Disabilities Forging a New Civil Rights Movement* (Three Rivers Press, 1994).

27. For our published narrative work on our family's experience with Sari's nursing home care toward the end of her life, see Eva Kahana, "Dreams of Hot Toast and Smiling Nurses: Toward a Model of Patient-Responsive Care in Nursing Homes," *Research in the Sociology of Health Care* 24, no. 1 (2006): 109.

28. Jay Magaziner, Sheryl Itkin Zimmerman, K. M. Fox, and B. J. Burns, "Dementia in United States Nursing Homes: Descriptive Epidemiology and Implications for Long-Term Residential Care," *Aging and Mental Health* 2, no. 1 (1998): 28–35.

29. Eva Kahana, Boaz Kahana, Loren Lovegreen, Jeffrey Kahana, Jane Brown, and Diana Kulle, "Health-Care Consumerism and Access to Health Care: Educating Elders to Improve Both Preventive and End-of-Life Care," in *Research in the Sociology of Health Care*, ed. Jennie Jacobs Kronenfeld (Emerald, 2011), 173–193.

30. Robert W. Kleemeier, "The Use and Meaning of Time in Special Settings: Retirement Communities, Homes for the Aged, Hospitals, and Other Group Settings," *Aging and Leisure* (1961): 273–308.

31. Goffman, *Asylums*.

32. Karen Davis, Stephen C. Schoenbaum, and Anne-Marie Audet, "A 2020 Vision of Patient-Centered Primary Care," *Journal of General Internal Medicine* 20, no. 10 (2005): 953–957; Moira Stewart, *Patient-Centered Medicine: Transforming the Clinical Method* (Radcliffe, 2003); Eva Kahana, Loren Lovegreen, and Boaz Kahana, "Long-Term Care: Tradition and Innovation," in *Handbook of Sociology of Aging* (Springer, 2011), 583–602.

33. Eva Kahana and Boaz Kahana, "Patient Proactivity Enhancing Doctor-Patient-Family Communication in Cancer Prevention and Care Among the Aged," *Patient Education and Counseling* 50, no. 1 (2003): 67–73.

34. Ibid.

35. Linda S. Noelker and Zev Harel, *Linking Quality of Long-Term Care and Quality of Life* (Springer, 2000).

36. SaraJane Brittis, "Sharing Destinies: Staff and Residents' Perspectives on Excellence in High Quality Nursing Homes in London, England and New York City, USA," Dissertation (Case Western Reserve University, 1996).

37. Jeanie Kayser-Jones, Ellen Schell, William Lyons, Alison E. Kris, Joyce Chan, and Renee L. Beard, "Factors that Influence End-of-Life Care in Nursing Homes: The Physical Environment, Inadequate Staffing, and Lack of Supervision," *The Gerontologist* 43, Suppl. 2 (2003): 76–84.

38. Kahana, Biegel, and Wykle, *Family Caregiving Across the Lifespan*; Jeffrey S. Kahana, "Reevaluating the Nursing Home Ombudsman's Role with a View Toward Expanding the Concept of Dispute Resolution," *Journal of Dispute Resolution* (1994): 217–233.

39. Shakespeare, *Disability Rights and Wrongs Revisited*.

40. Russell and Foreman, "Maintaining a Relationship with a Family Member in a Nursing Home."

41. Shapiro, *No Pity*.

42. Stewart, *Patient-Centered Medicine*.

43. Goffman, *Asylums*.

44. Jeanne A. Teresi, Douglas Holmes, and Marcia G. Ory, "The Therapeutic Design of Environments for People with Dementia: Further Reflections and Recent Findings from the National Institute on Aging Collaborative Studies of Dementia Special Care Units," *The Gerontologist* 40, no. 4 (2000): 417–421.

45. Cameron J. Camp, Jiska Cohen-Mansfield, and Elizabeth A. Capezuti, "Mental Health Services in Nursing Homes: Use of Nonpharmacologic Interventions Among Nursing Home Residents with Dementia," *Psychiatric Services* 53, no. 11 (2002): 1397–1404.

46. Joseph Angelelli, Vincent Mor, Orna Intrator, Zhanlian Feng, and Jacqueline Zinn, "Oversight of Nursing Homes: Pruning the Tree or Just Spotting Bad Apples?" *The Gerontologist* 43, Suppl. 2 (2003): 67–75.

47. Brittis, "Sharing Destinies."

48. Joel S. Savishinsky, *The Ends of Time: Life and Work in a Nursing Home* (Praeger, 1991); Vladeck, *Unloving Care*.

49. David Oliver and Sally Tureman, *The Human Factor in Nursing Home Care* (Routledge, 2013); Victoria E. Bumagin and Kathryn F. Hirn, *Helping the Aging Family: A Guide for Professionals* (Springer, 1989).

50. Kahana et al., "Innovations in Institutional Care from a Patient-Responsive Perspective."

51. Eva Kahana, "The Humane Treatment of Old People in Institutions," *The Gerontologist* 13, no. 3, Pt. 1 (1973): 282–289; Goffman, *Asylums;* Jules Henry, *Culture Against Man* (Vintage, 1965).

52. J. Neil Henderson, "The Culture of Care in a Nursing Home: Effects of a Medicalized Model of Long-Term Care," in *The Culture of Long-Term Care: Nursing Home Ethnography,* ed., J. Niel Henderson and Mario D. Vesperi (Greenwood, 1995), 37–54.

53. Abraham Harold Maslow, "A Theory of Human Motivation," *Psychological Review* 50, no. 4 (1943): 370–396.

54. Kahana, "Dreams of Hot Toast and Smiling Nurses."

55. Penny Simkin, "Birth Plans: After 25 Years, Women Still Want to Be Heard," *Birth* 34, no. 1 (2007): 49–51.

56. Kahana et al., "Innovations in Institutional Care from a Patient-Responsive Perspective."

57. Clifford Bennett, *Nursing Home Life: What It Is and What It Could Be* (Tiresias Press, 1980); Barbara K. Haight, Yvonne Michel, and Shirley Hendrix, "The Extended Effects of the Life Review in Nursing Home Residents," *The International Journal of Aging and Human Development* 50, no. 2 (2000): 151–168.

58. Jiska Cohen-Mansfield and Perla Werner, "The Effects of an Enhanced Environment on Nursing Home Residents Who Pace," *The Gerontologist* 38, no. 2 (1998): 199–208.

59. Gill Livingston, Kate Johnston, Cornelius Katona, Joni Paton, Constantine G. Lyketsos, and Old Age Task Force of the World Federation of Biological Psychiatry, "Systematic Review of Psychological Approaches to the Management of Neuropsychiatric Symptoms of Dementia," *American Journal of Psychiatry* 162, no. 11 (2005): 1996–2021.

60. Agich, *Autonomy and Long-Term Care.*

61. David O. Moberg, "Research in Spirituality, Religion, and Aging," *Journal of Gerontological Social Work* 45, nos. 1–2 (2005): 11–40.

62. Oliver and Tureman, *The Human Factor in Nursing Home Care.*

63. Jeanne Katz, Caroline Holland, and Sheila Peace, "Hearing the Voices of People with High Support Needs," *Journal of Aging Studies* 27, no. 1 (2013): 52–60.

64. Chris Gilleard and Paul Higgs, "Frailty, Disability and Old Age: A Reappraisal," *Health* 15, no. 5 2010: 475–490.

8

The Experience of Disability at the End of Life

What is it like to experience disability in late life? To answer this question, we must take into account the experiences of people living to the outer limits of life expectancy. Although late-life disability is not confined to those age eighty-five and over (the old-old), this fast-growing segment of the population has the highest rate of disability. As we consider the larger process of disablement in old age—and its similarities and differences to disability at other points during the life course—the question of how disability affects this old-old cohort of seniors is instructive. So, too, is the question of how these individuals include—or reject—disability in the narratives they construct for themselves about growing old.

The old-old, as well as many of the young-old (ages sixty-five to seventy-five), perceive and experience disability as an intrusion into their existing lives and a threat to their health and their broader sense of well-being. The concept of *well-being* refers to the meanings older persons give to their lives and the subjective ways in which they interpret their life experiences. Disability for older persons is usually a process of chronic disease progression that leads to the loss of functional abilities, rather than a single event such as an injury or acute illness.[1]

In this age cohort, disability is part of the aging process and a signifier that the person is nearing the end of life. Yet each individual understands this process in a unique way. In *How We Die* (1993), Sherwin B. Nuland explains the biology behind the weakening of the body in very old age, but also recognizes our subjective reactions against this process:

> Surrounded by it though we may be, there is for each of us that something within that turns the face of consciousness away from the reality of our own concomitant aging. Something within us will not accept the immediacy of awareness that, even as we bear witness to it in the obviously old, our own bodies are simultaneously and subtly undergoing the same inexorable process that will lead eventually to senescence and death.[2]

A person's subjective reaction to disability is mirrored by a societal ambivalence toward defining limitations in old age in terms of social barriers. Disability among the old-old has been viewed instead as a public health problem. But unlike the young-old, for whom the primary objective is to delay and compress disability,[3] the old-old cannot defer disability indefinitely. At this late point in the life course, disability is linked with mortality and is typically considered in the context of end-of-life health care, with a focus on cost-benefit analysis and the institutional arrangements for how this care should be delivered.[4] Rarely have scholars considered the issue of disablement during old age in terms of rights and social inclusion, or as primarily a product of person and environment interaction.

One significant feature of the old-old cohort is the dominance of women. At present there are 4.2 men for every 10.0 women in the eighty-five-and-older age group, compared with 8.5 men for every 10.0 women in their sixties. The implication of this gender imbalance among the old-old is that large numbers of elderly women are living alone. However, either gender may fear losing a spouse: "Worse than the fear of death is the fear of being left alone," observes philosopher Paul Arthur Schilpp in his essay "At 92" in Philip L. Berman's collection *The Courage to Grow Old* (1989).[5] The elderly also fear losing—and surviving—their friends. "More loneliness comes as your old friends disappear," warns Schilpp. "Although my wife . . . is alive, nearly ninety-five percent of my contemporaries are dead."[6] This loss of social connectedness and support heightens the impact of disabling conditions and environments.

This age group also utilizes nursing homes at a higher rate (18.2 percent) than the young-old. Yet even with higher rates of disability (55 percent and up for those age eighty-five and older), there is marked diversity in capability within this group. Researchers report that "approximately one-third of the oldest old are healthy enough to live independently in the community, one-third are functionally impaired, and one-third are extremely frail and disabled."[7]

Health and Disability

Although experts have noted that "disabled people are generally healthy,"[8] disability in old age is usually seen through the lens of health deficits. At first glance, this perspective seems to endorse a medical model of disability that diverges sharply from the social approach favored by disability scholars. But, closer examination reveals that, in the context of very old age, health is not simply about avoiding disease. The old-old strive to preserve health as a means of maintaining their independence in the community.

Health is an especially valuable resource for avoiding depending on others or ending up in a nursing home. For the very old, therefore, disability is not disease per se, but rather the interaction between available social and physiological resources. This interaction is what constitutes functional disability, defined as "a chronic health problem, either physical or mental, [that] produces a behavioral change in a person's capacity to perform the necessary tasks for daily living."[9]

The very old are usually facing not just one disease, but a combination of chronic ailments that interfere with their ability to manage activities of daily personal care (such as eating, bathing, toileting, and dressing) or the activities of managing a home (such as shopping, preparing meals, and housecleaning). The former are categorized as personal activities of daily living (PADLs or ADLs) and the latter as instrumental activities of daily living (IADLs).[10] It is important to note that both categories reflect an understanding of disability as essentially socially constructed rather than disease based.

To what degree is a person able to manage on his or her own? For the very old who live on their own and do not have access to family caregivers, disability is a combination of faltering ability and lack of support. These old-old individuals often live with multiple chronic conditions and require the assistance of another person. This is in contrast to the seventy-five to eighty-four age group, in which fewer than 10 percent require such help.[11] In a demographic sense, the oldest old face disability as a function of age. How chronic conditions impose functional limitations and become a major cause of disability among the very old is an important sociological question. The older person who cannot readily reach the toilet because of mobility impairments and who then falls trying to get to the toilet is an example of how seemingly mild impairments can cascade into a significant disability—and even lead to institutionalization. While not all such cases can be avoided, their numbers can be reduced if older persons have someone looking after them—and if physicians take a preventive (and holistic) approach to care that goes beyond simply treating medical conditions.[12]

The interplay between health conditions and social resources for those age eighty-five and older who live in the community sheds light on disability as a process that transcends disease and diagnosis. Without focusing narrowly on cognitive and bodily impairments as such, we should be attuned to the benefits of early intervention for conditions that can be effectively managed. This intervention encompasses medical treatments, environmental modifications, and social supports. For the very old, such interventions are too often delayed or not forthcoming at all, resulting in the cascading effect noted above, in which a mobility impairment and a nonmodified environment lead to a fall and a complete loss of independence.[13]

The precarious relationship between health and disability among the very old often centers on conditions that restrict mobility and functional capacity. Diseases that affect the joints and bones, such as osteoarthritis and osteoporosis, are especially common in this age group. Heart disease, vision problems, and cognitive impairments—both separately and in combination—can also restrict a very old person's mobility and impact daily functioning.[14]

This tenuous balance between health and disability means that for the very old, we must view the role of disease prevention and health promotion—and the equally important concept of health literacy—somewhat differently than we do for other age groups. We cannot narrowly focus on what the old-old should do to avoid illness; we must also address the question of how they can learn to live with chronic illness and disability. For example, how can we help them manage taking their (numerous) medications and avoid negative drug interactions? How can we modify their home environments to limit fall risks? How can we make sure they get rehabilitation services? Each positive intervention lessens the older person's disability.[15]

A disability model of aging does not diminish the role of health and illness issues. It does, however, highlight an urgent need to bring care and resources to the old-old so that they can live independently. For the very old, social processes are just as important risk factors for becoming disabled as are chronic disease processes—maybe even more so. And for the very old, the consequences of disability are more than simply the loss of health.

In the coming decades, more and more people will live to the age of eighty-five and older. The ideal that has emerged is to compress disability into the very last moments of life. This goal may well be desirable, but is it achievable? And even for those who take the best care of their bodies, what happens if Alzheimer's or Parkinson's disease strikes? The current framework of disease prevention and health promotion needs to expand to include a larger role for care and assistance in late life. Richard Fortinsky, a leading authority on aging and health, working with the British scholar Murna Downs, highlights the value of community based support in caring for individuals with dementia and their families.[16] We may also glean valuable lessons from the rights-oriented independent living movement, which disability activists started in the 1970s.[17]

Illness and Disability

Few older persons are prepared for the transition from health to illness or to address issues of disability in late life. A common thread is the desire to avoid confrontations with illness and loss. Writing at the age of seventy-six in another essay in *The Courage to Grow Old,* satirist Ira Wallach confesses: "I avoid those of my contemporaries whose idea of scintillating conversation is a recital of their physical woes."[18] Also writing in her late seventies in one more essay in Berman's collection, actress Rosemary DeCamp concludes that "the only courage that is necessary is the courage to grow old graciously—to forego complaints, to stifle symptom sharing."[19]

But the reality of illness—and the disabilities that accompany illness—is never far from the minds of the very old. "To see someone taking care of a wife or husband with Alzheimer's disease," wrote journalist John Tebbel, "opens the door to a particular kind of hell that must take extraordinary courage to confront every day. . . . The same can be said for cancer and other diseases whose outcome is known and inevitable, soon or late."[20] Such are the fears of illness and disability seen from a distance—as a plight that awaits the unlucky.

Yet we have much to learn from those who are unlucky but who nevertheless show us that illness and disability can confer great meaning on life, even amid great pain. The publisher William I. Nichols cared for his wife throughout her battle with Alzheimer's disease. In another essay in *The Courage to Grow Old*, written in the form of a letter to a former classmate who has also lost his wife after a long illness, Nichols describes how the pain and suffering actually strengthened his love for his mate: "Often toward the end, but when she could still walk, she would say: 'Let's look at OUR house!' Then, arm in arm, we would walk through each room, remembering the objects one by one."[21]

Such are the personal reflections—on life and death, well-being, and disability—of those living into old age. Previously we have examined the experience of the adventurous traveler, the older person who refuses to let age or disability interfere with cherished activities. But such opportunities become more limited as individuals move through old age into very old age. Indeed, as they approach the last period of life, they experience a documented diminishment in functioning. If the essays in *The Courage to Grow Old* have a single unifying theme, it is that the space of life occurs within smaller spheres as people reach advanced age. But within these spheres remains the opportunity for growth and engagement with life—with the ability to be creative, to love, and to change. Most important is the realization during old age that authenticity and self-acceptance are the basis for a meaningful life—and that disability does not diminish the capacity to find meaning at the end of life.

Death and Dying in Advanced Old Age

Advanced old age changes our relationship to time. Our sense of a future based on numerous possibilities gives way to a sense of limitations. It is not just that time affects our perspective, but that physical and social losses in later life restructure how we use time. The passage of time and the correlate of diminishing confidence in one's future health can lead, as Richard A. Kalish observes, to "death as an organizer of time."[22]

It is common for the very old to think in the immediate term and to detach themselves from any long-term future. When older individuals are in institutions such as hospitals or nursing homes, the physical restrictions of place further magnify the boundaries of time. Time presents a paradox in old age. Even as the personal meaning of time changes, the presence of time can seem excessive. What should an older patient in a hospital do with his or her time? How might a nursing home resident use the long stretches of time in the day? As time becomes limited in the long term, with the imminent approach of death, it also has less actual day-to-day meaning.[23]

Death has not figured prominently in disability studies. One exception is in connection with the right to die and the issue of the physician's role in end-of-life care. A possible explanation for this omission is that we associate death with illness and therefore with a medical model. Disability scholars and activists, however, see disability as something other than illness and usually consider it from the vantage point of social barriers to inclusion. Nevertheless, for many disabled people at the end of life—especially when degenerative illnesses are present—disability is inextricably linked with death.

Death occupies a more significant (albeit changing) place in the aging literature. Gerontologists, at first, placed death in a social context and recognized the "many meanings of death and dying" arising from "interactions with others."[24] Proximity to death involved more than just the dying process. They believed that a perceived nearness to death led younger people to avoid the aged and socially isolate them. The result was a mutual disengagement process—between the elderly and society—as older individuals internalized social attitudes toward death and those who were dying. Gerontologists saw this disengagement as having certain benefits for the dying person; Kalish, for example, hypothesized that it allowed the older person to cope better with death. Old age (and the lessening of attachments) served as a buffer to the stress of impending death.[25]

Early gerontological work on death and dying drew upon anthropological, philosophical (especially existentialist), and religious orientations. It explored the myriad meanings associated with death and dying—for dying individuals, their families, and those who cared for them.[26] Kalish's contribution to the field focused on understanding the meaning of death through cultural attitudes and values.[27] In more recent years, however, the trend in gerontology has moved away from such perspectives and toward a more scientific approach to death and dying. The 2011 *Handbook of Aging and the Social Sciences* calls for "valid and reliable scales to measure the impact of death and dying on individuals and families."[28]

The general absence of research on death by disability scholars and the emphasis on scientific and medical considerations in late life among gerontologists may reflect the greater uneasiness within the larger society surrounding the end of life. Death is not a topic that readily lends itself to analysis as either a civil rights issue for the disability community or as a scientific question for social scientists. Yet all people, when faced with a terminal illness, seek to die with dignity, without fear, and with the support of their loved ones.

An awareness of death also can play a role in awakening people to the possibilities that exist within their remaining available lives. The path toward death (whether long or short) can even unlock some of the mysteries of life. In fact, one might consider the period of old age and the experience of disability not so much as a journey toward the end of life, but as a road that leads away from youth and the impression that we can live our lives without experiencing tragic elements. To see things in this way does not require a religious predisposition or a commitment to a specific spirituality—but it does mean that we should pause and reflect upon ourselves as human beings and social actors.

The social meaning of death in advanced age has in some ways stayed the same and in other ways changed over the past two centuries. In the early nineteenth century, all ages commonly experienced death. But in his study of old age in America, historian W. Andrew Achenbaum finds that even then, "death loomed as the ultimate source of grief in old age."[29] It is not modern society that draws a connection between old age and death, but such a connection is an enduring social understanding of the life cycle. Still, the social meaning of death is not stable, but changes based on time and context.

Achenbaum's research about early America shows that older persons were valued for their experience and perspective on life. Achenbaum refers to the "usefulness of old age" and shows how the elderly were seen as examples of virtuous living. Death was just one more aspect of the life cycle that demonstrated their usefulness. An older generation taught a younger generation how to die and how to accept the "debilities" of late life. In death the generations could be further bound to each other, and an awareness of death taught the whole community that life should have a larger purpose beyond what we today might consider individual fulfillment.[30] Death—and the disabilities connected with it—could be made tolerable by incorporating older persons within a social system that valued them until, and through, death. The presence of social networks provided a source of comfort and validation as older persons sought to make sense of debility and approaching death.

Current research shows that psychosocial support helps older people navigate this phase of life. However, there may be no better illustration of how older individuals can come to accept the debilities of late life than we see in the correspondence between Thomas Jefferson and John Adams at the end of their lives. On several occasions, the two men—who died on the same day July 4, 1826—raised the issue of debility in old age and its relation to death. In 1816, when Jefferson was seventy-three, he answered Adams's question "Would I agree to live my 73 years over again for ever?" by saying that he would be willing to relive the period from twenty-five to sixty but not after that:

> For, at the latter period, with most of us, the powers of life are sensibly on the wane, sight becomes dim, hearing dull, memory constantly enlarging it's [sic] frightful blank and parting with all we have ever seen or known, spirits evaporate, bodily debility creeps in palsying every limb, and so faculty after faculty quits us and where then is life?[31]

Jefferson frankly expresses the linkage between old age and physical and mental debility. He felt that there is "a ripeness of time for death, regarding others as well as ourselves. . . . When we have lived our generation out, we should not wish to encroach on another." But when did this time occur? Jefferson admitted that he had not yet reached it: "I enjoy good health; I am happy in what is around me." But he also felt ready—that he had largely completed his life journey: "I am ripe for leaving all, this year, this day, this hour." The issue of debility is what he feared the most, and mental debility in particular: "Bodily decay is gloomy in prospect; but of all human contemplations, the most abhorrent is body without mind." He could nevertheless reassure Adams that his mind was well, and he mentioned his goal of reading fifteen volumes of "anecdotes and incidents" written by a well-known French writer, critic, and diplomat "before I go."[32]

Adams, too, reflected on death and debility in later life. At age eighty-seven, he wrote to Jefferson: "I cannot mount my Horse, but I can walk three miles over a rugged rockey Mountain." Yet he felt the creaks of age: "I feel when setting in my chair, as if I could not rise out of it, and when risen, as if I could not walk across the room; my sight is very dim; hearing pretty good; memory poor enough." He then took up the issue of death and answered Jefferson's query "Is Death an Evil?" by responding, "It is not an Evil. It is a blessing to the individual, and to the world. Yet we ought not to wish for it until life becomes insupportable; we must wait the pleasure and convenience of this great teacher."[33]

The idea of death as a teacher may be difficult to understand in our own time period. We aim to delay death as long as possible and to compress disability until as near death as possible. But this contemporary orientation may reflect a youth-centered outlook toward aging rather than the perspective of those who have experienced very old age. For Adams, death was the proper teacher for those pupils (like himself) who had succeeded in reaching very old age. In one of his last letters to Jefferson, he laid out a quandary that still exists for many people today. A man of religious convictions but also a liberal rationalist, Adams explained: "I am certainly very near the end of my life. I am far from trifling with the idea of Death which is a great and solemn event." Curious and perhaps even hopeful, he continued: "But I contemplate it without terror or dismay" because "either it is a transformation or it is the end." Adams "could not believe" it was the end, but if it was, he asked, "Why should I dread it?" If, however, death was a transformation, he told Jefferson, "I shall ever be under the same constitution and administration of Government in the Universe, and I am not afraid to trust and confide in it."[34]

The letters between Adams and Jefferson reveal that both men approached debility in old age and death "gracefully, exemplifying some of the better qualities that Cicero commended in his essay on the subject, *De Senectute*." The editor of their correspondence, Lester J. Cappon, offers three reasons for their contentment in old age: (1) both had returned to their homes and entered retirement from public affairs "from desire, not compulsion"; (2) both were "mentally active," and "keeping up with their correspondence and thus abreast of the outside world continually refreshed and stimulated the confinements of old age"; and (3) while both suffered from physical impairments, they also enjoyed "sound health" and in spite of limitations "continued [their] customary exercise" of walking and riding.[35]

These two men's acceptances of debility and death and their absence of fear affirm psychologist Sheldon Tobin's research showing that there is "something very different about the psychology of the very old" in relation to approaching death. Unlike the young who are in the midst of creating their self-identity, and the middle aged whose "task is to fulfill the self," the very old seek to "preserve the self." The letters between these extraordinary men epitomize Tobin's idea about the "preservation" of a lifetime of work and that work's associated social meaning. Yet Tobin states that people need not be "extraordinary" in their accomplishments to "persist in being themselves in the final years of their lives despite illness and losses that assault their personhood."[36]

Tobin interviewed the very old and learned that "death becomes acceptable when life's tasks are completed." The very old had already passed through family, work, and various other life-experiential components that constitute the early and middle parts of the life cycle. This completion helped make death acceptable, shifting their fears away from death itself to the dying process. Living fully, Tobin discovered, had immunized the very old from the five stages that Elizabeth Kübler-Ross describes in her 1969 book *On Death and Dying:* denial, anger, bargaining, depression, and acceptance. Tobin concludes that the Kübler-Ross's "stages are likely not to be relevant" for the very old individual. Rather, this person simply "wishes for an easy death" that avoids the pain and suffering of a prolonged illness, faced alone and in an institutional setting.[37]

When disability interferes with a normal or good death, the path toward acceptance becomes more complicated. For the very old, disability in late life evokes a unique fear, especially when that disability is associated with a prolonged dying process marked by pain and isolation, as with Alzheimer's disease.[38] Understanding the connection between late-life disability or degenerative illness and death will require more research—but it is important work that might explain why so many elderly people fear disability in ways that are distinct from the more positive attitudes of younger people.

Disability and death can become intertwined in other ways during late life. One scenario is when an older person is the parent of a disabled adult child, especially when that child is developmentally disabled. Because the older parent has substantial unfinished business in caring for that child, the parent is afraid to die out of concern for the child's future welfare. The other scenario is when a middle-aged person suffers from a degenerative condition that is ultimately terminal—a situation that can drain the physical and social resources of even the most resilient person. In his autobiography, *The Body Silent*, Robert Francis Murphy presents a firsthand account of such challenges and the lack of societal support for persons living with degenerative disabilities.[39] Murphy's account of his own response to disability—framed against the attitude of society—is a remarkable feat of self-construction. He knows that his paralysis and degenerative disability will ultimately lead to death, but he chooses to embrace his disability and his life.

His disability, in fact, becomes a self-conscious defense against death. At the end of his book, Murphy declares: "All of us dangle between loss of self and loss of others, . . . between life and death."[40]

A Life Interrupted:
Impairments and Their Cultural Meanings

Just as there is an emphasis in disability studies on separating disability from illness, there is an emphasis in gerontology on separating old age from illness. Conditions likely to lead to death among the very old—cardiovascular diseases, cancer, diabetes, neurological diseases—are deemed illnesses that are distinct from old age and are rarely considered from the vantage point of a disability paradigm. While numerous books focus on how to avoid illness, few provide guidance on how to live with both illness and disability. For the very old, the struggle between life and death often takes place at the outskirts of their own recognition of themselves as disabled. But even before such a final struggle, the encounter between old age and disability is characterized by the leitmotif of what anthropologist Samantha Solimeo and others have characterized as "biographical disruption."[41]

Older individuals living with Parkinson's and Alzheimer's disease—two degenerative ailments that typically strike older adults—provide a revealing look at the complex relationship between aging and disability. Both diseases can be difficult to diagnose and have symptoms that are associated with normal aging. Each condition, however, disrupts the expected trajectory of old age for individuals and their caregivers. The physical challenges of Parkinson's and the cognitive impairments of Alzheimer's lead to a loss of independence. They also fundamentally change the expectations of individuals and their families for what it means to grow old.[42]

Older individuals with Parkinson's experience mobility impairments, with early symptoms of "slowness, stiff movement, and stooped posture."[43] The subjective meanings they attach to this disease are as important as the somatic considerations. In her study, Solimeo emphasizes how progressive and deteriorating diseases "disrupt the essential values of the archetypal American self—independence, autonomy, individualism, self-control, and self-efficacy."[44] She found that to those affected by the disease, perceptions of what Parkinson's is—and means—varied by age group. Yet few considered themselves to be disabled or suffering from an illness. "Very few of the people I met would consider themselves to be anything but healthy people," Solimeo writes. "I was repeatedly assured that 'I feel great, except for the PD' [Parkinson's disease]."[45] It thus does not appear that the onset of this disease—even with its disruptive features—forced people to grapple with ideas about disability so much as to come to terms with an unexpected turn in the aging process.[46]

A similar pattern of self-perception—of becoming old rather than disabled—is evident in those suffering from Alzheimer's disease, a malady whose "primary cause has continued to elude scientists since the problem was first brought to medical attention in 1907."[47] The disease itself involves the "progressive degeneration and loss of vast numbers of nerve cells in those portions of the brain's cortex that are associated with the so called higher functions, such as memory, learning, and judgment."[48] While Alzheimer's can affect the younger old, it is "predominantly a problem of the oldest old" and is "strongly associated with increasing age among those 65 years of age and older."[49]

Over time—usually a long, arduous period for those suffering from the disease and for their caregivers—Alzheimer's robs people of their dignity and ultimately leads to death. In *The Caregiver: A Life with Alzheimer's* (1999), E. S. Goldman (writing under the pseudonym Aaron Alterra) recounts his experiences watching as his wife slowly (over a span of years) loses her cognitive abilities, her control over her own life, and finally her bodily functions. We see how difficult diagnosis of the disease is and how little support physicians provide in this process. Indeed, when Goldman first learns about the diagnosis, he realizes that Alzheimer's is a "caregiver's disease."[50]

Pointing out that medicine has a limited array of tools to combat this disease is not an indictment of medicine or a call for a curative approach. But it does shed light on the need to see the subject of illness and disability in old age through a social lens. In his foreword to *The Caregiver*, Arthur Kleinman—himself a caregiver as well as a noted psychiatrist and anthropologist—observes: "The critical knowledge of the illness experience does not reside in the medical profession. Expert knowledge of Alzheimer's belongs to spouses, children, friends, and the professional companions, aides, and nurses who do the actual caregiving . . . and just being there for people whose brain is no longer capable of letting them be independent."[51]

All too often, however, the primary caregiver for an older person with a degenerative disease is left standing alone. This caregiver—usually an elderly spouse or adult child—is getting only limited support from other family members who might live in other cities or be too busy or unwilling to help. The aloneness of these caregivers stems not only from physically doing the hard work by themselves, but from the stigma that is associated with disease and illness, especially in old age. This stigma seeps into the fearful way that other elderly people often view older persons living with impairments. It is for this reason that disease-specific support groups have formed, for those living with illnesses and for their caregivers.[52]

Diseases of a degenerative nature and those involving a loss of cognitive abilities affect the elderly in ways that threaten their independence. These diseases also raise the risk that an older person will face a difficult dying process—and one over which that individual has little control. This prospect creates anxiety for these older people and their families. At the same time, these types of diseases highlight the limits of medical solutions that hold out the ideal of a cure and have traditionally been society's first line of defense.

We do not want anyone to become sick or disabled in old age—yet when these conditions inevitably arise, we as a society do little to make life easier for elders living with disease or disability or for those caring for their loved ones.[53] Easing this burden is not simply a matter of arranging for needed medical and social services to support older persons and their family caregivers. It also goes beyond removing barriers and asserting rights—the issue at the center of disability discourse. Rather, providing meaningful help requires that we delve more deeply into an understanding of impairment among the very old, including its diverse cultural meanings and the ways it affects relationships between the older person and family members, especially those who are caregivers. In fact, impairment may serve as a bridge to guide us through the complicated terrain of aging and disability.[54]

By focusing on impairment and the social setting of old age, we can deepen our understanding of the meaning of old age and disability. Shifting views of old age—from a time of illness and decline (the perspective of gerontologists through the 1970s) to a time of health and vitality (the current perspective)—have reframed how we understand disability in late life. This shift is expressed in the language of successful aging. Scholars who focus on cognitive functioning and diseases such as dementia have embraced the view that vitality in the elderly is normative while its absence is non-normative.[55] This evolving professional view of what it means to be old has implications for how the elderly themselves perceive disease and disability.

A Social Response to Late-Life Disability

The standard approach to old age has been to view disability as a health correlate of advanced aging. The social category of youth is not associated with disability while the social category of very old age is statistically associated with impairment, disability, and death. Moreover, research on the aging of the very old has traditionally emphasized these connections. More recently, however, gerontologists have begun to emphasize wellness in old age. As Leonard Poon and others have shown, wellness is a multifaceted concept. It calls for psychological, physical, social, spiritual, and personality resources and also entails active agency by the older person. Yet both approaches— the older paradigm of illness and the newer paradigm of wellness—risk obscuring the social and cultural aspects of disability in old age.[56]

Aging and disability encompass universal experiences based on shared features and distinctive experiences based on human variations. Attention to social contexts and concrete experiences can help us appreciate this tension between the shared and the diverse, the general and the particular. In his groundbreaking work on the experiences of aged nursing home residents, Jaber F. Gubrium addresses this social science dilemma of reconciling the general and the particular. Gubrium alerts us to the difference in meaning between "the social" and what he terms "social worlds." His point is that how we think and how we conceptualize what constitutes social analysis can lead to differing questions and ways of understanding the lives of older persons.[57]

In gerontology, Gubrium states, "the leading set of concepts" comprise "an analytic vocabulary whose central concern is 'society' [and whose] associated concepts include social structure, status, and role." These concepts "are used by gerontologists to explain the actions of older people." Gubrium argues that while this approach has value in showing the effects of social influences, it also leads to a level of abstraction that can obscure the "everyday experiences" of older persons.[58] We need to understand these everyday experiences if we are to understand the diverse range of older people's abilities and disabilities, especially in the very old.

Gubrium advises supplementing this social approach with one that looks at the practical "worlds" of the aged as they actually live in specific and varied settings. Drawing on a social interactionist tradition, his concept of "social worlds" as plural "highlights the perspective that the social is organized fragments, not spun out of whole cloth."[59] To clarify his usage, Gubrium explains:

> Social worlds turn us to the possibility that one world, such as one's immediate family, might structure our status as older persons in a different way from how another world, such as a group of longtime friends, structures it. . . . The variegation offered by the concept is clear, as the social becomes a complex landscape of experiential occasions and diverse encounters with others.[60]

From the social world point of view, not only is the contextual landscape relevant—the places in which the person is connected—but so too is the temporal reference point of age itself.

Applying this social world orientation to disabled older people reveals that the story of aging with disability must be attuned to the constructs of person, place, and age. This story will vary, as we have explored in the preceding chapters, but if current research is confirmed the story reveals a tale of two quite different realities. In one, the elderly who are poorer, sicker, older, and with fewer personal and social resources can be endangered by continuing to live at home. In the other, the elderly who can negotiate their environment more effectively, even with health and functional limitations, are capable of living lives of meaning without losing their independence.

The first social world is the subject of a 2015 *New York Times* article that highlights a study published in *JAMA Internal Medicine*. Researchers found that close to 6 percent of Americans over the age of sixty-five (more than 2 million people) are effectively homebound, rarely or never leaving their homes. Added to this number are 6 million more who are classified as "semi-homebound"—individuals who encounter difficulty leaving their homes or who can leave only with assistance.[61]

Katherine Ornstein, lead author of the *JAMA Internal Medicine* paper, notes that these homebound individuals tend to be older, nonwhite, less educated, lower income, and in poorer health than other aging adults—with a large percentage of the completely homebound suffering from dementia (80 percent) or depression (60 percent). In her *New York Times* article, Paula Span writes that "while physical and mental health play key roles, the difference between those stuck at home and those able to participate in life beyond their front doors also depends on their environments and on assistance." Ornstein and her colleagues as well as other public health advocates worry that inhospitable home environments, outdoor physical obstacles such as steps, and poor access to services—to put it simply, place—are imperiling the lives of the very old. Span suggests that perhaps the ideal of "aging in place" has "inadvertently helped imprison" older adults. She reports that

Ornstein's team of researchers discovered that "people in assisted living facilities actually got outside more often than those in their own homes" because "aides, outings, vans, and single-floor designs probably promoted access to a broader world."[62]

Yet aging in place is the option that most seniors prefer. Research shows that the desire to live at home is a powerful one even for older persons with significant disabilities—and they understandably fear the path away from home toward assisted living and, ultimately, a nursing home. Most older persons strongly resist this trajectory, equating it with the surrender of their independence, followed soon after by death. The issues here are more than a tug-of-war between older persons who want to stay at home and health experts who worry that "remaining at home . . . gives older people a sense of control that may prove illusory."[63]

The way that the very old achieve this independence, even in the face of varying forms of disability, is the subject that Meika Loe outlines in her fascinating study *Aging Our Way* (2011). She concludes that today more people "are living longer and healthier, while avoiding or delaying severe disability."[64] From a disability perspective, it is worthwhile considering Loe's findings, based on her three-year investigation of thirty individuals aged 85 to 102 who mostly lived in their own homes near Albany in upstate New York. She says of them: "These elders are role models; they are typical of the aging populace as well as the 'aging in place' movement. They represent the vast majority of Americans who, for reasons of familiarity, ease, networks, and economic necessity, hope to—and are—aging in their own homes and communities."[65]

Awareness of Disability in the Very Old

In any discussion of old age and disability, not only is the contextual landscape relevant—the places where older persons live and the people with whom they are connected—but so too is the temporal reference point of age itself. Indeed, while age may be "diminishing in importance as a regulator of behavior,"[66] and few would wish to see age as a limiting category, we cannot ignore the fact that age influences self-presentation and social perception—especially when a person reaches very old age.

Family members, physicians, caregivers, and others make assumptions about disabled older persons and their capacity to act and to function at home and within their communities. Older persons also realize that age is a signifier of the possibilities and limits of life. This awareness colors how they understand and relate to their own illnesses and disabilities. At this point in their lives, the very old are no longer thinking about being adventurous travelers or about their status at work or in social circles.

In *Old Soul, Young Spirit* (2015), Adolfo Quezada writes, "Old age is not quitting time; but neither is it a time of acceleration. Rather, it is a time to gather ourselves as we prepare for the end of our life. It is a time to complete unfinished business, reconcile estrangements where appropriate, and enter into a deeper communion with God."[67] While not every older person embraces conventional religion, growing old leads often to a general spiritual awareness. "Growing old is more than just aging," explains Quezada. "Aging is what happens to our mind and body with the passing of time; *growing* old is what happens to us spiritually as we stay attentive to our moments and remain wide awake through this chapter of life."[68]

Earlier gerontological literature took notice of this inward focus and labeled this attitude "disengagement."[69] Most contemporary scholarship in gerontology has rejected the idea of disengagement and its suggestion of a roleless social status for the aged. But there may be a positive aspect to disengaging from roles, removing social masks that were previously worn, and embracing an authentic self. The last years of life are an opportunity, perhaps our last, to become who we truly are. By disengaging from assigned social roles and engaging with people and projects that are central to our being, we may lessen the social effects of disability and illness.[70]

Any attempt to address disability in very late life should thus aim to relate impairments and environmental contexts to an older person's specific self-understanding. Sociologist Herbert Blumer describes this self-understanding as the interpretive aspects of self-presentation: how a person within a social context "selects, checks, suspends, regroups, and transforms the meanings in light of the situation in which he is placed and the direction of his action."[71]

For Blumer and scholars like Erving Goffman and Irving Zola, who elaborated on his method, meaning is forged within a social context. It is derived through interactions between a person and others—social interactions that define how people see themselves and how others see them. In this context, disability involves self-understanding and social understanding and cannot be defined only in functional terms of what a person can and cannot do. To develop this idea of social meaning in the context of very old persons with disabilities, it may be useful to divide the concept of disability into two dimensions: (1) vulnerability (the fear and perception of looming disability); and (2) impairment (physical or intellectual) in relationship to social and physical environments.[72]

Disability and Vulnerability

The concept of vulnerability has not been fully developed in either the field of aging or the field of disability studies. Perhaps the closest analogue in aging is the paradigm of stress and coping.[73] For many older persons, vulnerability is linked to impending impairments, illness, and manifestations of disability (e.g., limits on functioning as measured by ADL and IADL). Gerontologist and octogenarian Elias Cohen has determined based on actuarial tables that he can expect to live for 2,000 more days, and this realization has led him to observe that "the sense of risk and vulnerability loom larger and larger in the long and short range decision-making of everyday life."[74]

We can think of vulnerability as an older person's subjective understanding of threats to his or her well-being. Such awareness is not brought on by age alone, but reflects a prior set of attitudes toward illness, disability, and larger dangers to oneself. Here, Cohen guides us from his own perspective: "As I see it, each of the ordinary decisions relative to planning and maintaining my life in these last 2000 days will increasingly be made in a risk-benefit context, with 'risks' having an increasingly heavy thumb on the scale."[75] In Cohen's calculation, how much an older person chooses to do is subject not only to that person's actual impairment and functional disability, but also to his or her personal sense of vulnerability.

In other words, vulnerability is the shadow cast by both old age and disability, whether that disability is already present or whether the person is simply apprehensive that it may emerge in the near future. Older individuals who have recovered from major surgery, who have cancer that is in remission, or who have any number of chronic diseases may be especially prone to feelings of vulnerability.[76] These feelings can be minor, or they can represent a major impediment to social and physical functioning. The practical effect of this condition occurs when older persons seek regular medical consultations not only to address existing conditions, but also so that doctors or other health professionals can assure them of their physical well-being. Vulnerability, independent from disability, thus becomes a stressor for the elderly.[77]

Vulnerability is also implicated in anxiety and higher rates of depression for very old persons.[78] Another way to think of vulnerability is that it is the fear that one's health and independence are under constant threat—and this fear induces a high level of self-monitoring behavior as the individual seeks signs indicating that the threat is not present or looks for information about how it might be neutralized. Avoiding foods, physical and social environments, and people who are perceived as elevating the risk of illness and disability becomes a major focus of energy and thought.

The concept of vulnerability and the associated understanding of risks are not, however, universal concerns for the very old. While most older people recognize their own limitations and the dangers that certain activities pose for them, many elderly individuals may nevertheless choose to downplay the risks and continue in their everyday activities as if these threats were not present. In a way, this attitude of denial confirms their status as nondisabled—but it also serves a functional purpose. By limiting excessive preoccupation with vulnerability and impending death, these older people protect themselves against inaction and withdrawal from the world. This active renunciation of vulnerability and the perception of risk may explain why many of these very old individuals, even when physically limited by disability, remain in their family homes and do not arrange to modify the physical layout or bring in help to manage their environment.[79]

Drawing on the stress and coping model, we can see that such forms of distancing oneself from the threat of one's own vulnerabilities become a coping strategy. The older person copes with this threat by trying to defend an older identity against the intrusions of this newer more diminished one. For the elderly living with disability, such a course of action (or inaction) may seem reasonable in their own minds when counterbalanced against their fear of losing their home and independence if their children or health care providers force them to go to a safer institutional type of environment.[80]

An older person's attempt to manage the inner self-perception of vulnerability may coincide with an ongoing effort to manage the outward appearance of illness or disability—a process that allows the person to maintain social status. It is a common practice for the elderly to downplay or neglect to mention all of their problems in their interactions with physicians. Likewise, in social interactions with their peers, older persons may go to great lengths to preserve a healthy image—that they are still able to drive, swim, or play tennis—as a way of symbolically rejecting the attribution of "in decline" as applied to them.[81]

What, then, is vulnerability among the aged? Perhaps it is the feeling of standing on a precipice, knowing that at some point you will fall and become disabled to a greater or lesser degree—and yet feeling hopeful that you can delay or perhaps even avoid the descent.

Disability and Impairment

The ways in which vulnerability becomes enmeshed with impairment and functionality to produce a type of disability that is unique to old age is a subject that requires substantial attention from scholars in both aging and disability studies. Up to now, researchers have not studied exactly how and when vulnerability limits functional activities. We believe that disablement represents a process that is triggered by degree of impairment, environmental context, and subjective assessments. An older person who has lost a leg to diabetes, who has suffered a stroke, or who is experiencing dementia or some form of degenerative disease such as Parkinson's must reorient his or her life around the reality of this impairment. These types of severe impairments also prompt a reassessment of self and identity. Yet ironically, the reality of living with such an impairment often diminishes the older person's previous fears about the threat of disability. In fact, research has found that older persons with disabilities do not rate their quality of life as lower than do their nondisabled peers.[82]

Research and personal accounts related to physical disability in late life note the great importance that older people place on health and well-being—and the threat that disability poses to them. "It is exposure to increased risk and increased vulnerability to our physical well-being," Cohen relates, that "is most prominent in our perception of change in our lives."[83] The very old understand that diminished health and well-being lead to dependency. In this older population, the connection between disability and poor health is much greater than in a younger population where a person may be disabled but in overall good health.[84]

The shift away from being able to manage one's life without help to requiring assistance is central to how the older person understands disability. In fact, this is what is measured in typical ADL and IADL inventories that assess functional disability. The inability to care for oneself in areas such as dressing, toileting, bathing, and getting around the house is what is meant by disability, rather than the specific impairment or disease condition that contributes to such limitations. When an older person needs help with these daily routines, the issue raised is almost always whether this individual can live alone or whether this person requires care in an institutional setting. This framework of thinking about disability in old age grows out of policy systems that have not made independent living a priority for seniors.

For the very old, disability is a measure of diminished health and personal capability that does not fully take into account environmental and social contexts. The concept of functional disability places a great deal of weight on physiological resources and less weight on compensatory systems. Most importantly, it does not recognize a role for personal assistance within the home environment as a primary means to minimize disability. In a practical sense, disability for the very old comes down to those who can find and afford help and social support that enables them to live at home versus those who cannot and therefore find that they require care in a nursing home.

The implications of functional disability rather than disability based on a specific type of impairment is thus central to our assessment and understanding of disability in old age. Younger people's response to disability has typically centered on fighting for accommodations that reshape the environment of public facilities, workplaces, and home. Yet these systematic efforts to gain inclusion have generally not addressed situations of overarching health decline, as most younger people with disabilities have stable health.

Disability in very late life presents the closest analogue to Zola's ideal of universalizing disability—the idea that disability is not a state that is distinct from normal life.[85] Disability during this final stage of life also reveals the multiple meanings and varied interpretations that scholars and those who experience disability ascribe to it. In this chapter, we have explored the ways in which disability is configured in very late life. Unlike for younger and middle-aged persons, disability for the elderly has a broad medical and illness component. Various categories of impairments create different levels of disability, especially as they intersect with environments and social resources. Moreover, the experience of old age itself can become its own form of disability as a person struggles with feelings of vulnerability and as social and personal resources become exhausted. Even so, we should be mindful of Florida Scott-Maxwell's admonition in *The Measure of My Days* (1968): "We who are old know that age is more than a disability. It is an intense and varied experience, almost beyond our capacity at times, but something to be carried high."[86]

Notes

1. The way that illness interacts with selfhood varies with a person's age. In old age there is a subjective expectation that disability is part of a typical trajectory, a "part of life" and thus part of the older person's embodiment of self. This understanding serves to establish an identity as an aged person rather than a person living with disability. See Kathy Charmaz, *Good Days, Bad Days* (Rutgers University Press, 1993), 76–77; Samantha Solimeo, *With Shaking Hands* (Rutgers University Press, 2009), 15–16.

2. Sherwin B. Nuland, *How We Die: Reflections of Life's Final Chapter* (Vintage, 1995), 50.

3. J. F. Fries, "Aging, Natural Death, and the Compression of Morbidity," 245–250.

4. Kenneth G. Manton and Beth J. Soldo, "Disability and Mortality Among the Oldest Old: Implications for Current and Future Health and Long-Term Care Service Needs," in *The Oldest Old,* ed. by Richard M. Suzman, David P. Willis, and Kenneth G. Manton (Oxford University Press, 1992). The authors observe that "the current public policy concern with the increase in the number of the oldest old is motivated, in part, by the expected impact of this trend on levels of federal expenditures, particularly for chronic health services." Ibid.

5. Paul Arthur Schilpp, "At 92," in *Courage to Grow Old,* ed. Phillip L. Berman (Ballantine, 1989), 313.

6. Ibid.

7. Leonard W. Poon, Yuri Jang, Sandra G. Reynolds, and Erick McCarthy, "Profiles of the Oldest-Old," in *Cambridge Handbook of Age and Ageing,* ed. Vern L. Bengtson, Peter B. Coleman, and Thomas B. L. Kirkwood (Cambridge University Press, 2006), 348.

8. Ronald J. Berger, *Introducing Disability Studies* (Lynne Rienner, 2013), 137. Berger notes that despite being generally healthy, the disabled have "health care needs that are typically greater than those of the non-disabled population." Ibid.

9. Sally Bould, Beverly Sanborn, and Laura Reif, *Eighty-five Plus: The Oldest Old* (Wadsworth, 1989), 52.

10. Ibid.

11. Lisa F. Berkman, "The Changing and Heterogeneous Nature of Aging and Longevity: A Social and Biomedical Perspective," in *Annual Review of Gerontology and Geriatrics,* ed. M. Powell Lawton and George L. Maddox (Springer, 1988), 37–68.

12. Acute and chronic diseases often "go untreated much longer in the very old because they do not report their symptoms to health providers. Elderly persons living in the community may be concealing as many as half their symptoms." Ibid., 57.

13. The very old often reside in nursing homes not only because of medical needs, but also for lack of a social support system in combination with multiple chronic ailments. These institutionalized individuals are also more likely than the old-old living in the community to have cognitive impairments and to require help with toileting. Ibid., 54.

14. Ibid., 59–66, 72.

15. Idid., 68–74.

16. Richard H. Fortinsky and Murna Downs, "Optimizing Person-Centered Transitions in the Dementia Journey: A Comparison of National Dementia Strategies," *Health Affairs* 33, no. 4 (2014): 566–573; Richard H. Fortinsky, "Coordinated, Comprehensive Community Care and the Older Americans Act," *Generations* 15, no. 3 (1991): 39–42.

17. Deborah Stone, *The Samaritan's Dilemma: Should Government Help Your Neighbor?* (Nation, 2008).

18. Ira Wallach, "Strolling Toward the Finish Line," in *The Courage to Grow Old,* ed. Phillip L. Berman (Ballantine Books, 1989), 157.

19. Rosemary DeCamp, "From the Dragonfly to the Old Lady," in *The Courage to Grow Old,* ed. Phillip L. Berman (Ballantine Books, 1989), 178.

20. John Tebbel, "Life on a Shrinking Island," in *The Courage to Grow Old,* ed. Phillip L. Berman (Ballantine Books, 1989), 163.

21. William I. Nichols, "Letter to a Friend," in *The Courage to Grow Old,* ed. Phillip L. Berman (Ballantine Books, 1989), 231–232.

22. Richard A. Kalish, "Death and Dying in a Social Context," in *Handbook of Aging and the Social Sciences,* ed. Robert H. Binstock and Ethel Shanas (Van Nostrand Reinhold, 1976), 483–486.

23. Ibid., 486–487.

24. Ibid., 483, 485.

25. Kalish argued that how the elderly understand death (whether as a form of punishment or transcendence) and approach it (e.g., fear and denial) is different from how younger persons do. "The older person who is dying, who has suffered a loss, or who is concerned with finitude may not always respond in the same fashion as a comparable younger person." Ibid., 485–486, 504.

26. Herman Feifel, *The Meaning of Death* (McGraw-Hill, 1965); Ernest Becker, *The Denial of Death* (Free Press, 1997); Robert J. Kastenbaum, *Death, Society and Human Experience* (Routledge, 2011).

27. Richard A. Kalish, *Death, Dying, Transcending: Views from Many Cultures* (Baywood 1980); Richard A. Kalish, *Death, Grief, and Caring Relationships* (Brooks/Cole, 1981).

28. Deborah T. Gold, "Late-Life Death and Dying in 21st-Century America," in *Handbook of Aging and the Social Sciences,* ed. Robert H. Binstock, Linda K. George, Stephen J. Cutler, Jon Hendricks, and James H. Schulz (Academic, 2011), 245. Gold's work represents an important synthesis of the current approach by gerontologists and reflects the shift to a medical and public health point of view.

29. W. Andrew Achenbaum, *Old Age in the New Land: The American Experience Since 1790* (Johns Hopkins University Press, 1978), 30.

30. Ibid., 9–25. The idea that life experience formed the basis for common sense was a distinctive feature of this period. Common sense was the ultimate guide to both behavior and an idealized moral sense. The apprehension of death and experience with debility and loss helped shape communal attitudes that made both death and disability acceptable rather than deviant.

31. Lester J. Cappon, *The Adams-Jefferson Letters* (University of North Carolina Press, 1988), 483–484.

32. Ibid., 484. Jefferson is referring to *La Correspondance littéraire, philosophique et critique* (1813–1814), by Friedrich Melchior, Baron von Grimm.

33. Ibid., 579.

34. Ibid., 613.

35. Ibid., 552–553.

36. Sheldon S. Tobin, *Preservation of the Self in the Oldest Years: With Implications for Practice* (Springer, 1999), xi, 1–2.

37. Ibid., 16, 119–125, 131. Tobin's psychological view of death as a time of "withdrawal" is similar to Kalish's view of death as "disengagement." Death marks the endpoint of a journey across the life cycle.

38. In *How We Die*, Nuland provides a clinical view of the many ways in which people die, and he shows that few people achieve a good death. His chapter "Three Score and Ten" is a superb autoethnographic encounter between Nuland and his grandmother who helped raise him after his mother died when he was eleven years old. Although his grandmother's death was caused by a stroke, his larger point is that she died of old age. He observes that "there is plenty of evidence that life does have its natural, inherent limits." Nuland, *How We Die*, 43–63, 70.

39. Robert F. Murphy, *The Body Silent: The Different World of the Disabled* (Norton, 2001).

40. Ibid., 229.

41. Solimeo, *With Shaking Hands*, 61. The unique contribution of Solimeo's book is to examine how the experience of living with Parkinson's disease influences a person's perceptions of aging.

42. The challenges of diagnosing, treating, and caring for these individuals exist even though Alzheimer's primarily affects cognition and Parkinson's primarily affects physical functioning. Additionally, with both illnesses, individuals can experience a feeling of failure—of having not succeeded in aging successfully. See Kara Bottiggi Dassel, "Aging and Parkinson's Disease: Personal Identification, Embodiment, and Experience with a Degenerative Disease," *The Gerontologist* 49, no. 5 (2009): 720–723.

43. As the disease progresses, the person may experience incontinence, dysphagia, dementia, and depression. Because the symptoms can vary, can present in mild form, and can be mistaken for the signs of normal aging, diagnosis is difficult. Solimeo, *With Shaking Hands*, 18–20.

44. Ibid., 61.

45. Ibid., 82. Solimeo's life course model did reveal that "younger PD sufferers . . . emphasized how PD symptoms sped up the process of social and somatic aging." In contrast, "sufferers in their seventies focused on the interplay of these conditions with normal aging" while those "in their eighties and older emphasized how older age and normal aging was a greater condition on their lives than were individual PD symptoms." Ibid., 83.

46. Solimeo had previously observed that Parkinson's disease "is experienced as a condition that both reflects and reproduces the belief that the story of growing older is one of growing sicker." Ibid., 44.

47. Nuland, *How We Die*, 91.

48. Ibid.

49. Denis A. Evans, Paul A. Scherr, Nancy R. Cook, Marilyn S. Albert, H. H. Funkenstein, Laurel A. Beckett, Liesi E. Hebert, et al., "The Impact of Alzheimer's Disease in the United States Population," in *The Oldest Old*, ed. Richard Suzman, David P. Willis, and Kenneth G. Manton (Oxford University Press, 1992), 283–284. These authors note that much remains unknown about Alzheimer's, including whether it is a "heterogeneous category" and if in its early presentation it forms a "continuum with normal cognitive functioning." The disease "will place substantially increased demands on the delivery of long-term care services to older persons in the United States and other developed countries experiencing similar demographic changes." Ibid., 295.

50. Aaron Alterra, *The Caregiver: A Life with Alzheimer's*, 2nd ed. (Cornell University Press/ILR Press, 2007), 50. Alterra describes Alzheimer's as "a warren of unexpected nuances that those who have been caregivers try to prepare others for." Ibid., 26.

51. Ibid., xi. Critical resources that are needed to address Alzheimer's include family members who are willing to help as caregivers, offer relief to the primary caregivers, or provide financial assistance to hire aides and professional helpers (as Medicare does not provide coverage for these services). This lack of resources represents a gaping hole in Alzheimer's policy. Ibid., 166–181.

52. Jesse F. Ballenger notes the "peculiar dread" surrounding dementia and the larger "stigma" it has historically pinned on the entire aging process. Jesse F. Ballenger, *Self, Senility, and Alzheimer's Disease in Modern America: A History* (Johns Hopkins University Press, 2006), 1, 10. That the elderly can adopt negative self-views based on social standards follows from the analysis in Sander L. Gilman, *Disease and Representation: Images of Illness from Madness to Aids* (Cornell University Press, 1988).

53. Ballenger provides a historical rationale for emphasizing a caregiving agenda as a means of normalizing the aging process for all older persons, both those who are living with dementia-based diseases and disability and those who are not. Ballenger, *Self, Senility, and Alzheimer's Disease in Modern America*.

54. Mark Sherry, "A Sociology of Impairment," *Disability and Society* 31, no. 6 (2016): 729–744.

55. Jennifer A. Margrett, Benjamin T. Mast, Maria C. Isales, Leonard, W. Poon, and Jiska Cohen-Mansfield, "Cognitive Functioning and Vitality Among the Oldest Old: Implications for Well-Being," in *Understanding Well-Being in the Oldest Old,* ed. Leonard W. Poon and Jiska Cohen-Mansfield (Cambridge University Press, 2011), 186–212. The authors reject the "stereotypes" and "myths" that "cognitive decline in the very old is inevitable and there is nothing we can do about it." Ibid., 186. They urge the adoption of "the concept of cognitive vitality" as a means to evaluate the resources that are available to the very old to meet the needs of "day-to-day living," linking their concept to John Rowe and Robert Kahn's 1987 model of "successful aging." Ibid., 188. Interestingly, Margrett et al. argue that cognitive vitality can exist with cognitive deficits and even dementia. Yet their framework envisions "normative" and "non-normative" changes in cognition. The former comprise typical age-related changes while the latter include "dementia-related" changes. Ibid., 191–194. See also John W. Rowe and Robert L. Kahn, "Human Aging: Usual and Successful," *Science* 237, no. 4811 (1987): 143–149.

56. For the older view, see Evan C. Hadley, "Causes of Death Among the Very Old," in *Oldest Old*, ed. Suzman, Willis, and Manton, 183–195; Manton and Soldo, "Disability and Mortality Among the Oldest Old," 199–245. For the newer focus, see Jiska Cohen-Mansfield, "The Shifting Baseline Theory of Well-Being: Lessons from

Across the Aging Spectrum," in *Understanding Well-Being in the Oldest Old,* ed. Poon and Cohen-Mansfield, 51; Lee Hyer and Catherine A. Yeager, "Posttraumatic Stress Disorder and Its Treatment at Late Life," in *Understanding Well-Being in the Oldest Old,* ed. Poon and Cohen-Mansfield, 100; Margrett et al. "Cognitive Functioning and Vitality Among the Oldest Old," 198–201; Howard Litwin, "Social Relationships and Well-Being in Very Late Life," in *Understanding Well-Being in the Oldest Old,* ed. Poon and Cohen-Mansfield, 213–215; Alex J. Bishop, "Spirituality and Religiosity Connections to Mental and Physical Health Among the Oldest Old," in *Understanding Well-Being in the Oldest Old,* ed. Poon and Cohen-Mansfield, 227–228.

57. Jaber F. Gubrium, "The Social Worlds of Old Age," in *Cambridge Handbook of Age and Ageing,* ed. Malcolm Johnson, Vern L. Bengtson, Peter G. Coleman, and Thomas B. L. Kirkwood (Cambridge University Press, 2005), 310–315. Gubrium highlights how his own views were informed by other works: Anselm L. Strauss, *Mirrors and Masks: The Search for Identity* (Free Press, 1959); Barney G. Glaser and Anselm L. Strauss, *Awareness of Dying* (Aldine, 1965); and David R. Unruh, *Invisible Lives: Social Worlds of the Aged* (Sage, 1983).

58. Gubrium, "Social Worlds of Old Age," 310.

59. Erving Goffman, *Stigma: Notes on the Management of Spoiled Identity* (Simon and Schuster, 1963).

60. Gubrium, "Social Worlds of Old Age," 311.

61. Paula Span, "At Home, Many Seniors Are Imprisoned by Their Independence," *New York Times,* June 19, 2015; Katherine A. Ornstein, Bruce Leff, Kenneth E. Covinsky, Christine S. Ritchie, Alex D. Federman, Laken Roberts, Amy S. Kelley, Albert L. Siu, and Sarah L. Szanton, "Epidemiology of the Homebound Population in the United States," *JAMA Internal Medicine* 175, no. 7 (2015): 1180–1186. The reported number of homebound older Americans excludes the 1.4 million who live in nursing homes. The data is based on the 2011 National Health and Aging Trends Study.

62. Span, "At Home, Many Seniors Are Imprisoned by Their Independence."

63. Ibid.

64. Meika Loe, *Aging Our Way: Lessons for Living from 85 and Beyond* (Oxford University Press, 2011), 5.

65. Ibid., 6. While Loe is not concerned with the causes of the longevity of this group, she does note that recent research suggests that "very old people . . . are still with us because they have lived conscientiously," embracing a "spirit of prudence and persistence, coupled with meaningful social connections." The research Loe refers to is Howard S. Friedman and Leslie R. Martin, *The Longevity Project: Surprising Discoveries for Health and Long Life from the Landmark Eight-Decade Study* (Hudson Street Press, 2011).

66. B. L. Neugarten and G. O. Hagestad, "Age and the Life Course," in Robert H. Binstock and Ethel Shanas, *Handbook of Aging and the Social Sciences* (Van Nostrand Reinhold, 1976), 53.

67. Adolfo Quezada, *Old Soul, Young Spirit: Reflections of Growing Old* (Self-publish, 2015), 8.

68. Ibid., 5, emphasis in original.

69. Elaine Cumming and William Earl Henry, *Growing Old, the Process of Disengagement* (Basic Books, 1961).

70. Laura L. Carstensen articulates elements of this viewpoint in "Social and Emotional Patterns in Adulthood: Support for Socioemotional Selectivity Theory," *Psychology and Aging* 7, no. 3 (1992): 331–338.

71. Herbert Blumer, *Symbolic Interactionism: Perspective and Method* (Prentice Hall, 1969), 5.

72. The creation of self-identity differs for younger and older persons based on their interactions within a social context of family and peers. See Rosalyn Benjamin Darling, *Disability and Identity: Negotiating Self in a Changing Society* (Lynne Rienner, 2013).

73. Benjamin L. Hankin and John R. Z. Abela, *Development of Psychopathology: A Vulnerability-Stress Perspective* (Sage, 2005).

74. Elias Cohen, *The Last 2000 Days* (unpublished manuscript in possession of authors); see also Elias Cohen, "The Last 2000 Days," *The Gerontologist* 57, no. 1 (2017): 116–120.

75. Cohen, *The Last 2000 Days.*

76. Andrea Luciani, Gilda Ascione, Cecilia Bertuzzi, Desirè Marussi, Carla Codecà, Giuseppe Di Maria, Sarah Elisabeth Caldiera, et al., "Detecting Disabilities in Older Patients with Cancer: Comparison Between Comprehensive Geriatric Assessment and Vulnerable Elders Survey-13," *Journal of Clinical Oncology* 28, no. 12 (2010): 2046–2050.

77. Zev Harel and Phyllis Ehrlich, *The Vulnerable Aged: People, Services, and Policies* (Springer, 1990).

78. Poon et al., "Profiles of the Oldest-Old," 346–353.

79. George Agich, *Dependence and Autonomy in Old Age: An Ethical Framework for Long-Term Care* (Cambridge University Press, 2003).

80. Carsten Wrosch and Richard Schulz, "Health-Engagement Control Strategies and 2-Year Changes in Older Adults' Physical Health," *Psychological Science* 19, no. 6 (2008): 537–541. The growing rates of elder abuse, including patterns of family members seeking to take advantage of older persons who are vulnerable by taking control of their finances, gives such fears a foundation in fact and a legitimacy that we cannot simply ignore. Shlomo Breznitz, *The Denial of Stress* (International Universities Press, 1983).

81. Laura C. Hurd, "'We're Not Old!': Older Women's Negotiation of Aging and Oldness," *Journal of Aging Studies* 13, no. 4 (2000): 419–439.

82. Linda K. George, "Perceived Quality of Life," in *Handbook of Aging and the Social Sciences,* 6th ed., ed. Robert H. Binstock and Linda K. George (Academic Press, 2006), 321–333.

83. Cohen, *The Last 2000 Days.*

84. Kenneth G. Manton, "Past and Future Life Expectancy Increases at Later Ages: Their Implications for the Linkage of Chronic Morbidity, Disability, and Mortality," *Journal of Gerontology* 41, no. 5 (1986): 672–681.

85. Irving Kenneth Zola, *Missing Pieces: A Chronicle of Living with Disability* (Temple University Press, 1982).

86. Florida Scott-Maxwell, *The Measure of My Days* (Knopf, 1968), 5.

9

Toward Better Public Policies

How we define and understand the concept of disability with respect to younger versus older persons is reflected in distinct public policy patterns. In political discussions disability and aging are treated as separate issues, with different constituencies and advocacy organizations. Disability and aging have also found little common ground in our culture. Despite these cleavages, mutual concerns do exist. This chapter considers the potential for improved public policies for the disability and aging communities.

On one level, aging and disability are associated with each other because old age is accompanied by greater risk for diseases and frailty that may lead to varied forms of physical and cognitive impairments. But when such impairments set in, we tend to identify them with getting older, rather than with becoming disabled. On another level, there are key variations between how public policy addresses aging and how it addresses disability. This situation results not from a failure of policy, but from a blend of historical, sociological, and cultural factors that relate to the social and political construction of aging and disability.

Let us consider the hypothetical example of a sixty-five-year-old man who needs a knee replacement and who may have limited ability to navigate a work setting that requires walking and stair-climbing. When he consults with a physician, physical therapist, or other health professional, the explanation as to what is wrong is typically that these limitations are the result of old age. He may even be told that he should not expect to keep up with younger folks. Rarely does the older person—or his health care provider—view the issue from a social or environmental perspective.[1] The man likely assumes that his problem is a normative one (i.e., just what it means to "get old"), and one that he must manage or surmount through his own individual efforts or through surgery and physical therapy. In this sense, he does not see aging with disability as a political or societal issue.

This chapter was coauthored with Michael R. Slone, a Case Western graduate student.

Yet that is precisely how a younger woman with a physical impairment that limits her mobility would see the same situation. She may actively identify as a "Crip"—a term that connotes a certain pride in having to contend with a permanent mobility challenge—and would seek ways to have her employer or school make adjustments that would enable her to do her job or get to class, notwithstanding the impairment. Disability thus connotes to her—and society—something beyond the impairment itself. It suggests a social and political identity that is shaped by having a permanent physical or intellectual impairment.

In terms of self-identity—how people view themselves—the older and younger person with impairments may have the same physical limitations, but in fact they see themselves differently. Older individuals—and gerontologists—construe disability in a way that aims to mitigate disability.[2] This approach has led to a policy agenda disjunction between younger people who are disabled and older people who have impairments but generally eschew being identified as disabled. First and foremost, disabled younger people and their advocates seek inclusion in all social and economic settings. Older people make few such demands and have few advocates claiming these rights on their behalf.[3]

From a very early age, today's younger people with disabilities are socialized to believe that they have the right to receive an education in the least restrictive environment.[4] This environment includes, for example, help provided by a personal aide who can facilitate interactions with typical individuals and who can support the student in navigating a school setting that might be impossible to manage without assistance.[5] In contrast, when older persons were growing up, they were not socialized to view disability as acceptable or empowering. Quite the contrary: they were taught to see disability as a social stigma and usually continue to hold this belief. Many elderly people thus choose to opt out of being considered disabled. Such a view of themselves is threatening to their core identity as nondisabled.[6]

Challenges in Care-Getting for Older Adults with Disabilities

This divergence in outlook between younger and older individuals about the meaning of disability naturally leads to different types of public policies. It also explains why developing a "care-getting" model for seniors has proved to be so challenging. By learning how to initiate requests for assistance, older adults enhance their long-term ability to remain independent in their communities.[7] Younger individuals with disabilities have usually spent many years as care-getters, and they have much that they can share with the elderly about how to approach care-getting without loss of dignity.

The realm of personal meaning filters how we interpret disability in the context of younger versus older persons living with physical and cognitive impairments. In *Politics of Disablement* (1990), Michael Oliver captures these differences in his "social theory of disability," which he says "must be located within the experience of disabled people themselves and their attempts, not only to redefine disability but also to construct a political movement amongst themselves and to develop services commensurate with their own self-defined needs."[8]

This claim goes even further for Oliver as well as those who make the strongest case for the social basis of disability. In distinguishing between impairment and disability, Oliver distances "disability" from "biological pathology" and the individual, and he "locates the causes of disability squarely within society and social organization."[9] Oliver's social theory of disability rests on a clear distinction between impairment and disability, as outlined in 1976 by the Union of the Physically Impaired Against Segregation (UPIAS), an influential British disability activist group: "Impairment [means] lacking all or part of a limb, or having a defective limb, organism or mechanism of the body. Disability [is] the disadvantage or restriction of activity caused by a contemporary social organization which takes no or little account of people who have physical impairments and thus excludes them from the mainstream of social activities."[10]

Not all disability scholars accept such a stark separation between impairment and disability. Tom Shakespeare, for example, cautions against replacing biological determinism with a purely socially determined view of disability.[11] Nevertheless, Oliver makes a compelling point when he states: "The kind of society that one lives in will have a crucial effect on the way the experience of disability is structured."[12]

Public policies offer a window on how society frames disability for both younger and older persons. Such policies are tied to current public opinion and the accumulation of past policies that persist into the present. These past policies, in turn, reflect the political contexts that originally gave shape to them and continue to sustain them today. What we can clearly see through this window on society is that the politics of disability—and specifically, of the disability rights movement—has little in common with the politics of aging.

The Politics and Policies of Disability and Aging

Disability emerged as a "cause" through a long struggle by the disabled and their allies for civil and human rights and for inclusion in society. Discrimination, exclusion, and dependence are common threads in the lives of disabled persons. The public policy of using laws to combat discrimination, promote inclusion, and support independence represents a "cause" policy agenda. But there are other disability policy agendas as well. Certain public policies provide care to the disabled, while others promote cures through medical interventions. The celebration of disability—disability pride—is the most recent item on the disability policy agenda. Dana Lee Baker presents a taxonomy of these four different policy agendas toward persons living with disability—cause, care, cure, and celebration—and shows that while each approach has legitimacy, together they are often in tension or even competition with one another.[13]

According to Baker, different policy agendas may be more relevant to different categories of people living with disabilities. For example, the balance between seeking independence (cause) and needing assistance (care) varies based on the type of disability. Those with physical impairments may be on the cause end of the spectrum while those with intellectual impairments are more likely to find themselves on the care end. Baker points out that the ideal of finding a cure animates much research spending, even though for most disabled individuals receiving care represents the greater need. She also notes that the celebration agenda can minimize the challenges and suffering faced by many people living with disabilities.[14] Different bodies and minds, as Tom Shakespeare reminds us, present different needs and require different social policies.[15]

The question of human needs—what they are, and how society should respond to them—lies at the heart of the politics and policies of both disability and aging. How we understand these needs leads to "the development of specialized categorical programs designed to limit the numbers and types of beneficiaries."[16] These categories are used to include some people and exclude others from entitlements, rights, and services. Whether a policy objective is focused on cause, care, or cure depends on the category of the type of person the policy is intended to help. Social Security, Medicare, Medicaid, and a variety of disability-oriented legislation, programs, and government agencies—including the Individuals with Disabilities Act (IDEA), the Americans with Disabilities Act, Social Security Disability Insurance (SSDI), Vocational Rehabilitation and Employment (VR&E), and the Office of Workers' Compensation Programs (OWCP)—are structured around societal assumptions about group-based needs. A younger person's needs are likely to be defined in terms of education and rehabilitation while an older person's needs are typically defined in terms of income maintenance and medical care.[17]

The effects of categorization are twofold. First, varied service organizations and advocacy groups arise around specific categories, resulting in separate aging and disability networks with distinctive objectives based on cause (disability) and care/cure (aging). Second, the responses by aging advocates and disability groups have differed in ways that are consistent with the cause versus care/cure distinction. Elias S. Cohen notes that aging advocates have emphasized an "organizational/financing strategy" while disability advocates have pursued a "litigation/legislation strategy."[18]

Cohen points to the deinstitutionalization agenda that disability advocates pursued after the *Olmstead* decision in 1999, contrasting their agenda with the efforts by aging advocates to establish an independent organizational presence in the years after the passage of the Older Americans Act (OAA) in 1965. By using the ADA to challenge institutional service models, especially for those with developmental disabilities, the disability movement brought greater attention to the need for community-based programs.[19] In contrast, the "strategy of the aging movement," says Cohen, "has shied away from confrontation and challenge to fundamental policy."[20] Accordingly, aging advocates used the OAA to create a policy presence that is distinct from both the existing federal Social Security bureaucracy and state and local welfare agencies.

The Administration on Aging (AoA) was established to serve as the administrative arm of the OAA, and it embraced expansive programs that covered "*all* older Americans" and an identity that was free from association with the Social Security Administration and welfare.[21] Aging advocates pursued a similar goal of independence from the existing welfare-oriented bureaucracy at the state level.[22] The resulting State Units on Aging (SUAs) have been largely independent of other service programs, and like their federal counterpart in the AoA, they have not wielded much power within state government.[23]

We can see a divergence between the approaches that disability and aging advocates have used to pursue their policy goals—as well as the goals themselves. The disability community has focused on the issues of deinstitutionalization and inclusion, using a civil rights strategy. The aging community has pursued the goal of obtaining services for all seniors (discussed in greater detail below) and has emphasized organizational strategies. While disability focuses on a common identity among people with different impairments, aging has eschewed a common age-based identity out of concern that this approach would encourage ageism. Aging advocates apparently believe that their goal of broadly advancing the interests of all older persons precludes a simultaneous focus on aging as a general category of vulnerability and social need.[24]

Understanding this reluctance to frame a specific aging agenda requires a brief overview of the complex relationship between aging and US politics.

Aging and Politics

There is a recognized politics of disability that seeks inclusion for disabled people in various aspects of their private and public lives. There has not, however, been a recognized politics of aging—despite assumptions that seniors carry outsized political clout with lawmakers. The question of why older persons do not represent a major political force was raised and answered by political scientist Robert Binstock in the 1970s. Even though "contemporary trends" showed an increase in the number of older persons, Binstock (and others) found that "there is no 'aging vote' [because] the political attachments of the aged are diverse and notable for their stability."[25]

A person's previous life "experiences and attachments" persist into old age and present "a multitude of sources for group identification and perceptions of special interests" that are separate from old age.[26] Moreover, age is not a core political identity because many older persons do not consider themselves to be old. To be labeled "old" carries negative connotations, and even social prejudice, that older adults seek to avoid.[27] A heterogeneous older population with a desire to retain a non–old age identity weighs against a general political identity based on old age and a political agenda that focuses on the special needs of the elderly.

This diversity of "political attitudes and partisan attachments" among the elderly—and their lack of a specific age-based identity—does not mean that old age is without political significance or that the elderly lack political power.[28] A growing body of research highlights the complex nature of elder power and its impact on public policy. The first wave of research on the politics of aging focused on a broad interest group approach.[29] Elder political power, according to this view, is expressed primarily through mass-membership organizations such as AARP. These organizations provide older persons with "access to public officials," offer "public platforms" to voice concerns, and are perceived as powerful voting blocs by elected officials.[30]

More recently, however, the varied dimensions—real and perceived—of elder political power have received attention. Andrea Campbell's research shows that older voters have exercised their political power to protect Social Security benefits.[31] We can expect this use of power to expand with the aging of the baby boomer generation.[32] But it remains unclear whether such power will be used to advance other policy concerns such as promoting policies focused on care for disabled seniors. This agenda has not been a priority in the politics of aging or for policymakers.

Policy-Relevant Criteria for Disability

From a contemporary policy perspective, what we call "disability" is not the same as impairment or illness. Many people with varied impairments, illnesses, or both are not disabled. This distinction is especially relevant for seniors who experience mounting mobility difficulties, declines in sensory perception, and overall greater challenges in getting around—what has been described as "diminishment"—and yet who neither see themselves nor are considered for policy purposes as disabled.[33]

As a matter of policy, disability is a legal and administrative category that is used to assign public benefits to those who meet certain formal requirements. When we consider who is disabled and what policies are available to them, we are addressing what the political scientist Deborah Stone refers to as the "distributive dilemma." This is "the problem of how to help people in need without undermining the basic principle of distribution according to work."[34] In the context of aging, such policies have been designed largely as universal benefits available to everyone who attains a preset age: sixty for the Older Americans Act and sixty-five for Medicare benefits.

Eligibility for accommodations and benefits under the ADA and SSDI—the two centerpieces of US disability policy—is determined by meeting standards of physical or cognitive limitations in one or more domains of functioning. Broadly speaking, the ADA prevents discrimination based on a fluid definition of disability, and it requires accommodations based on a blend of the legal, biological, medical, and economic factors that make up disability.[35] SSDI provides payments to those deemed to have met a medical, legal, or administrative standard of disability. This standard is also based on functional criteria and allows these individuals to withdraw from the labor system under a structured compensation model.[36]

Policy systems for the elderly and the disabled have thus historically been separate; they are motivated by different values and supported by independent interests. This is true at the federal and state levels. In light of such divergences, the ability to connect the aging and disability systems is crucial if the needs of older disabled individuals are to be met. Yet Michelle Putnam, who acknowledges both the policy imperatives and challenges of "crossing network lines," believes that "a complex history of cultural ideology, social and economic forces, and policy interventions constructs two distinct realms of age and disability in the United States."[37]

Those concerned with the intersection between disability and aging policies should keep in mind the value convergence that defines how policymakers view the elderly and the disabled. Both are treated as groups deserving of social accommodation and economic benefits. Thus, few critics of welfare policy have sought to restrict benefits to either seniors or the disabled—in marked contrast to popular efforts to curb or even end welfare based solely on economic need.[38]

As important as this claim is on the public's sympathy, the resulting willingness to commit to the causes of the elderly and the disabled is, ironically, what has created the real division between these two groups. While age is easily encompassed at the categorical level (there is usually little doubt about when someone was born), disability is informed by gradations that are both large and small. Who should be counted as deaf or blind or mobility impaired? What constitutes an intellectual disability? Whose disabilities are severe enough that they disqualify them from the workforce? Surely, these and myriad other questions suggest that a universal standard of disability for purposes of making public policy is unattainable. Deborah Stone is right to emphasize that the policy concept of disability—how law and government define disability—"represents a politically fashioned compromise at any given time and place about the legitimacy of claims to social aid."[39]

The American policy framework that provides benefits and care to older people is built on the pillars of the New Deal and the Great Society.[40] It includes pensions through Social Security and medical coverage through Medicare for people age sixty-five and older who have participated in the labor force.[41] Both programs are popular with people of all ages despite concerns about their future funding, but neither is focused on the daily care needs of seniors living with disabilities.[42] In contrast, the Medicaid program provides medical services to seniors who meet an income eligibility test. Because this program is part of the welfare system, it is less popular than the other two entitlement programs. "Medicare was buoyed by popular approval and the acknowledged dignity of Social Security," writes historian Paul Starr, while "Medicaid was burdened by the stigma of public assistance."[43]

The stigma of Medicaid has hindered its policy effectiveness. However, demographic trends are such that the need for Medicaid-type care programs will increase with the growth of the eighty-five-and-older population. These old-old individuals experience chronic illnesses and disabling conditions that are not amenable to cure. Disability for members of this age group arises from multiple factors, including illness, physical environments that do not meet their needs, loss of social support, and a limited ability to effectively advocate for themselves and exercise agency. The key resources that these elders need are personal assistance and support, not medical treatment—yet these needs remain largely unmet for many seniors. For this reason, the issue of care will emerge as a major public policy challenge.[44]

Old-Age Policy as Cure

The Medicare program was instituted in 1965 as an amendment to the Social Security Act. Medicare covers individuals who are age sixty-five and older, and the program currently serves more than 40 million older Americans.[45] A key aspect of Medicare coverage is patient improvement.[46] For this reason, Medicare does not typically cover long-term care costs or generally cover nonskilled home health care services (home health aides)— the very services most needed by the sickest older people who are living with disabilities, including individuals with such disabling conditions as Parkinson's and Alzheimer's disease.[47]

In his account of caring for his wife (Stella) who suffered from Alzheimer's disease, Elliot Stanley Goldman (using the pen name Aaron Alterra) explains that he had assumed that "Medicare and its supplement would pick up the main cost." The initial costs—for testing to confirm that Stella's condition was in fact Alzheimer's—were covered by Medicare. However, "inasmuch as it was Alzheimer's, Medicare did not cover anything after the diagnosis—not a dime's worth, nothing. Any investment in time and postage to pin down that fact and its illogical ramifications was simply wasted." Stella's cascade of disability was only amplified by a Medicare policy that covered "medical costs that were the consequence of Alzheimer's—breaks from fall, pneumonia, bed sores—but none of the costs of Alzheimer's care that prevented such costly consequences."[48]

Old-Age Policy as Care

Medicaid offers the most substantial medical and home health care benefits for disabled older persons and pays for nearly 60 percent of all nursing home care.[49] To qualify, however, one must first meet income criteria that are close to the poverty level. Restrictions on Medicaid eligibility are set by each state, with both an income and an asset test.[50] Even for seniors who do qualify, the stigma of participating in a welfare program combined with bureaucratic admission barriers have resulted in the underutilization of Medicaid. Fewer than half of the elderly who qualify actually participate in the program. Such low rates of participation raise larger questions about why so many older people avoid seeking help.[51]

A majority of older persons will require assistance with care and home help needs as they get older. This population will have a broad spectrum of needs—and persons with disabilities, whose numbers are expected to reach 20 million by 2040—will have the greatest care needs. How policymakers prepare for this rising need represents a key social policy challenge. The solutions that they devise will be constructed in the context of a great demographic shift that inverts the population paradigm underlying aging policies (i.e., a large pool of younger working persons and a smaller pool of older nonworkers). This demographic tilt has implications beyond the funding of social and medical programs and includes the availability of service providers to care for the growing disabled elderly population.[52]

Demographic and social forces will likely continue to solidify Medicaid's primary role in caring for the disabled (and impoverished) elderly. An increase in life expectancy, coupled with employment mobility, have resulted in larger numbers of vulnerable seniors and fewer children to provide care and support for them. The high costs of long-term care for these elders have led to some important policy innovations, such as Medicaid's Home and

Community-Based Services (HCBS) waiver program that is intended to give elderly Medicaid-eligible recipients access to home care (if costs are below the going rates of long-term care facilities). Working within broad federal guidelines, states provide waivers to pay for support services that enable seniors to remain at home and in their communities in spite of chronic illnesses and disabilities. The HCBS waiver program is notable for the breadth of care that it provides. As Carol Cox notes, these services go well beyond Medicare and "include case management, homemaker, home health aide, personal care, adult day health services, rehabilitation, transportation and respite care." In addition to these services, "Medicaid waivers also permit states to offer personal services (PCS)" aimed at allowing the elderly to function within their home environments—specifically, to help with activities of daily living.[53] However, the waiver program is currently only a secondary component of Medicaid expenditure and lags well behind the 70 percent spent on nursing home care.[54]

The model of the waiver program shows how a supportive policy can significantly lessen disability for the most vulnerable elderly population. The expansion of this program is not currently a significant part of the aging policy agenda. The rising costs of Medicaid spending in a funding-restrictive political environment is one barrier.[55] The availability of family caregivers and the stigma associated with seeking public assistance have meant that family members are providing most of the services that disabled seniors receive. AARP has estimated the economic value of this care (as of 2013) at $470 billion, and it estimates that by 2040 family and friend caregivers will be assisting more than 11 million disabled seniors.[56]

Ideologically, the emphasis on voluntary family caregivers, when combined with a strong desire on the part of older persons to live independently in the community, suggests a long-term tension between what people want and what is possible. At some point, greater public resources will be needed to allow older persons with disability to remain in their community—especially in light of the *Olmstead* decision and the momentum toward placement in a least restrictive environment. Recent calls for older persons to embrace a rights-oriented agenda may lead to the use of legal measures to restrict the funding available to nursing homes. A shortage of family caregivers may also force the children of elderly disabled parents and the elderly themselves to advocate for public support for community-based care programs.

The Aging Network

Area Agencies on Aging (AAAs) and their associated aging network comprise the policy system that is most germane to assisting seniors with independence as they age and encounter impairments in later life. There are around 655 AAAs across the country. These entities are perhaps the least well-known aspect of our nation's old-age policy, and they are minor players when measured by the amount of federal funds spent on them compared with Social Security and Medicare. Yet they are the first line of defense when it comes to providing social support to seniors and their families—and to connecting both with community resources that address a wide range of elder needs.

AAAs and their associated community of service providers emerged out of the Older Americans Act, a grant-in-aid program that Congress enacted in 1965. The purpose of the law was to provide support for seniors so that they could remain independent in their communities. The original aim of the law was (overly) ambitious, as evidenced by its Declaration of Objectives.[57] Passage of the OAA, as well as its amendments in the 1970s, reflected the government's overall social interventionist approach at that time. This positive view of social intervention by government coalesced with the public's special sympathy for the needs of the elderly who "were seen as poor, frail, socially dependent, objects of discrimination and, above all, deserving."[58]

However, as with many new welfare programs designed in the 1960s, limited federal funds were made available to support the broad aspirations and scope of the OAA. Over the ensuing years, this imbalance between grand objectives and minuscule funding levels has grown, posing challenges to program implementation.[59] Moreover, with each new reauthorization of the act, additional goals have been added in response to public concerns and newly identified needs—but without the commensurate addition of federal resources.

This situation has led to varied criticisms of the act for being unrealistically ambitious and lacking in clear standards and proof of effectiveness. Critics also argue that the OAA is more likely to serve the interests of providers and researchers—the aging enterprise—rather than the aged themselves.[60] Despite these criticisms, the act and the service organizations it supports have endured and even grown during periods when commitment to scaling back government services ran high.[61]

The aging network functions as the best advocate within the current policy system for seniors and helps coordinate needed services, especially to underserved communities. The services of AAAs are available to all persons age sixty and older. At the national level the Administration on Aging, which was established under the OAA, provides a voice for senior interests. The OAA also created State Units on Aging in each state. Thus, there is a cakelike layering with representation and responsibility for the aged at the federal, state, and local levels.[62]

It is important to understand that AAAs are not frequently engaged in the actual delivery of services. They usually are simply a conduit for federal and state funds, which are distributed broadly to local service agencies. In this connection, Title III: Grants for State and Community Programs on Aging receives about 70 percent of the OAA budget of about $1.4 billion. It provides the federal funding for nutrition sites (42.0 percent); supportive services such as transportation and senior centers (19.0 percent); family caregiver support, including limited respite care for family caregivers (7.9 percent); and disease prevention and health promotion such as arthritis and diabetes management and classes in nutrition (1.0 percent).[63]

While it is true that the AAAs often fall short of their formal objectives, they nevertheless retain substantial potential to influence national, state, and local policymakers because of their unique knowledge of the needs of seniors.[64] They are also a first line of defense when it comes to addressing crises in the lives of individuals and their families—and have the most complete grasp of community service resources that can support seniors in living independent lives.[65] Finally, they are a key intermediary between seniors and both providers and policymakers, especially at the state and local level.

The development of service programs and priorities by AAAs has changed over time to reflect the perceived needs of seniors and the evolving priorities of aging policy. In the early 1970s, national concern focused on the unmet nutritional needs of seniors, and this attention led to a significant rise in funding for OAA activities under the Richard Nixon administration. The development of long-term care ombudsman programs in the late 1970s reflected a growing awareness of nursing home abuses. In the early 1980s, funding for AAAs began to significantly lag behind inflation. As a result, by the latter part of the decade, the majority of federal funds for the elderly were directed toward priority services for poor and vulnerable seniors.

In the 1990s, the issue of Alzheimer's disease gained national attention through the experience of former president Ronald Reagan's family, and in 2000 the AAAs added family caregiver support—a major concern to families caring for loved ones with dementia—to their mandate. During the next decade, issues of long-term care and civic engagement emerged as the twin bookends in framing public policy across the aging continuum. For the eligible oldest seniors, the goal was to offer community-based long-term care (using both the aging network and Medicaid funds) while for the newest seniors—those in the baby boom cohort—the objective was to tap into their potential for community service by enhancing civic engagement opportunities.[66]

The structure of these agencies, along with their emphasis on developing alternative funding sources and public-private partnerships, has meant that most resources are devoted to the neediest older adults. In this sense, the universal ideal of programming for all seniors age sixty and over has been refocused on individuals with the greatest needs. This shift does not mean that AAAs do not engage in providing innovative services for all seniors. Services geared toward promoting health and limiting disease are potentially a major way for AAAs to address disability from an aging perspective. In the next section, we review findings from a 2006–2008 study sponsored by the National Institute on Aging that coauthor Jeffrey Kahana conducted with Lawrence Force and Valerie Capalbo through the Center on Aging and Policy at Mount Saint Mary College.[67]

Service Innovation: Perspectives on Area Agencies on Aging

All 655 directors of AAAs were invited to participate in an online survey, which 181 of them completed. Given the limited research on the roles of AAAs in health promotion and disease prevention, and the association between disease and disability among the elderly, the data offer a preliminary vantage point for understanding how policymakers at the local level are responding to the issues of aging and health in later life within the restrictive budgetary confines they are allotted under Title III of the OAA.

Few directors singled out disability services as a key area of innovation in connection with their agency's health promotion and disease prevention programming. Usually, disability is seen within gerontology as a marker for morbidity and mortality. As Kenneth Land and Yang Yang note, "Measures of disability actually function quite well as indicators of illness in older populations and thus are good measures for morbidity."[68] Thus, it is useful to think of the health promotion and disease prevention policy model of the OAA as a proactive means of avoiding or limiting disability in later life. Once again, the connection between illness and disability comes to the fore in older populations in ways that are quite different from younger populations where disability is often independent of illness.

In response to the question "Does your AAA provide any innovative services for disease prevention and health promotion?" 111 agencies responded yes (63.89 percent) and 65 agencies responded no (36.11 percent) out of 180 total responses to this question. The survey further asked those who responded yes to describe the types of service that were provided. In keeping with the mandate and funding of the AAAs, much of what these agencies described relates to information sharing with seniors, including the widespread adoption of the Stanford University model of chronic disease self-management.[69]

Agencies reported disseminating information to homebound seniors on health and wellness through brochures, pamphlets, and flyers. They also reported that blood pressure screenings, walking programs, yoga, and tai chi are popular services provided by AAAs. Diabetes testing and self-management programs, along with fall prevention information and classes, have also been widely implemented. Some AAAs offer geriatric depression screening and counseling programs, and many provide nutrition counseling and advisers—in some cases, including visits to homebound seniors who score high on nutritional risk. Senior centers are usually the sites for activity programs such as lectures, group exercise, and Wii games. Notable areas of innovation include mental health and dental health services and support programs that specifically target Alzheimer's needs.[70]

AAAs also provide services to special needs populations, but the OAA's mandate to serve all seniors age sixty and older has meant that such services are usually available based on age; they are not specially targeted to those with special needs. In our survey, 54.44 percent ($n = 92$) of respondents reported that their agencies provided services for developmentally disabled individuals while 45.56 percent ($n = 77$) reported that they did not. A similar number, 52.94 percent ($n = 90$), answered that they served the mentally ill, and 47.06 percent ($n = 80$) reported that they did not. A much smaller number, 35.40 percent ($n = 57$), provided services to those with HIV/AIDS while 52.66 percent ($n = 89$) reported offering services to those with terminal illness.[71]

Most services to special needs populations fall into the domain of informational and referral services. When someone receives direct services, it is usually as a result of qualifying for a Medicaid waiver program that covers community-based services to those who meet income and health eligibility standards. The HCBS waiver program includes personal care, home-delivered meals, adult day care, homemaker services, medical equipment and supplies, assistance with chores, social worker and nutritional counseling, and other services designed to maintain seniors in their home setting. As with Medicaid, qualification for the program is based on age (sixty and older), maximum income level ($1,500 per month), and medical needs that meet the state's eligibility requirements for care in a nursing home. The allowable payments may not be greater than 60 percent of what the state would pay for a nursing home, and a physician must agree that the plan is appropriate for the needs and ability of the individual.

We should note that the Medicaid system is tiered to meet different needs across the age spectrum, according to specific needs and policy objectives. Services are available to the disabled not only through state units on aging, but also through state units concerned with developmental disabilities and those that offer assistance with jobs and family services. As with services covered by Medicaid waivers through the HCBS program, these other services for the disabled are available in the person's home and community setting, whereas under the traditional program, they would be provided in a hospital or nursing home.

There is, however, a notable gap in coverage for the types of disabilities that impact an older person's daily activities but for which services are not typically available (or funded), as opposed to the types of disabilities that require long-term care approaches (e.g., services that are covered by Medicaid waivers for those who meet income eligibility criteria). In a sense, the system is geared to respond to health and illness concerns, rather than those related to the social or environmental aspects of disability. To put it differently, the OAA has not paid sufficient attention or provided adequate funding to help disabled individuals who happen to be older remain safe and integrated into their own communities as they age.

Such services would likely include transportation for medical, social, and consumer purposes; assistance with homemaking and food preparation; help with certain activities of daily living, such as bathing and personal care; and opportunities for social support. While these types of services are offered to those who meet a very low-income eligibility standard (under Medicaid), many seniors of even modest incomes do not qualify.

There is likely a connection between the health-based research agenda of aging and the public policy system that has not prioritized aging-based needs for care services. We can accept the basic tenets of the successful aging model while also making room at the table for older persons who have disabilities—and addressing the question of how to validate and support them into their older years.[72] By seeing disability as something other than a failure of either bodily functions or lifestyle choices, we can become attuned to the environmental and social aspects of disability that affect disabled individuals of all age groups. This shift in focus might also encourage policymakers to expand funding and support for AAAs.

This new perspective, however, calls for us to bear in mind that many older adults persist in viewing themselves as nondisabled even when they have suffered significant impairments.[73] Kenneth Ferraro points out the "paradox that despite the fact that older people are more likely to have chronic diseases and higher disability, the may actually be somewhat more optimistic in rating their health."[74] And most older individuals prefer a doctor-centered (and cure-oriented) clinical model when it comes to addressing disability. Unless seniors themselves demand an alternative model to address disability in old age, it is unlikely that policymakers will implement changes to address the needs of disabled elders for a social model of support that can enhance their lives in the community. The question of why seniors are not inclined to adopt a disability identity is critical for future efforts to develop such a model.[75]

From Policy to Practice

It is at the personal, family, and community levels that the subject of aging with disability has gained greatest visibility—even if policymakers have not yet fully responded to these issues. What happens when older people can no longer live independently in their home setting because of increasing levels of impairment? What services are they eligible for, and who will guide the older individuals and their spouses, children, or other relatives through the maze of services and resources that might allow them to remain independent? As career and family often take children to distant cities, and as their parents continue to live in the family home well into old and old-old age, this reality will call for meaningful consideration of joint action between families and policymakers.

Current policy is based on the presumption that the seniors are capable of making key decisions and can access the necessary information to connect effectively with care providers. But research shows that many seniors lack the communication skills and experience of self-advocacy. This inadequacy is especially true in their interactions with physicians. Moreover, they are reluctant to seek help from friends and family since they worry about being or becoming a burden to others. As a result, many seniors are poorly equipped to seek out services or marshal the social resources that would enable them to function longer within their communities, especially after they have begun to experience the adverse health events and conditions that cause disability.[76]

The existing aging network must help disabled seniors develop these skills—and these seniors, in turn, must develop a desire to advocate for themselves. These skills, however, are not sufficient to address the changing nature of the aging population whose members are likely to experience disability at some point, usually upon reaching very advanced age. Such individuals, we must recognize, will have suffered a series of losses that have culminated in a level of disability that interferes with independent living. From a policy standpoint, the question we must ask is: How do we conceptualize and implement a care-based system—but one that is not necessarily long-term care—to support older individuals living in a home-based environment?[77]

Notes

1. Debra J. Sheets, "Aging with Disabilities: Ageism and More," *Generations* 29, no. 3 (2005): 37–41.
2. James F. Fries, "Aging, Natural Death, and the Compression of Morbidity," *New England Journal of Medicine* 303, no. 3 (1980): 130–135.
3. Sheets, "Aging with Disabilities."
4. Jean B. Crockett and James M. Kauffman, *The Least Restrictive Environment: Its Origins and Interpretations in Special Education* (Routledge, 2013).
5. Joseph P. Shapiro, *No Pity: People with Disabilities Forging a New Civil Rights Movement* (Three Rivers Press, 1994).
6. Those who engage in such concealment of their disabilities, as Irving Kenneth Zola has observed, "may inadvertently have negatively affected their own

conditions." Irving Kenneth Zola, "Toward the Necessary Universalizing of a Disability Policy," *Millbank Quarterly* 67, no. 2, Pt. 2 (1989): 419.

7. Eva Kahana, Boaz Kahana, and May Wykle, "'Care-Getting': A Conceptual Model of Marshalling Support Near the End of Life," *Current Aging Science* 3, no. 1 (2010): 71–78.

8. Michael Oliver, *The Politics of Disablement: A Sociological Approach* (St. Martin's Press, 1990), 11.

9. Ibid.

10. Oliver, *The Politics of Disablement* citing the definitions presented in Union of the Physically Impaired Against Segregation (UPIAS), *Fundamental Principles of Disability* (UPIAS, 1976). The group was founded in 1972 and disbanded in 1990.

11. Tom Shakespeare, "Disability Studies Today and Tomorrow," *Sociology of Health and Illness* 27, no. 1 (2005): 138–148.

12. Oliver, *The Politics of Disablement*, 11.

13. Dana Lee Baker, *The Politics of Neurodiversity: Why Public Policy Matters* (Lynne Rienner, 2011). In chapter 2, Baker presents her taxonomy of policy agendas. In chapters 3–8, she analyzes the various tensions among these competing agendas (e.g., "Securing Civil Rights vs. Providing Care"; "Providing Care vs. Finding a Cure") and highlights the aggregate significance of each agenda.

14. Ibid.

15. Shakespeare, "Disability Studies Today and Tomorrow."

16. Elias S. Cohen, "Social, Economic and Political Realities of Cross-Network Partnerships and Coalitions," in *Aging and Disability: Crossing Network Lines,* ed. Michelle Putnam (Springer, 2007), 93.

17. These categories are problematic because they create fragmentation within social welfare systems. Programs that serve similar populations are severed and separated. This is the case for educational programs and children's services; mental health and disability programs; the Older Americans Act and long-term care; and, most broadly, disability and aging. Ibid., 94.

18. Ibid., 95.

19. Ibid., 104–107. According to Cohen, federal efforts have been "substantial" while state responses have been inadequate. See also Judith Gran, Max Lapertosa, and Ruthie Beckwith, *Olmstead: Reclaiming Institutionalized Lives* (National Council on Disability, 2003).

20. Cohen, "Social, Economic and Political Realities of Cross-Network Partnerships and Coalitions," 107.

21. The independence of aging within the larger federal bureaucracy—and its very broad mandate—has come at a high price. The AoA's budget has been "miniscule," according to Cohen, and the agency has had minimal influence over major policy programs such as Medicare and Medicaid, Supplemental Security Income (SSI), NIH research, and veterans' services. Cohen, "Social, Economic and Political Realities of Cross-Network Partnerships and Coalitions," 108–109. See also Fernando Torres-Gil, *The New Aging: Politics and Change in America* (Auburn House, 1992).

22. Cohen recounts his own role in this process at the 1961 White House Conference on Aging (WHCoA): "As chair of the WHCoA working committee on organization of state units, I presided over vigorous arguments against any arrangements that were not independent of existing state agencies." Cohen, "Social, Economic and Political Realities of Cross-Network Partnerships and Coalitions," 109.

23. On the role of the state units and their many activities, see National Association of State Units on Aging, *40 Years of Leadership: The Dynamic Role of*

State Units on Aging (National Association of State Units on Aging, 2004). Because these agencies are relatively small and not well funded, "one longtime observer . . . has characterized their efforts as 'a mile wide, and an inch deep,' not as a critical comment, but rather as a reflection on the breadth of the interest and concern and the limited political and financial clout required to take programs to the level that Title I of the OAA sets out as objectives." Cohen, "Social, Economic and Political Realities of Cross-Network Partnerships and Coalitions," 111 (quoting E. Ansello, personal communication with the author, May 24, 2005).

24. Jake Epp, *Achieving Health for All: A Framework for Health Promotion* (Canada Ministry of Supply and Services, 1987); Carroll L. Estes, *The Aging Enterprise* (Jossey-Bass, 1979).

25. Robert H. Binstock, "Aging and the Future of American Politics," *Annals of the American Academy of Political and Social Science* 415, no. 1 (1974): 200, 202.

26. Ibid., 203.

27. Binstock reports that many older persons "apparently . . . wish to avoid identification as aged because they feel that it would lead others to regard them as old, different, and perhaps deviant." Ibid. See also Sheets, "Aging with Disabilities," 38–39.

28. Binstock, "Aging and the Future of American Politics," 202.

29. See Robert H. Binstock, "Interest-Group Liberalism and the Politics of Aging," *Gerontologist* 12, no. 3, Pt. 1 (1972): 265–280.

30. Binstock, "Aging and the Future of American Politics," 209–210.

31. Andrea Louise Campbell, "Self-Interest, Social Security, and the Distinctive Participation Patterns of Senior Citizens," *American Political Science Review* 96, no. 3 (2002): 565–574; Andrea Louise Campbell, *How Politics Makes Citizens: Senior Political Activism and the American Welfare State* (Princeton University Press, 2003).

32. Michael S. Lewis-Beck et al., *The American Voter Revisited* (University of Michigan Press, 2008), 354–356. See also Robert B. Hudson, "Politics and Policies of Aging in the United States," in *Handbook of Aging and the Social Sciences*, 8th ed., ed. Linda George and Kenneth Ferraro (Academic, 2015), 444–446.

33. Elias S. Cohen, "The Elderly Mystique: Constraints on the Autonomy of the Elderly with Disabilities," *Gerontologist* 28, Suppl. (1988): 24–31.

34. Deborah A. Stone, *The Disabled State* (Temple University Press, 1986), 15.

35. The antidiscrimination aspects of disability policy have been pivotal in defining not only policy, but the focus of the disability rights movement. See Harlan Hahn, "Disability Policy and the Problem of Discrimination," *American Behavioral Scientist* 28 (1985): 293–318; Harlan Hahn, "Antidiscrimination Laws and Social Research on Disability: The Minority Group Perspective," *Behavioral Sciences and the Law* 14, no. 1 (1996): 41–59. Richard Scotch and Kay Schriner have in recent years called for a more nuanced and multilayered approach to addressing disability as an aspect of "human variation." See Richard K. Scotch and Kay Schriner, "Disability as Human Variation: Implications for Policy," *ANNALS of the American Academy of Political and Social Science* 549 (1997): 148–159.

36. Edward D. Berkowitz, *Disabled Policy: America's Programs for the Handicapped: A Twentieth Century Fund Report* (Cambridge University Press, 1989).

37. Michelle Putnam, "Moving from Separate to Crossing Aging and Disability Service Networks," in *Aging and Disability: Crossing Network Lines*, ed. Michelle Putnam (Springer, 2007), 7.

38. Lori Simon-Rusinowitz and Brian F. Hofland, "Adopting a Disability Approach to Home Care Services for Older Adults," *Gerontologist* 33, no. 2 (1993): 159–167; Sheets, "Aging with Disabilities."

39. Stone, *The Disabled State*, 27.
40. Paul B. Baltes and Jacqui Smith, "New Frontiers in the Future of Aging: From Successful Aging of the Young Old to the Dilemmas of the Fourth Age," *Gerontology* 49, no. 2 (2003): 123–135; Peter Uhlenberg, "Population Aging and Social Policy," *Annual Review of Sociology* 18, no. 1 (1992): 449–474.
41. Medicare Part A covers hospital care, skilled nursing facility care, hospice care, and most skilled home health care services. It is funded through the Federal Insurance Contributions Act (FICA) payroll tax (most of which pays for Social Security) that is split between employers and employees. Part A is free to anyone who has paid FICA tax for at least ten years. Medicare Part B is supplementary medical insurance that covers doctor's visits, outpatient surgeries, lab work and X-rays, preventive services, durable medical equipment, and some skilled home health care services. Part B is funded through the premiums that beneficiaries pay, but is also heavily government subsidized (75 percent) through general revenues. Medicare Part D covers prescription drugs and is funded according to the same formula as Part B. Medicare Part C allows private health insurance companies to offer premium-based Medicare Advantage plans that provide Parts A and B benefits and may also include Part D benefits. See Marilyn Moon, "Organization and Financing of Health Care," in *Handbook of Aging and the Social Sciences,* 8th ed., ed. Linda George and Kenneth Ferraro (Academic, 2015), 399. See also "What Does Medicare Cover (Parts A, B, C, and D)?" Medicare Interactive, www.medicareinteractive.org/get-answers/introduction-to-medicare/explaining-medicare/what-does-medicare-cover-parts-a-b-c-and-d.
42. One reason for the intergenerational popularity of these programs is the indirect help they provide to younger family members of those covered. Medicare "took the burden of grandma's hip replacement, and grandpa's cataract operation, off the back of their families." Lawrence M. Friedman, *A History of American Law,* 3rd ed. (Simon and Schuster, 2005), 562.
43. Paul Starr, *The Social Transformation of American Medicine* (Basic Books, 1982), 370. Starr also notes that "while Medicare had uniform national standards for eligibility and benefits, Medicaid left states to decide how extensive their programs would be." Ibid.
44. See Carole B. Cox, *Social Policy for an Aging Society: A Human Rights Perspective* (Springer, 2015), 79–97.
45. Marilyn Moon, "Organization and Financing of Health Care," in *Handbook of Aging and the Social Sciences,* 8th ed., ed. Linda George and Kenneth Ferraro, (Academic, 2015), 398.
46. Muriel R. Gillick, "Medicare Coverage for Technological Innovations—Time for New Criteria?" *New England Journal of Medicine* 350, no. 21 (2004): 2199–2201.
47. "What's Not Covered by Part A & Part B?" Medicare, www.medicare.gov/what-medicare-covers/not-covered/item-and-services-not-covered-by-part-a-and-b.html.
48. Aaron Alterra, *Caregiver: A Life with Alzheimer's* (Steerforth, 1999), 166. Not only does Medicare not support home health assistance that can prevent costly medical interventions but, under the Balanced Budget Act of 1997, those who suffer from degenerative diseases such as Parkinson's can access only limited assistance for outpatient therapy (e.g., physical, occupational, and speech-language therapy). Medicare provides only $1,940 per calendar year for physical therapy and speech-language therapy (combined) and $1,940 per calendar year for occupational therapy. All additional services must be paid for out of pocket unless the services are deemed

"medically necessary." See "Government Benefits and Insurance," Michael J. Fox Foundation, nd, www.michaeljfox.org/understanding-parkinsons/living-with-pd/topic/government-benefits.

49. Cox, *Social Policy for an Aging Society,* 83.

50. Because of the federalism governance model in the United States, each state can set its own Medicaid eligibility cutoffs. Per person spending allocations also vary significantly among the states. A person's annual income must be at or below the federal poverty level (around $12,000), and the asset cap is set at $2,000–$4,000 for a single person and $3,000–$6,000 for a couple. A useful overview of past and recent developments in the organization and financing of Medicaid (and Medicare) is provided in Marilyn Moon, "Organization and Financing of Health Care," in *Handbook of Aging and the Social Sciences,* 6th ed., ed. Robert H. Binstock and Linda K. George (Academic, 2006), 380–396; Marilyn Moon, "Organization and Financing of Health Care," in *Handbook of Aging and the Social Sciences,* 7th ed., ed. Robert H. Binstock and Linda K. George (Academic, 2011), 295–307; and Marilyn Moon, "Organization and Financing of Health Care," in *Handbook of Aging and the Social Sciences,* 8th ed., ed. Linda K. George and Kenneth Ferraro (Academic, 2016), 397–417.

51. See Kenneth Howse, Shah Ebrahim, and Rachael Gooberman-Hill, "Help-Avoidance: Why Older People Do Not Always Seek Help," *Reviews in Clinical Gerontology* 14, no. 1 (2005): 63–70.

52. Robyn I. Stone, "The Direct Care Worker: The Third Rail of Home Care Policy," *Annual Review of Public Health* 25 (2004): 521–537.

53. Cox, *Social Policy for an Aging Society,* 84.

54. Ibid.; see also Centers for Medicare and Medicaid Services, *Medicaid Expenditures for Long-Term Services and Supports (LTSS) in FY 2014: Managed LTSS Reached 15 Percent of LTSS Spending.* 2016. Retrieved from https://www.medicaid.gov/medicaid/ltss/downloads/ltss-expenditures-2014.pdf.

55. Medicaid expenditures in 2017 are estimated to be approximately $674 billion.

56. AARP, "Family Caregivers Provide Staggering $470 Billion in Unpaid Care According to AARP Study" (AARP, July 2015).

57. Robert H. Binstock, "From the Great Society to the Aging Society—25 Years of the Older Americans Act," *Generations* 15, no. 3 (1991): 11–18.

58. Ibid. See also Robert Morris, Robert H. Binstock, and Martin Rein, *Feasible Planning for Social Change* (Columbia University Press, 1966).

59. Carroll L. Estes and Karen W. Linkins, "Devolution and Aging Policy: Racing to the Bottom in Long-Term Care," *International Journal of Health Services* 27, no. 3 (1997): 427–442.

60. Elizabeth A. Kutza and Sharon M. Keigher, "The Elderly 'New Homeless': An Emerging Population at Risk," *Social Work* 36, no. 4 (1991): 288–293; Estes, *The Aging Enterprise.*

61. This endurance and growth were due especially to the commitment of Arthur S. Flemming during the period 1973–1978. Flemming had been secretary of health, education and welfare under President Dwight Eisenhower and was appointed commissioner on aging by President Richard Nixon. Flemming oversaw the expansion of the aging services network and, in particular, the Area Agencies on Aging. See Binstock, "From the Great Society to the Aging Society."

62. See Carol V. O'Shaughnessy, "Aging and Disability Resource Centers (ADRCs): Federal and State Efforts to Guide Consumers Through the Long-Term Services and Supports Maze," Background Paper No. 81, National Health Policy Forum, Washington, DC, November 2010.

63. Administration for Community Living, *Title III—Grants for State and Community Programs on Aging*, August 2016, https://acl.gov/About_ACL/Allocations/docs/OAA/T3-2016.pdf.

64. Stephanie Whittier, Andrew Scharlach, and Teresa S. Dal Santo, "Availability of Caregiver Support Services: Implications for Implementation of the National Family Caregiver Support Program," *Journal of Aging and Social Policy* 17, no. 1 (2005): 45–62; Barry D. Lebowitz, Enid Light, and Frank Bailey, "Mental Health Center Services for the Elderly: The Impact of Coordination with Area Agencies on Aging," *Gerontologist* 27, no. 6 (1987): 699–702.

65. Richard H. Fortinsky, "Coordinated, Comprehensive Community Care and the Older Americans Act," *Generations* 15, no. 3 (1991): 39–42.

66. Laura B. Wilson, *Civic Engagement and the Baby Boomer Generation: Research, Policy, and Practice Perspectives* (Routledge, 2006).

67. Lawrence Force, Jeffrey S. Kahana, and Valerie Capalbo, "The Role of AAAs in Promoting Health for Seniors: A Preliminary Research Report," *Open Longevity Science* 4 (2010): 30–35.

68. Kenneth C. Land and Yang Yang, "Morbidity, Disability, and Mortality," in *Handbook of Aging and the Social Sciences*, 6th ed., ed. Robert H. Binstock and Linda K. George (Academic, 2006), 41.

69. Force, Kahana, and Capalbo, "The Role of AAAs in Promoting Health for Seniors."

70. Ibid.

71. Ibid.

72. John W. Rowe and Robert L. Kahn observe that "successful aging is dependent upon individual choices and behaviors." John W. Rowe and Robert L. Kahn, *Successful Aging* (Pantheon Books, 1998), 37. We should not dismiss their point as relating merely to personal choices in such areas as how people live and what they eat. The question of lifestyle has been repeatedly linked to both health and quality of life. This is especially true as people grow old. See Jon Hendricks and Laurie Russell Hatch, "Lifestyle and Aging," in *Handbook of Aging and the Social Sciences*, 6th ed., ed. Robert H. Binstock and Linda K. George (Academic, 2006), 303–319. But we should also be careful not to conclude "that older adults with disability . . . are aging unsuccessfully." Linda K. George, "Perceived Quality of Life," in *Handbook of Aging and the Social Sciences*, 6th ed., ed. Robert H. Binstock and Linda K. George (Academic, 2006), 322.

73. Kenneth F. Ferraro, "Self-Ratings of Health Among the Old and the Old-Old," *Journal of Health and Social Behavior* 21, no. 4 (1980): 377–383.

74. Kenneth F. Ferraro, "Health and Aging," in *Handbook of Aging and the Social Sciences*, 6th ed., ed. Robert H. Binstock and Linda K. George (Academic, 2006), 246.

75. Jessica Kelley-Moore, "Disability and Ageing: The Social Construction of Causality," in *The Sage Handbook of Social Gerontology*, ed. Dale Dannefer and Chris Phillipson (Sage, 2010), 96–110.

76. Eva Kahana and Boaz Kahana, "Patient Proactivity Enhancing Doctor-Patient-Family Communication in Cancer Prevention and Care Among the Aged," *Patient Education and Counseling* 50, no. 1 (2003): 67–73; Banghwa Lee Casado, Kimberly S. van Vulpen, and Stacey L. Davis, "Unmet Needs for Home and Community-Based Services Among Frail Older Americans and Their Caregivers," *Journal of Aging and Health* 23, no. 3 (2011): 529–553.

77. Zola, "Toward the Necessary Universalizing of a Disability Policy."

10

The Promise of Convergence in Gerontology and Disability Studies

The individual and societal graying of disability is a historic process that began in the mid- to late twentieth century in most Western societies. This growth of the elder population—and the rapid rise in those age eighty-five and over—suggests that not only are Americans aging, but the existing policy infrastructure and academic frameworks laid in the 1960s and 1970s are aging as well.[1] These twin developments can lead to a greater convergence in gerontology and disability studies—and to opportunities for both fields to learn from each other.

What is the effect of this aging boom on the prospects for elders who are experiencing disability for the first time in later life? Many of these individuals entered adulthood at a time when disability was far from accepted. It is worth recalling that Irving Kenneth Zola initially found his own disability—the consequence of childhood polio—to threaten his self-image. It took many years and his experience at Het Dorp for him to begin to reclaim his own positive identity as a disabled person.

Zola's memoir reveals that it's not just society that "denigrates, stigmatizes, and distances . . . those with disabilities."[2] Disabled people often stigmatize themselves—and may even choose to distance themselves from what it means to be disabled. Zola recounts the efforts he made to fit in so as to avoid being perceived by others or seeing himself as disabled. Our goal in this book is to understand and support elders who hold attitudes toward disability that are not consistent with the pride that animates the disability rights movement. For elders, disability can pose a threat to their identity, sense of security, and vision for their future. Change is possible—both for the individual older person and for society—only from a place of self-understanding and acceptance.[3]

Disability in old age results from an interaction between a person's environment and either physical or cognitive impairments or both. But it is also a personal experience. The issue of adjustment to changes in one's ability—and corresponding changes to self-identity—provide a personal context to disability. We should therefore consider both what constitutes disability and what disability means to a person of a certain age and generational affiliation.

Finally, we should recognize that disability in late life may represent a series of disconcerting transitions that lead away from independence: from home to an assisted living (or nursing) facility, from mobility to reliance upon others for transportation, and ultimately from life to death.[4] Especially in the United States, these transitions take place within a social context that treats old age as a health problem rather than a social process. From the medical specialists to the hospitals that treat acute illness to the nursing home (and the public-pay systems of Medicare and Medicaid that underwrite such treatments), the "social world" of the older person is rooted in a medical otherness. To be an older person, especially when living with an illness-related impairment, is to find that much of one's time is spent under the management of physicians—and to live in fear of becoming sick and disabled. As we noted in Chapter 8, these fears create a synchronism between age, frailty, and vulnerability that can be disabling regardless of any physical or cognitive impairment.

Throughout this book we have examined the lived experience of older persons with disabilities. The elderly are rooted in a place—within family relationships, friendships, and residential neighborhoods. These connections, as much as disease and impairment, affect how an older person experiences disability. Beyond physical or cognitive impairment, a leading factor in nursing home admission is the collapse of an older person's formal and informal social support systems. We hope that in the future, Area Agencies on Aging (AAAs) and the network of service agencies they connect can bolster social supports—a process that is under way with the creative use of Medicaid vouchers. If the need for supportive services becomes a political issue that receives attention from seniors and their families, the likelihood will increase that community-based programs will become a normative alternative to the nursing home.

What Is Disability in Old Age?

For those who approach disability from an aging perspective, disability constitutes a measurable deficit in health or functional ability. The view of disability scholars and activists is quite different. It is not the "physical or mental impairment, but rather the link of such impairments with the social, attitudinal, architectural, medical, economic and politic environment" that constitutes disability.[5] But looking primarily at factors that are external to the individual presents as incomplete a picture of disability as the medical model's essentialist view. What makes our understanding of disability so elusive is that we cannot separate its experiential aspect from a person's unique life history. Only by linking the physical component to the social and the personal can we see the many (and at times conflicting) dimensions of disability in old age.

Our earlier chapters have shown that we cannot define disability on the basis of impairment and disease alone, although these do play a large role. How older persons reshape their environment, how they choose to live, and whether they find joy in lifelong and newer pursuits all affect morale and influence functioning. Some older people have no impairments, yet are functionally disabled as a result of social isolation and the absence of support. Going hand in hand with these social losses are the long-identified issue of depression in old age and the newer recognition of addiction among the elderly. We also cannot minimize the gender component of disability in old age. Because women are more likely than men to live to very old age, they make up a much larger percentage of the elderly population. As these women reach old age—alone—they are more susceptible to the combination of environment-related disability and morale-based impairment.

Disability is a complex topic at any age and even more so in old age, when the cumulative losses of social and physical resources limit compensatory systems. With fewer connections to work, community, and friends—and often without a spouse or children to provide social support—many elderly people are not equipped to handle the manifold challenges of late life. For older persons, the inability to marshal support from others and to find meaning in late life contribute in key ways to disability.

How Do Elders Understand Disability?

Sociologists and other scholars of aging have shown considerable interest in generational differences in the way people experience old age. Meika Loe's fascinating study of independently living elders offers a window into aspects of disability in very old age. Loe shows that members of the Greatest Generation, who came of age during the privations of the Great Depression, are resilient as they face numerous hardships in their eighties and nineties.[6] How the baby boomers will experience disability in late life is a question on the minds of academics and policymakers.[7]

But no matter which generation we observe as its members grow old, if we wish to gauge how elders understand disability, we must listen to the narratives they construct to connect the life they once lived without disability to the life they are now living with disability. What Jaber Gubrium calls an older person's "life story" can "communicate what life was in relation to what it has become."[8] This longer view of the life course allows for a plurality of perspectives about what disability means to the individual. When considered within the context of a person's life course, disability in old age is not a discrete condition. Rather, it assumes meaning in relationship to that individual's past life experiences—and how that person perceives it as shaping his or her current and future life.[9]

But for older persons with severe disability, the distinction between their current experiences and their lives, as they understand them, may diverge. To such a person, "life can be separated from experience."[10] In other words, how the elderly understand what is happening to them on a daily basis (*how they are*) can be distinct from how they understand their lives (*who they are*). How older persons relate to others and envision their life with disability is thus biographically informed; their current experience can feel either divorced from their past or integrated into it.[11]

Scholars can enrich their studies of disability in old age by reaching beyond social context and even congruence models, which account for both person and environment, to grapple with the subjective construction of disability by older persons. The anthropological literature on aging provides a valuable framework for supplementing these useful approaches by situating disability within an evolving understanding of the self and its efforts to create a subjective sense of meaning across the many experiences of old age.[12]

Transitions in Late Life

For a person who becomes disabled in late life, the experience of disability is different from that of the person who is born with an impairment or acquires it at an earlier stage of life. The elderly person often experiences an erosion rather than a breakdown of functional and cognitive ability; gerontologists refer to this process in terms of *decrements*. But while adaptation and adjustment of resources in late life can enhance functioning and limit decrements, they do not prepare the whole person for the transition brought about by late-life disability.

In late life the ideal of avoiding disability becomes more problematic than it is for younger people. We know that impairments of body, mind, or both; diminishment in personal strength and capacity to function; and the breakdown of social supports mean that disability is an experience that will inevitably affect most elderly persons. But what is less clear are the subjective transition points that mark the road along this journey. The older person's strong desire to preserve a nondisabled identity can limit help-seeking behavior, and this avoidance can be disabling too. Additionally, in response to survey questions, older persons with disabilities may underestimate their reliance on accommodations.[13]

In navigating issues of disability in later life, how people live—whether in cities, suburbs, or rural areas—and how they prioritize their time and resources can be as important as their type of impairment. In Chapter 6, we examined how modifications to the home environment can create a more livable space for elders with disability. Considerable research shows that even minor adjustments to the home—as environmental gerontology advocates—can have major payoffs for aging in place in late life, even for elders with disabilities.[14] Stephen M. Golant argues that "conventional places of residence . . . must help their older occupants compensate for the effects of their chronic health problems, physical and cognitive limitations, and absent social supports."[15] The wider community also has the potential and obligation to create more livable spaces for older people with disabilities.

Our own research working with AAAs has shown older people's self-reported benefits of social support and engagement. The powerful and capacity-promoting effects of social relationships have long been documented. In their landmark 1988 article in *Science,* House, Landis, and Umberson found that "social relationships, or the relative lack thereof, constitute a major risk factor for health."[16] The work of Gene Cohen in aging and creativity has also extended our understanding of benefits that accrue to those who stay mentally stimulated and socially engaged in later life.[17] Furthermore, the increasing use of technology offers a new frontier for aging in place among older adults living with disabilities.[18]

Yet the challenges to remaining active and engaged in the face of medical issues, the loss of spouse and friends, the inability to drive (especially in rural and suburban areas), and the lack of family social supports can be formidable. For older people who are not impaired, isolation significantly increases their risk of future disability; for those who are impaired, the lack of social contact raises the risk that the severity of their disability will increase.[19]

The movement linking physical space (home) with a sense of social place (family and community) will need to grow stronger to ensure that older persons can continue to live safely in their own homes. We will also need to keep exploring the role of social relationships and networks in the context of residential life.[20] Even if elders are aging in place, they are living socially isolated rather than integrated lives if they lack these foundational relationships. For this reason, Golant has proposed "aging in the right place" as a meaningful alternative goal.[21]

A broad understanding of place within an environmental framework of aging illuminates the ways in which social relationships assume such high importance for elders living with impairments.[22] Having family and friends who can provide instrumental and social support can make it possible for an older person with impairments to live at home—and even more importantly, maintain the desire and determination to continue living independently.[23]

Gerontology and Disability Studies

In this book we have highlighted the current focus on health and aging by gerontologists. Kenneth Ferraro sums up its significance: "The study of health has been *the* issue that has generated the most social science research on aging during the last 50 years." The reason for this focus is that "health is a critical part of the aging process, and . . . the ultimate goal is that discoveries related to health and aging will enhance the quality of life over the life course, thereby reducing the likelihood of premature morbidity, disability, and death."[24]

The relationship between health and aging is a complex interaction that is affected by a person's chronological age and socioeconomic status plus a host of other factors. Clearly, the change in health status brought about by a physical or cognitive disability is a turning point in an older person's life. Gerontologists, we believe, will continue to study the ways in which older people lose their health as well as the specific processes of disablement. However, the idea that disability in old age is an unexceptional event and not a tragedy—that it is a natural human condition affecting many elderly people and not the result of deficient health behavior—awaits greater attention from the aging and public health research communities.

Younger disabled people interact with the concept of disability by making disability a story about us rather than them. Disability is part of who they are, even as they seek to integrate into society. For these individuals, disability is about identity and politics—and about who they are as people. Using disability as a means of empowerment rather than a negative descriptive category has served to strengthen their identity and allowed them to make claims for greater access and inclusion within society.[25] Moreover, many younger people living with disability have adopted a perspective that goes beyond the mere demand for change; it encompasses their sense of pride, dignity, and self-worth. Whether disability makes disabled people give up or try harder can be just as important a determinant of impairment as the physiological or environmental factors that define what constitutes disability. If we consider disability from this vantage point, we can examine how the fields of gerontology and disability studies might develop a dialogue, given their different perspectives.

Are we on the cusp of a new era in the relationship between these two academic disciplines? For some time now, scholars have contended that the distance between the fields is shrinking. "A convergence of interests between age and disability," writes W. Andrew Achenbaum, "may be imminent, thanks to policy initiatives at the federal level."[26] In a recent study of the intersection between aging and disability, Michelle Putnam envisions a future of greater cooperation between the policy systems of aging and disability.

In *Physical Disability: A Psychosocial Approach,* Beatrice Wright offers a useful framework that can be applied to older persons living with disability. She imagines the possibility that disability might enlarge meaning in life.[27] Wright also argues that, unlike traditions that see social stigma and devaluation as the plight of the disabled, an attitude of acceptance of their own disabilities allows the disabled to reprioritize their life goals. By letting go of normal standards, disability makes room for itself and can be lived on its own terms.

This acceptance of disability does not mean that a person living with disability leads life on the same terms as a nondisabled person does. But to say that one set of terms is different from another does not imply that it is of lesser worth. According to Wright, accepting the condition of "disability as non-devaluating" leads to changes that broaden our values, limit the effects of disability, subordinate the physical self to the true self, and transform how people view themselves in comparison to others.[28] In the case of older persons, this process may take the form of a reorientation toward the present and a focus on what matters most for them as they look toward the future.

For anyone who experiences the transition from nondisability to disability, as conventionally understood, the change and the loss can prove jarring. Although many paths may lead to such a loss—the primary loss may be physical or cognitive—the path forward is the same in each case. The disabled person must acknowledge the pain of loss and be able to mourn for it—and then overcome his or her defenses against accepting these new life circumstances. This process may take time as well as help and support from others—but leading life as if there has been no change can be more disabling than the impairments that the person is now experiencing.

Loss allows new values to replace old ones—a process that can ease suffering. The individual can now distill what matters in life, discovering an appreciation of friendship, family, and service to others, as well as resources he or she once took for granted—such as free time, creative expression, and new experiences. "Enlarging the scope of values" in this way allows the individual to move from mourning to personal acceptance and then to take the next step—becoming aware of others who have also suffered losses that resulted in disability.[29]

Wright also shows how an awareness of the disability of others permits disabled persons to gain a truer appreciation of the abilities they still possess.[30] This awareness does not mean that disabled persons should allow their own disability to affect how they see themselves or how others see them. According to Wright, we must stop relying on the prowess of the body (in appearance and in functional ability) to stand as a signifier of a person's worth. By deemphasizing the physical being—"subordinating physique"—and discovering inner attributes of character and personality, disabled people can gain new control over their lives. "Nonphysique values such as kindness, wisdom, effort, and cooperativeness" can compensate for lost physical assets. Empathy and actions that show concern for others can replace physique as a means of validation.[31] Wright focuses on physical disabilities, but the same analysis applies to cognitive disabilities—the prowess of a person's mind should not function as a signifier of worth.

Equally important for maintaining personal integrity in the face of impairment is what Wright calls "containing disability effects." Disability should not define the whole person.[32] If, for example, an older woman cannot walk without assistance, that impairment does not imply that she is unable to manage her own affairs or accomplish cognitive tasks or even other physical ones.

In a relational framework, when a person with a disability interacts with a nondisabled person, they may both reach conclusions based on societal norms, or standards. But Wright posits that every person has an intrinsic worth that is not dependent on how he or she measures up to others. When we think of other people only in a comparative sense (who is smarter, better looking, stronger), we are using "comparative values" based on standards "along a scale of better to worse."[33] We see this comparative valuation in the concepts of normal versus non-normal aging and successful versus unsuccessful aging.

Wright argues that this comparative framework devalues the disabled person and the interaction. She proposes replacing comparative values with "asset values" based on inherent qualities: "What matters is the object of the judgment in a setting that has its own intrinsic purposes and demands. The person's reaction is then based upon how appropriately the situational demands are fulfilled rather than on a comparison with a predetermined standard."[34] Impairment-based differences—for example, one person is in a wheelchair and the other is ambulatory—need not define a social interaction (as they often do). The person in the wheelchair may be a professor teaching a biology class or a lawyer taking a deposition or a physician examining a patient; the fact that this person is in a wheelchair has little bearing on the situational demands. However, it does color the nature of the social interaction and the way that both the disabled person and the nondisabled person interpret it.

The distinction between comparative and asset values reminds us that disability is not an intrinsic feature of a person. It is a situational condition that can be altered by education and training, well-designed and accessible community settings, and adaptive technologies—all of which can enable those with impairments to succeed in the areas of life that confer asset value. No one would deny Stephen Hawking's understanding of advanced physics—an asset value—because he happens to have various physical impairments. Yet all too often, comparative values are used to grade elders' ability—as evident in ADL and IADL functional scores.

By replacing comparative values with asset values, disabled people can transform the way they view themselves and their own disabilities. Let's consider the example of an elderly woman with varied physical impairments that make leaving home difficult and create a high degree of dependence on family members. This individual might find her situation depressing and might even feel anger toward family members she perceives as less than helpful or even neglectful. From her point of view, she is a poor housebound elder, and these younger persons are capable of doing much more for her than they are willing to do.

But if this elderly woman can turn herself into an asset to her family, she may be able to change how family members see her and how she perceives herself. To do so, she could write notes or e-mails to her grandchildren, read to them and tell them stories about her own childhood, teach them songs and jokes, bake cookies with them, help with childcare, or just lend a sympathetic ear. In general, she can present to those around her a positive attitude of gratitude that she is alive and still enjoying life. By presenting herself in this way, her interactions with her family will be organized around pleasant experiences, despite her impairments. She will feel better about herself, and her family will find her company enjoyable and helpful. By paying attention to needs of family members, an opportunity for true reciprocity becomes possible. No longer must she see herself and have others view her only through the lens of her disabilities.

One might argue that this scenario places too much of a demand on a disabled elderly person to reach out to others. But Wright is telling us that this person's disabling condition is not her actual physical impairments. By shifting her attitude so that she takes an interest in others (the family), by containing the disability effects through positive engagement, and by becoming an asset in the situational setting of the family, this person has the potential to transcend her physical limitations. "The person with a disability," says Wright, "has much to gain psychologically if he can look upon physique in terms of its inherent or essential characteristics—that is, what it permits him to do and what it restricts him in doing—without basing his evaluation on comparison with other individuals or with his previous nondisabled state."[35] Seeing all that is left, rather than what is missing, enables the pieces of life to come together so that the whole person becomes greater than the sum of his or her parts.

In her research for *Aging Our Way: Lesson for Living from 85 and Beyond,* Meika Loe found this same pattern. Those elders who maintained their independence into their eighties and nineties generally made a practice of developing a positive attitude, even when they had impairments. They did not allow their limitations to define them as persons; they subscribed to the philosophy that they were assets for others and even did what they could to act as caregivers notwithstanding their own needs.[36]

210 Disability and Aging

Despite the half-century between the first edition of Wright's *Physical Disabilities* and Loe's book, both scholars look at disability from the vantage point of ability—what people can (still) do—arguing that who we are as individuals is not determined by our functional capabilities. Yet those who seek to understand disability in old age cannot ignore society and the social context that informs ideas and values about disability. Today disability in old age is viewed as the opposite of health and well-being. It is rarely characterized as a source of empowerment or as an opportunity to expand inner resources and appreciate the gifts of life that remain. In fact, disability in old age is rarely examined as part of the aging experience. It exists outside the main theoretical frameworks of gerontologists and is equally missing from the narratives of disability scholars.[37]

The "disjuncture"—to use disability studies scholar Carol J. Gill's term[38]—faced by the elderly with disabilities is separating and invalidating because seniors do not regard disability as a positive concept that can lead to change. They grew up during a time when to be disabled was to be stigmatized, when disability carried a moral badge of inferiority, and when they encountered few disabled people in the normal walks of life. Disability was something hidden away, not generally talked about in public, and those who were disabled often lived their lives confined to institutions. The social, political, and legal rights movements for the disabled would come much later—beginning in the 1970s—leading to a cultural transformation in society's view of disability.

These older individuals typically do not understand disability as a path leading to services that can lessen social and environmental barriers. Their views on this subject are also influenced by current policies that result in fragmented services for the disabled elderly. Understandably, many worry about the financial costs for health-related services now that they are on Medicare and no longer covered under their employers' group insurance policies. Imagine how much the psychological outlook of disabled elders—and their lives in general—would improve if they did not have to worry about Medicaid spend downs and could obtain in-home support as a universal entitlement.

The word "disability" strikes fear in the minds of many seniors because it does not serve to foster meaning in their lives. Elders see disability not as an opportunity to discover personal integrity in late life and to constructively reprioritize goals and objectives, but instead as a path leading away from true selfhood and into a frightening world of institutional care. Thus disability becomes synonymous with the loss of personal independence, financial security, and social standing. For those seeking to advance the cause of the older disabled, the first goal is to change how seniors think of disability—to help them see that disability is not a concept to fear or a condition that detracts from who they are as normal people. The second goal is to call for a broader public dialogue about how nondisabled society can more fully accept all persons with disability.

But even after older disabled persons have transformed their own thinking about disability, in social interactions they must constantly justify themselves as capable and act to disarm those who carry negative stereotypes or even feelings of anxiety about disability. Disability studies scholars are familiar with such behaviors by wheelchair users and other disabled people as well as their family members.[39] All too often, especially with the elderly, one or more impairments can lead to limitations in functional abilities and losses of independence (such as driving), which then leads to a social demotion in the eyes of others. Adult children may now interact differently with an elderly parent and even discuss (in front of the parent) ideas for a safer but more restrictive living environment, such as an assisted living facility.

For elders, the need to prove their capability—and reassure those who question it—is a routine experience when dealing with health care professionals and relatives. Older people will frequently say they are fine, even when they are not. They are reluctant to share their true concerns because they want to maintain their dignity and lessen the burden on their family. To acknowledge their disability to others would mean letting them into their world, with all its challenges, and reevaluating themselves in ways that might prove uncomfortable when they are struggling with self-acceptance.[40]

Carol J. Gill worries that this divide between "the worlds of disability and nondisability" is deep—a "troubling disjuncture" that "many disabled individuals find central to their social experience."[41] Yet her emphasis on the "transformative power of the disability experience" also provides a way forward for elders. Gill finds (confirming Wright) that "in response to permanent disability, individuals stretch the boundaries of what is important to them. They place greater value on areas of life that are open to exploration and that they may have underappreciated before acquiring an impairment." In looking at the experiential writing of those with disabilities, Gill also concludes that "in addition to a transformation of *values,* . . . many disabled people undergo a crucial cognitive or *conceptual* transformation. They change the way they understand and think about disability." She notes that "this transformation becomes an essential part of their identity and connects them to others with similar experiences."[42]

Toward a New Normal for the Aged Living with Disabilities

Those who see disability as just one aspect of what it is to be a normal person might be considered idealists. After all, why should society—or any individual—readily accept the pain and suffering of disability as normal when it is easier to place disability in a corner of the human experience and label it as exceptional? Disability has existed in this corner for most of history, including the twentieth century. Separation and segregation have been the dominant historical motifs, leading to social isolation and stigmatization for various groups of people living with disabilities.[43] When set aside from the rest of normal experience in this way, disability has been explained as a consequence of either bad luck or poor choices.[44] Yet if we are being honest with ourselves, whether disabled or not, we have a responsibility to acknowledge that disability is part of the life course—and, like pain, loss, and death, it is fundamental to the human experience.

The literature on disability reveals that from an autobiographical point of view, few disabled persons despair as a result of their disability. These individuals remain strong in spirit—they are even grateful for what they have—and they are capable of accepting and adjusting to their situation. This is what it means to speak, as Wright and Gill do, of the transformation that takes place within the person, notwithstanding pain, impairments, and lack of social acceptance. Throughout his career, disability historian Paul Longmore showed that the human spirit can triumph over physical impairments—but also that society, through its public policies, has been responsible for demeaning this same spirit. Seared into the minds of a generation of scholars is the image of Longmore burning his highly acclaimed book on George Washington to avoid losing his disability benefits by earning too much income in royalties.[45] And as political scientist Harlan Hahn documented over the course of his career, society and its prejudicial attitudes create obstacles that make it difficult for disabled persons to actually accomplish what they are capable of achieving.[46] But even with these socially imposed barriers, disabled persons find an inner capacity to accept themselves and often do so in ways that help others. They become advocates and empathizers who share their perspective on what it means to be human.

In Chapter 2, we described a matrix of disability across the life course and pointed to key differences in the way the timing of the onset of disability shapes the disability experience. As we conclude our book, we call attention to key dimensions of convergence through shared humanity and through social connectedness between persons experiencing disability during different phases of the life course. We also emphasize the benefits of greater interaction and constructive exchanges of ideas among scholars focused on aging and disability. We lamented the lack of previous interactions between gerontologists and disability scholars. We now also acknowledge the promise of greater connectedness through taking an interest in each other's contributions that is increasingly evident in our fields.[47]

Is there something specific to being older that makes disability in old age a unique experience, whether seen as a prelude to death or as a painful condition that confers suffering without corresponding meaning? One dimension in particular that calls for further attention is the stress that disability places on activity, productivity, and success in old age.

The stress that disability places on activity, productivity, and success may account for the widespread use of the concept of liminality in connection with older persons, especially those living with multiple disabilities in nursing homes. Renée Shield explains "liminality" as a state of limbo between the shedding of an old identity or role and the adoption of a new one: "It is the time when a person is in neither one role nor another." In the case of the nursing home residents, "they have been separated from their statuses as viable adults in the community, and not having died, they remain in the transition."[48] The problem with liminality is that the person is stuck without a social identity or role—just as the nursing home occupies a space between life and death without clearly demarcating the boundary between the two spaces.[49]

In *Number Our Days,* a sympathetic study of a community of aging Jewish seniors in Venice Beach, California, Barbara Myerhoff offers a fuller exploration of the idea of liminality within the aging experience. Although the anthropological term is related to the concept of marginal status, Myerhoff found that specific ritualistic and cultural forms of liminality provided a type of shield that protected community members from the marginality that accompanies poverty, illness, and nearness to death.[50] In the words of Shmuel the tailor, who has lost much, yet is enduring into old age: "The wise man searches, but not to find. He searches because even though there is nothing to find, it is necessary to search."[51]

Suggesting that disability can alert older persons to a new responsibility to search for meaning in life may strike some as overly optimistic and even idealistic. But as a character in Johann Wolfgang van Goethe's *Wilhelm Meister's Apprenticeship* observes: "If we take people as they are, we make them worse. If we treat them as if they were what they ought to be, we help them to become what they are capable of becoming." This proposition—a dictum that Victor Frankl and other existentialist psychotherapists have embraced—reflects a belief in the transformative possibility within each person—and therefore within society.[52]

The question of how older persons can maintain lives of integrity in their communities is a pressing one. This is more than an academic question. People are dealing with this challenge on a daily basis—as individuals, within families, and in local community settings. It is a point of connection rather than disjunction that binds the generations together, even if academic specialties seek to maintain their formal distance from one another. It is a mainstream question that calls for practical solutions—yet one that an age of bureaucracy, with its competing service and research systems, has kept in check. That is why advocates for change call for an act of movement, a crossing of frontiers and barriers, to approach the problems of old age and disability in a spirit of cooperation. Can the force of a graying society be the impetus for such cooperation? Only time will tell.

Notes

1. In 1900, the average life expectancy in the United States was 47.3 years old; by 1950, it had reached 68.2; and, in 2013, it was 76.4 for men and 81.2 for women. Christopher J. L. Murray, Theo Vos, Rafael Lozano, Mohsen Naghavi, Abraham D. Flaxman, Catherine Michaud, Majid Ezzati, et al., "Disability-Adjusted Life Years (DALYs) for 291 Diseases and Injuries in 21 Regions, 1990–2010: A Systematic Analysis for the Global Burden of Disease Study 2010," *The Lancet* 380, no. 9859 (2013): 2197–2223.

2. Irving Kenneth Zola, *Missing Pieces: A Chronicle of Living with a Disability* (Temple University Press, 2003), 239.

3. The goal should be to demystify disability and to embark on a path of acceptance for all people. See ibid., 420.

4. For an early effort to place old age in an environmental context, see Jaber F. Gubrium, *Late Life: Communities and Environmental Policy* (Charles C. Thomas, 1974).

5. Zola, *Missing Pieces,* 401.

6. Meika Loe, *Aging Our Way: Lessons for Living from 85 and Beyond* (Oxford University Press, 2011).

7. Eva Kahana and Boaz Kahana, "Baby Boomers' Expectations of Health and Medicine," *Medicine and Society* 16 (2014): 380–384.

8. Jaber F. Gubrium, "Perspective and Story in Nursing Home Ethnography," in *The Culture of Long Term Care: Nursing Home Ethnography,* ed. J. Neil Henderson and Maria D. Vesperi (Bergin and Garvey, 1995), 30.

9. For many years gerontologists debated a model of activity as opposed to disengagement, trying to correct a view of aging as a time when individuals did less and minimized past relationships. They replaced this disengagement perspective with one that stressed the benefits of continuing to engage in earlier life patterns—what came to be called an activity model. While for some individuals the idea of continuing to do what they have been doing is a good fit for their personality and circumstances, for others it is not. As people age, their ability to structure a life according to personal priorities—whether continuing to work, to change careers and foster a new passion, or to assume an interfamilial role as an engaged grandparent—will vary. No one-size-fits-all approach is useful. Raphaël Trouillet, Kamel Gana, Marcel Lourel, and Isabelle Fort, "Predictive Value of Age for Coping: The Role of Self-Efficacy, Social Support Satisfaction and Perceived Stress," *Aging and Mental Health* 13, no. 3 (2009): 357–366.

10. Jaber F. Gubrium, "Perspective and Story in Nursing Home Ethnography," 31.

11. In an interview, a resident in a nursing home commented about her experiences at the home, but then stated that these did not matter "because my life is over." This distinction between experience and life led Jaber F. Gubrium "to consider the possibility that life was not just something lived, but might be a thing, like a cherished heirloom . . . that one could look upon, inspect, think back on, look ahead to, close off, and open up to experience." Jaber F. Gubrium, "Perspective and Story in Nursing Home Ethnography," 23–36.

12. See for example Erving Goffman, *Stigma: Notes on the Management of Spoiled Identity* (Touchstone, 1986); Jules Henry, *Culture Against Man* (Random House, 1963); and Samantha Solimeo, *With Shaking Hands: Aging with Parkinson's Disease in America's Heartland* (Rutgers University Press, 2009).

13. Thomas M. Gill, Susan E. Hardy, and Christianna S. Williams, "Underestimation of Disability in Community-Living Older Persons," *Journal of the American Geriatrics Society* 50, no. 9 (2002): 1492–1497.

14. Stephen M. Golant, "Conceptualizing Time and Behavior in Environmental Gerontology: A Pair of Old Issues Deserving New Thought," *The Gerontologist* 43, no. 3 (2003): 628–637; Stephen M. Golant, "Commentary: Irrational Exuberance for the Aging in Place of Vulnerable Low-Income Older Homeowners," *Journal of Aging and Social Policy* 20, no. 4 (2008): 379–392; Stephen M. Golant, "Aging in Place Solutions for Older Americans: Groupthink Responses Not Always in Their Best Interests," *Public Policy and Aging Report* 19, no. 1 (2009): 1, 33–39.

15. Stephen M. Golant, "The Changing Residential Environments of Older People," in *Handbook of Aging and the Social Sciences,* 7th ed., eds. Robert H. Binstock and Linda K. George (Academic, 2011), 208.

16. James S. House, Karl R. Landis, and Debra Umberson, "Social Relationships and Health," *Science* 241, no. 4865 (1988): 541.

17. Gene D. Cohen, *The Creative Age: Awakening Human Potential in the Second Half of Life* (Harper Collins, 2001); Gene D. Cohen, Susan Perlstein, Jeff Chapline, Jeanne Kelly, Kimberly M. Firth, and Samuel Simmens, "The Impact of Professionally Conducted Cultural Programs on the Physical Health, Mental Health, and Social Functioning of Older Adults," *The Gerontologist* 46, no. 6 (2006): 726–734.

18. Sarinnapha Vasunilashorn, Bernard A. Steinman, Phoebe S. Liebig, and Jon Pynoos, "Aging in Place: Evolution of a Research Topic Whose Time Has Come," *Journal of Aging Research* (2012): 1–6.

19. Debra Umberson and Jennifer Karas Montez, "Social Relationships and Health: A Flashpoint for Health Policy," *Journal of Health and Social Behavior* 51, no. 2 (2010): S54–S66.

20. Neale Krause, "Social Relationships in Late Life," in *Handbook of Aging and the Social Sciences,* 6th ed., ed. Robert H. Binstock and Linda K. George (Academic, 2006), 181–200.

21. Stephen M. Golant, *Aging in the Right Place* (Health Professions Press, 2015).

22. Frank Oswald and Hans-Werner Wahl, "Dimensions of the Meaning of Home in Later Life," in *Home and Identity in Late Life: International Perspectives,* ed. Graham D. Rowles and Habib Chaudhury (Springer, 2005), 21–45.

23. Phyllis Moen and Mary Ann Erickson, "Chapter 3 Decision-Making and Satisfaction with a Continuing Care Retirement Community," *Journal of Housing for the Elderly* 14, nos. 1–2 (2001): 53–69.

24. Keneth F. Ferraro, "Health and Aging," in *Handbook of Aging and the Social Sciences,* 6th ed., ed. Robert H. Binstock and Linda K. George (Academic, 2006), 238–256.

25. Ronald J. Berger, *Introducing Disability Studies* (Lynne Rienner, 2013).

26. W. Andrew Achenbaum, *Crossing Frontiers: Gerontology Emerges as a Science* (Cambridge University Press, 1995), 266.

27. Beatrice A. Wright, *Physical Disability: A Psychosocial Approach* (Harper and Row, 1960).

28. Ibid., 222–224, 396.
29. Ibid., 163, 191.
30. Ibid., 163–170.
31. Ibid., 171.
32. Ibid., 172.
33. Ibid., 179. See also Tamara Dembo, Gloria Ladieu Levitan, and Beatrice A. Wright, "Adjustment to Misfortune: A Problem of Social-Psychological Rehabilitation," *Artificial Limbs* 32, no. 2 (1956): 4–62.
34. Wright, *Physical Disability,* 129.
35. Ibid., 130.
36. Loe, *Aging Our Way.*
37. Meredith Minkler and Pamela Fadem, "'Successful Aging': A Disability Perspective," *Journal of Disability Policy Studies* 12, no. 4 (2002): 229–235.
38. Carol J. Gill, "Divided Understandings: The Social Experience of Disability," in *Handbook of Disability Studies,* ed. Gary L. Albrecht, Katherine D. Seelman, and Michael Bury (Sage, 2001), 352.
39. See, for example, Spencer E. Cahill and Robin Eggleston, "Managing Emotions in Public: The Case of Wheelchair Users," *Social Psychology Quarterly* 57, no. 4 (1994): 300–312.
40. Carol J. Gill explains the experiential divide between disabled and nondisabled in this way: "A significant part of the disability experience centers on disabled persons' tireless efforts to set the record straight and to reestablish their real identities." In so doing, they demonstrate "their impressive industry in bridging the divide between their self-views and public perceptions of them, between their inner and outer worlds." Gill is careful to note, however, that there is no one "disability experience"—a point that is germane to seniors who may not be able to connect to the experiences of younger persons with disabilities. There are, she says, "various group, subgroup, and individual experiences." Gill, "Divided Understandings," 353.
41. Ibid., 352.
42. Ibid., 363–364, emphasis in original.
43. Lesley Chenoweth and Daniela Stehlik, "Implications of Social Capital for the Inclusion of People with Disabilities and Families in Community Life," *International Journal of Inclusive Education* 8, no. 1 (2004): 59–72.
44. Christa Van Kraayenoord, "The Media's Portrayal of Mothers with Disabilities," *International Journal of Disability, Development and Education* 49, no. 3 (2002): 221–224.
45. See Paul K. Longmore, *Why I Burned My Book and Other Essays on Disability* (Temple University Press, 2003).
46. Harlan Hahn, "The Politics of Physical Differences: Disability and Discrimination," *Journal of Social Issues* 44, no. 1 (1988): 39–47.
47. There are promising interactions between the Disability and Society and the Aging and the Life Course sections of the American Sociological Association reflected in shared program sessions in recent years.
48. Renée Rose Shield, *Uneasy Endings: Daily Life in an American Nursing Home* (Cornell University Press, 1988), 21–22.
49. As Renée Rose Shield puts it, "In transition between adulthood and death, the nursing home resident is perceived as 'other'—neither adult nor dead." These elders will not return to their homes, yet they are not prepared for death, and Shield observes the paradox that "instead of enabling the resident to prepare for death, the nursing home setting shushes the entire subject of death." It is this condition of lacking a direction between the points of "what is" to "what should be" that pres-

ents a fundamental challenge to the subjective experience of life in a kind of limbo—and this is why "the nursing home existence has an unreal, timeless quality to it." Ibid.

50. Barbara G. Myerhoff, *Number Our Days: A Triumph of Continuity and Culture Among Jewish Old People in an Urban Ghetto* (Simon and Schuster, 1980).

51. Ibid., 74.

52. The observation appears in Book VIII, Chapter 4, of Johann Wolfgang van Goethe's *Wilhelm Meister's Apprenticeship*. Viktor E. Frankl quotes Goethe's "remark" twice (using slightly different wording) and describes it as "the finest maxim for any kind of psychotherapy." See Viktor Emil Frankl, *The Doctor and the Soul: From Psychotherapy to Logotherapy,* 3rd ed., trans. Richard Winston and Clara Winston (Vintage Books, 1986), 8.

Bibliography

AARP. "Family Caregivers Provide Staggering $470 Billion in Unpaid Care According to AARP Study." AARP, July 16, 2015. www.aarp.org/about-aarp/press-center /info-07-2015/family-caregivers-provide-470-billion-in-unpaid-care-aarp-study .html.

Ablon, Joan. "Stigmatized Health Conditions." *Social Science and Medicine. Part B: Medical Anthropology* 15, no. 1 (1981): 5–9.

Abramson, Corey M. *The End Game.* Harvard University Press, 2015.

Achenbaum, W. Andrew. *Crossing Frontiers: Gerontology Emerges as a Science.* Cambridge University Press, 1995.

———. *Old Age in a New Land: The American Experience Since 1790.* Johns Hopkins University Press, 1978.

Administration of Community Living. *Title III—Grants for State and Community Programs on Aging.* August 25, 2016. https://acl.gov/About_ACL/Allocations /docs/OAA/T3-2016.pdf.

Agich, George J. *Autonomy and Long-Term Care.* Oxford University Press, 1993.

———. *Dependence and Autonomy in Old Age: An Ethical Framework for Long-Term Care.* Cambridge University Press, 2003.

Albrecht, Gary L. *The Disability Business: Rehabilitation in America.* Sage, 1992.

Albrecht, Gary L., Katherine D. Seelman, and Michael Bury. *Handbook of Disability Studies.* Sage, 2001.

Alterra, Aaron. *The Caregiver: A Life with Alzheimer's.* Cornell University Press/ILR Press, 2007.

Altman, Barbara, and Sharon Barnartt. *Environmental Contexts and Disability,* vol. 8. Emerald Group, 2014.

Altman, Irwin. *The Environment and Social Behavior: Privacy, Personal Space, Territory, and Crowding.* Brooks/Cole, 1975.

Angelelli, Joseph, Vincent Mor, Orna Intrator, Zhanlian Feng, and Jacqueline Zinn. "Oversight of Nursing Homes: Pruning the Tree or Just Spotting Bad Apples?" *The Gerontologist* 43, Suppl. 2 (2003): 67–75.

Atchley, Robert C. "Continuity, Spiritual Growth, and Coping in Later Adulthood." *Journal of Religion, Spirituality and Aging* 18, nos. 2–3 (2006): 19–29.

———. "Continuity Theory, Self, and Social Structure." In *The Self and Society in Aging Processes,* edited by Carol D. Ryff and Victor W. Marshall, 94–121. Springer, 1999.

Baker, Dana Lee. *The Politics of Neurodiversity: Why Public Policy Matters.* Lynne Rienner, 2011.

Ballenger, Jesse F. *Self, Senility, and Alzheimer's Disease in Modern America: A History.* Johns Hopkins University Press, 2006.

Baltes, Margret M. *The Many Faces of Dependency in Old Age.* Cambridge University Press, 1996.

Baltes, Paul B., and Margret M. Baltes. "Psychological Perspectives on Successful Aging: The Model of Selective Optimization with Compensation." *Successful Aging: Perspectives from the Behavioral Sciences* 1, no. 1 (1990): 1–34.

Baltes, Paul B., and Jacqui Smith. "New Frontiers in the Future of Aging: From Successful Aging of the Young Old to the Dilemmas of the Fourth Age." *Gerontology* 49, no. 2 (2003): 123–135.

Baynton, Douglas C. *Forbidden Signs: American Culture and the Campaign Against Sign Language.* University of Chicago Press, 1996.

Becker, Ernest. *The Denial of Death.* Free Press, 1997.

Bengtson, Vern L., Glen H. Elder Jr., and Norella M. Putney. "The Life Course Perspective on Ageing: Linked Lives, Timing, and History." In *Adult Lives: A Life Course Perspective*, 9–17. University of Chicago Press, 2012.

Bennett, Clifford. *Nursing Home Life: What It Is and What It Could Be.* Tiresias Press, 1980.

Bennett, Ruth, and Lucille Nahemow. "Institutional Totality and Criteria of Social Adjustment in Residences for the Aged." *Journal of Social Issues* 21, no. 4 (1965): 44–78.

Ben-Shlomo, Yoav, and Diana Kuh. "A Life Course Approach to Chronic Disease Epidemiology: Conceptual Models, Empirical Challenges and Interdisciplinary Perspectives." *International Journal of Epidemiology* 31, no. 2 (2002): 285–293.

Berger, Ronald J. *Introducing Disability Studies.* Lynne Rienner, 2013.

Berkman, Lisa F. "The Changing and Heterogeneous Nature of Aging and Longevity: A Social and Biomedical Perspective." In *Annual Review of Gerontology and Geriatrics*, 37–68. Springer, 1988.

Berkowitz, Edward D. *Disabled Policy: America's Programs for the Handicapped: A Twentieth Century Fund Report.* Cambridge University Press, 1989.

Berman, Phillip L. *The Courage to Grow Old.* Ballantine Books, 1989.

Bigby, JudyAnn. *Cross-Cultural Medicine.* ACP Press, 2003.

Binstock, Robert H. "Aging and the Future of American Politics." *Annals of the American Academy of Political and Social Science* 415, no. 1 (1974): 199–212.

———. "The Emergence of the Oldest Old: Challenges for Public Policy." In *The Future of Age-Based Public Policy*, edited by Robert B. Hudson. Johns Hopkins University Press, 1997.

———. "From the Great Society to the Aging Society—25 Years of the Older Americans Act." *Generations* 15, no. 3 (1991): 11–18.

———. "Interest-Group Liberalism and the Politics of Aging." *The Gerontologist* 12, no. 3, Pt. 1 (1972): 265–280.

———. "Old-Age Policies, Politics, and Ageism." *Generations* 29, no. 3 (2005): 73–78.

———. "The War on 'Anti-Aging Medicine.'" *The Gerontologist* 43, no. 1 (2003): 4–14.

Binstock, Robert H., and Linda K. George, with Stephen J. Cutler, Jon Hendricks, and James H. Schulz. *Handbook of Aging and the Social Sciences*, 7th ed. Elsevier/Academic Press, 2011.

Binstock, Robert H., and Jeff Kahana. "Setting Limits: Medical Goals in an Aging Society." *The Gerontologist* 28, no. 3 (1988): 424–426

Binstock, Robert H., and Ethel Shanas, with Vern L. Bengtson, George L. Maddox, and Dorothy Wedderburn. *Handbook of Aging and the Social Sciences.* Van Nostrand Reinhold, 1976.

Birren, James E. *Handbook of Aging and the Individual.* University of Chicago Press, 1959.

Black, Helen K., and Robert L. Rubinstein. "Themes of Suffering in Later Life." *Journals of Gerontology Series B: Psychological Sciences and Social Sciences* 59, no. 1 (2004): S17–S24.

Blair-Loy, Mary, and Amy S. Wharton. "Employees' Use of Work-Family Policies and the Workplace Social Context." *Social Forces* 80, no. 3 (2002): 813–845.

Blanck, Peter David. *Employment, Disability, and the Americans with Disabilities Act: Issues in Law, Public Policy, and Research.* Northwestern University Press, 2000.

Boerner, Kathrin. "Adaptation to Disability Among Middle-Aged and Older Adults: The Role of Assimilative and Accommodative Coping." *Journals of Gerontology Series B: Psychological Sciences and Social Sciences* 59, no. 1 (2004): P35–P42.

Borawski, Elaine A., Jennifer M. Kinney, and Eva Kahana. "The Meaning of Older Adults' Health Appraisals: Congruence with Health Status and Determinant of Mortality." *Journals of Gerontology Series B: Psychological Sciences and Social Sciences* 51, no. 3 (1996): S157–S170.

Bould, Sally, Beverly Sanborn, and Laura Reif. *Eighty-five Plus: The Oldest Old.* Wadsworth, 1989.

Bowling, Ann. "Enhancing Later Life: How Older People Perceive Active Ageing?" *Aging and Mental Health* 12, no. 3 (2008): 293–301.

Breen, Leonard Z. "The Aging Individual." In *Handbook of Social Gerontology: Societal Aspects of Aging,* edited by Clark Tibbitts, 381–388. University of Chicago Press, 1960.

Breznitz, Shlomo. *The Denial of Stress.* International Universities Press, 1983.

Brittis, SaraJane. "Sharing Destinies: Staff and Residents' Perspectives on Excellence in High Quality Nursing Homes in London, England and New York City, USA." Dissertation, Case Western Reserve University, 1996.

Burnett, John J., and Heather Bender Baker. "Assessing the Travel-Related Behaviors of the Mobility-Disabled Consumer." *Journal of Travel Research* 40, no. 1 (2001): 4–11.

Butler, Robert N. *The Longevity Revolution: The Benefits and Challenges of Living a Long Life.* PublicAffairs, 2010.

———. *Why Survive? Growing Old in America.* Harper and Row, 1975.

Butz, William P., and Barbara Boyle Torrey. "Some Frontiers in Social Science." *Science* 312, no. 5782 (2006): 1898–1900.

Cahill, Spencer E., and Robin Eggleston. "Managing Emotions in Public: The Case of Wheelchair Users." *Social Psychology Quarterly* 57 (1994): 300–312.

———. "Reconsidering the Stigma of Physical Disability." *Sociological Quarterly* 36, no. 4 (1995): 681–698.

Calasanti, Toni M. "Bringing in Diversity: Toward an Inclusive Theory of Retirement." *Journal of Aging Studies* 7, no. 2 (1993): 133–150.

Camp, Cameron J., Jiska Cohen-Mansfield, and Elizabeth A. Capezuti. "Mental Health Services in Nursing Homes: Use of Nonpharmacologic Interventions Among Nursing Home Residents with Dementia." *Psychiatric Services* 53, no. 11 (2002): 1397–1404.

Campbell, Andrea Louise. *How Policies Make Citizens: Senior Political Activism and the American Welfare State.* Princeton University Press, 2003.

————. "Self-Interest, Social Security, and the Distinctive Participation Patterns of Senior Citizens." *American Political Science Review* 96, no. 3 (2002): 565–574.

Cappon, Lester J. *The Adams-Jefferson Letters: The Complete Correspondence Between Thomas Jefferson and Abigail and John Adams.* UNC Press Books, 2012.

Carstensen, Laura L. "Social and Emotional Patterns in Adulthood: Support for Socioemotional Selectivity Theory." *Psychology and Aging* 7, no. 3 (1992): 331–338.

Casado, Banghwa Lee, Kimberly S. van Vulpen, and Stacey L. Davis. "Unmet Needs for Home and Community-Based Services Among Frail Older Americans and Their Caregivers." *Journal of Aging and Health* 23, no. 3 (2011): 529–553.

Centers for Medicare and Medicaid Services. *Medicaid Expenditures for Long-Term Services and Supports (LTSS) in FY 2014: Managed LTSS Reached 15 Percent of LTSS Spending.* 2016. https://www.medicaid.gov/medicaid/ltss/downloads /ltss-expenditures-2014.pdf.

Charmaz, Kathy. *Good Days, Bad Days: The Self in Chronic Illness and Time.* Rutgers University Press, 1991.

Chenoweth, Lesley, and Daniela Stehlik. "Implications of Social Capital for the Inclusion of People with Disabilities and Families in Community Life." *International Journal of Inclusive Education* 8, no. 1 (2004): 59–72.

Clarke, Laura Hurd, and Alexandra Korotchenko. "Aging and the Body: A Review." *Canadian Journal on Aging/La Revue Canadienne Du Vieillissement* 30, no. 3 (2011): 495–510.

Clarke, Philippa, and Sandra E. Black. "Quality of Life Following Stroke: Negotiating Disability, Identity, and Resources." *Journal of Applied Gerontology* 24, no. 4 (2005): 319–336.

Cohen, Elias S. "The Elderly Mystique: Constraints on the Autonomy of the Elderly with Disabilities." *The Gerontologist* 28, Suppl. (1988): 24–31.

————. "The Last 2000 Days." *The Gerontologist* 57, no. 1 (2017): 116–120.

————. "Social, Economic, and Political Realities of Cross-Network Partnerships and Coalitions." In *Aging and Disability: Crossing Network Lines,* edited by Michelle Putnam, 91–160. Springer, 2007.

Cohen, Gene D. *The Creative Age: Awakening Human Potential in the Second Half of Life.* Harper Collins, 2001.

Cohen, Gene D., Susan Perlstein, Jeff Chapline, Jeanne Kelly, Kimberly M. Firth, and Samuel Simmens. "The Impact of Professionally Conducted Cultural Programs on the Physical Health, Mental Health, and Social Functioning of Older Adults." *The Gerontologist* 46, no. 6 (2006): 726–734.

Cohen-Mansfield, Jiska, and Perla Werner. "The Effects of an Enhanced Environment on Nursing Home Residents Who Pace." *The Gerontologist* 38, no. 2 (1998): 199–208.

Cole, Thomas R. *The Journey of Life: A Cultural History of Aging in America.* Cambridge University Press, 1992.

————. "The Prophecy of *Senescence:* G. Stanley Hall and the Reconstruction of Old Age in America." *The Gerontologist* 24, no. 4 (1984): 360–366.

Cottrell Jr., L. S. "Adjustment of the Individual to Age/Sex Roles." *American Sociological Review* 7 (1942): 617–620.

Cox, Carole B. *Social Policy for an Aging Society: A Human Rights Perspective.* Springer, 2015.

Crenshaw, Kimberlé. "Demarginalizing the Intersection of Race and Sex: A Black Feminist Critique of Antidiscrimination Doctrine, Feminist Theory and Antiracist Politics." *University of Chicago Legal Forum* 140 (1989): 139–167.

Crimmins, Eileen M., Yasuhiko Saito, and Dominique Ingegneri. "Trends in Disability-Free Life Expectancy in the United States, 1970–90." *Population and Development Review* 23, no. 3 (1997): 555–572.

Crockett, Jean B., and James M. Kauffman. *The Least Restrictive Environment: Its Origins and Interpretations in Special Education.* Routledge, 2013.

Crosnoe, Robert, and Glen H. Elder. "Successful Adaptation in the Later Years: A Life Course Approach to Aging." *Social Psychology Quarterly* 65, no. 4 (2002): 309–328.

Cumming, Elaine, and William Earl Henry. *Growing Old, the Process of Disengagement.* Basic Books, 1961.

Dannefer, Dale. "Age, the Life Course, and the Sociological Imagination: Prospects for Theory." In *Handbook of Aging and the Social Sciences*, 7th ed., edited by Robert H. Binstock and Linda K. George, 3–16. Springer, 2011.

———. "Cumulative Advantage/Disadvantage and the Life Course: Cross-Fertilizing Age and Social Science Theory." *Journals of Gerontology Series B: Psychological Sciences and Social Sciences* 58, no. 6 (2003): S327–S337.

Darling, Rosalyn Benjamin. *Disability and Identity: Negotiating Self in a Changing Society.* Lynne Rienner, 2013.

———. "Toward a Model of Changing Disability Identities: A Proposed Typology and Research Agenda." *Disability and Society* 18, no. 7 (2003): 881–895.

Darling, Rosalyn B., and D. Alex Heckert. "Orientations Toward Disability: Differences over the Lifecourse." *International Journal of Disability, Development and Education* 57, no. 2 (2010): 131–143.

Dassel, Kara Bottiggi. "Aging and Parkinson's Disease: Personal Identification, Embodiment, and Experience with a Degenerative Disease." *The Gerontologist* 49, no. 5 (2009): 720–723.

Davis, Karen, Stephen C. Schoenbaum, and Anne-Marie Audet. "A 2020 Vision of Patient-Centered Primary Care." *Journal of General Internal Medicine* 20, no. 10 (2005): 953–957.

DeFriese, Gordon H., and Marcia G. Ory. *Self Care in Later Life: Research, Program, and Policy Issues.* Springer, 1998.

Dembo, Tamara, Gloria Ladieu Leviton, and Beatrice A. Wright. "Adjustment to Misfortune: A Problem of Social-Psychological Rehabilitation." *Artificial Limbs* 32, no. 2 (1956): 4–62.

Demiris, George, Marilyn J. Rantz, Myra A. Aud, Karen D. Marek, Harry W. Tyrer, Marjorie Skubic, and Ali A. Hussam, "Older Adults' Attitudes Towards and Perceptions of 'Smart Home' Technologies: A Pilot Study." *Medical Informatics and the Internet in Medicine* 29, no. 2 (2004): 87–94.

Denton, Margaret. "The Linkages Between Informal and Formal Care of the Elderly." *Canadian Journal on Aging/La Revue Canadienne Du Vieillissement* 16, no. 1 (1997): 30–50.

Diamond, Timothy. *Making Gray Gold: Narratives of Nursing Home Care.* University of Chicago Press, 2009.

Dillaway, Heather E., and Mary Byrnes. "Reconsidering Successful Aging: A Call for Renewed and Expanded Academic Critiques and Conceptualizations." *Journal of Applied Gerontology* 28, no. 6 (2009): 702–722.

Dittmann-Kohli, Freya. "The Construction of Meaning in Old Age: Possibilities and Constraints." *Ageing and Society* 10, no. 3 (1990): 279–294.

Dixon, Guy, Everard W. Thornton, and Carolyn A. Young. "Perceptions of Self-Efficacy and Rehabilitation Among Neurologically Disabled Adults." *Clinical Rehabilitation* 21, no. 3 (2007): 230–240.

Dowd, James J., and Vern L. Bengtson. "Aging in Minority Populations an Examination of the Double Jeopardy Hypothesis." *Journal of Gerontology* 33, no. 3 (1978): 427–436.
Drews, Wolfgang, and Christiane Schemer. "eTourism for All? Online Travel Planning of Disabled People." In *Information and Communication Technologies in Tourism 2010,* edited by Ulrike Gretzel, Rob Law, and Marrhias Fuchs, 507–518. Springer, 2010.
Elder, Glen H., Jr., Monica Kirkpatrick Johnson, and Robert Crosnoe. "The Emergence and Development of Life Course Theory." In *Handbook of the Life Course,* edited by Jeylan T. Mortimer and Michael J. Shanahan, 3–19. Springer, 2003.
Ellis, Carolyn. *Revision: Autoethnographic Reflections on Life and Work.* Routledge, 2009.
Emlet, Charles A., Shakima Tozay, and Victoria H. Raveis. "'I'm Not Going to Die from the AIDS': Resilience in Aging with HIV Disease." *The Gerontologist* 51, no. 1 (2010): 101–111.
Epp, Jake. "Achieving Health for All: A Framework for Health Promotion." Canada Ministry of Supply and Services, 1987.
Erikson, Erik H. *Childhood and Society.* Norton, 1950.
Erikson, Erik H., and Joan M. Erikson. *The Life Cycle Completed,* extended version. Norton, 1997.
Estes, Carroll L. *The Aging Enterprise.* Jossey-Bass, 1979.
Estes, Carroll L., and Karen W. Linkins. "Devolution and Aging Policy: Racing to the Bottom in Long-Term Care." *International Journal of Health Services* 27, no. 3 (1997): 427–442.
Estes, Carroll L., and James H. Swan. *The Long Term Care Crisis: Elders Trapped in the No-Care Zone.* Sage, 1993.
Evans, Denis A., Paul A. Scherr, Nancy R. Cook, Marilyn S. Albert, H. H. Funkenstein, Laurel A. Beckett, Liesi E. Hebert, et al. "The Impact of Alzheimer's Disease in the United States Population." In *The Oldest Old,* edited by Richard Suzman, David P. Willis, and Kenneth G. Manton, 283–299. Oxford University Press, 1992.
Falvo, Donna. *Medical and Psychosocial Aspects of Chronic Illness and Disability.* Jones and Bartlett, 2013.
Fausset, Cara Bailey, Andrew J. Kelly, Wendy A. Rogers, and Arthur D. Fisk. "Challenges to Aging in Place: Understanding Home Maintenance Difficulties." *Journal of Housing for the Elderly* 25, no. 2 (2011): 125–141.
Feifel, Herman. *The Meaning of Death.* McGraw-Hill, 1965.
Ferraro, Kenneth F. "Health and Aging." In *Handbook of Aging and the Social Sciences,* 6th ed., edited by Robert H. Binstock and Linda K. George, 238–256. Springer, 2006.
Ferraro, Kenneth F., and Melissa M. Farmer. "Double Jeopardy, Aging as Leveler, or Persistent Health Inequality? A Longitudinal Analysis of White and Black Americans." *Journals of Gerontology Series B: Psychological Sciences and Social Sciences* 51, no. 6 (1996): S319–S328.
Ferrell, Bruce A., Betty R. Ferrell, and Lynne Rivera, "Pain in Cognitively Impaired Nursing Home Patients." *Journal of Pain and Symptom Management* 10, no. 8 (1995): 591–598.
Fillenbaum, Gerda G., and Michael A. Smyer. "The Development, Validity, and Reliability of the OARS Multidimensional Functional Assessment Questionnaire." *Journal of Gerontology* 36, no. 4 (1981): 428–434.
Fisk, Arthur D., Wendy A. Rogers, Neil Charness, Sara J. Czaja, and Joseph Sharit.

Designing for Older Adults: Principles and Creative Human Factors Approaches, 2nd ed. CRC Press, 2009.

Force, Lawrence, Jeffrey S. Kahana, and Valerie Capalbo. "The Role of AAAs in Promoting Health for Seniors: A Preliminary Research Report." *Open Longevity Science* 4 (2010): 30–35.

Forlin, Chris, Graham Douglas, and John Hattie. "Inclusive Practices: How Accepting Are Teachers?" *International Journal of Disability, Development and Education* 43, no. 2 (1996): 119–133.

Fortinsky, Richard H. "Coordinated, Comprehensive Community Care and the Older Americans Act." *Generations* 15, no. 3 (1991): 39–42.

Fortinsky, Richard H., and Murna Downs. "Optimizing Person-Centered Transitions in the Dementia Journey: A Comparison of National Dementia Strategies." *Health Affairs* 33, no. 4 (2014): 566–573.

Fox, Renee C. "The Medicalization and Demedicalization of American Society." *Daedalus* 106, no. 1 (1977): 9–22.

Frank, Arthur W. "Reclaiming an Orphan Genre: The First-Person Narrative of Illness." *Literature and Medicine* 13, no. 1 (1994): 1–21.

Frankl, Viktor Emil. *The Doctor and the Soul: From Psychotherapy to Logotherapy,* 3rd ed., translated by Richard Winston and Clara Winston. Vintage Books, 1986.

Freedman, Vicki A. "Disability, Functioning, and Aging." In *Handbook of Aging and the Social Sciences,* 7th ed., edited by Robert H. Binstock and Linda K. George, with Stephen J. Cutler, Jon Hendricks, and James H. Shulz, 57–71. Elsevier/Academic Press, 2011.

Freedman, Vicki A., Linda G. Martin, Robert F. Schoeni, and Jennifer C. Cornman. "Declines in Late-Life Disability: The Role of Early- and Mid-Life Factors." *Social Science and Medicine* 66, no. 7 (2008): 1588–1602.

Freidson, Eliot. "Client Control and Medical Practice." *American Journal of Sociology* 65, no. 4 (1960): 374–382.

Fried, Linda P., Luigi Ferrucci, Jonathan Darer, Jeff D. Williamson, and Gerard Anderson. "Untangling the Concepts of Disability, Frailty, and Comorbidity: Implications for Improved Targeting and Care." *Journals of Gerontology Series A: Biological Sciences and Medical Sciences* 59, no. 3 (2004): M255–M263.

Friedemann, Marie-Luise, Rhonda J. Montgomery, Clementine Rice, and Linda Farrell. "Family Involvement in the Nursing Home." *Western Journal of Nursing Research* 21, no. 4 (1999): 549–567.

Friedman, Howard, and Leslie R. Martin. *The Longevity Project: Surprising Discoveries for Health and Long Life from the Landmark Eight-Decade Study.* Hay House, 2011.

Friedman, Lawrence M. *A History of American Law,* 3rd ed. Simon and Schuster, 2005.

Fries, J. F. "Aging, Natural Death, and the Compression of Morbidity." *New England Journal of Medicine* 303 (1980): 130–135.

Garland-Thomson, Rosemarie. "Disability Studies: A Field Emerged." *American Quarterly* 65, no. 4 (2013): 915–926.

Gaugler, Joseph E., K. A. Anderson, Steven H. Zarit, and Leonard I. Pearlin. "Family Involvement in Nursing Homes: Effects on Stress and Well-Being." *Aging and Mental Health* 8, no. 1 (2004): 65–75.

Gaugler, Joseph E., Leonard I. Pearlin, and Steven H. Zarit. "Family Involvement Following Institutionalization: Modeling Nursing Home Visits over Time." *International Journal of Aging and Human Development* 57, no. 2 (2003): 91–117.

Gawande, Atul. *Being Mortal: Medicine and What Matters in the End.* Macmillan, 2014.

Gelfand, Donald E. *The Aging Network: Programs and Services.* Springer, 2006.

George, Linda K., and Kenneth Ferraro. *Handbook of Aging and the Social Sciences,* 8th ed. Academic Press, 2015.

George, Linda K., and George L. Maddox. "Social and Behavioral Aspects of Institutional Care." In *Ageing and Health Care: Social and Policy Perspectives,* edited by Marcia Ory and Kathleen Bond. Routledge, 1989.

George, Linda K., and Frank. J. Whittington. "Well-Being in the Oldest of Old: An Oxymoron? No!" *The Gerontologist* 52, no. 6 (2012): 871–875.

Gignac, Monique A. M., Cheryl Cott, and Elizabeth M. Badley. "Adaptation to Chronic Illness and Disability and Its Relationship to Perceptions of Independence and Dependence." *Journals of Gerontology Series B: Psychological Sciences and Social Sciences* 55, no. 6 (2000): P362–P372.

Gilbert, Clare, and Allen Foster. "Childhood Blindness in the Context of VISION 2020: The Right to Sight." *Bulletin of the World Health Organization* 79, no. 3 (2001): 227–232.

Gill, Carol J. "Divided Understandings: The Social Experience of Disability." In *Handbook of Disability Studies,* edited by Gary L. Albrecht, Katherine D. Seelman, and Michael Bury. Sage, 2001.

Gill, Thomas M., Evelyne A. Gahbauer, Ling Han, and Heather G. Allore. "Trajectories of Disability in the Last Year of Life." *New England Journal of Medicine* 362, no. 13 (2010): 1173–1180.

Gill, Thomas M., Susan E. Hardy, and Christianna S. Williams. "Underestimation of Disability in Community-Living Older Persons." *Journal of the American Geriatrics Society* 50, no. 9 (2002): 1492–1497.

Gilleard, Chris, and Paul Higgs. "Frailty, Disability and Old Age: A Re-appraisal." *Health* 15, no. 5 (2010): 475–490.

Gillick, Muriel R. "Medicare Coverage for Technological Innovations—Time for New Criteria?" *New England Journal of Medicine* 350, no. 21 (2004): 2199–2201.

Gitlin, Laura N. "Conducting Research on Home Environments: Lessons Learned and New Directions." *The Gerontologist* 43, no. 5 (2003): 628–637.

Gitlin, Laura N., Laraine Winter, Mary Corcoran, Marie P. Dennis, Sandy Schinfeld, and Walter W. Hauck. "Effects of the Home Environmental Skill-Building Program on the Caregiver–Care Recipient Dyad: 6-Month Outcomes from the Philadelphia REACH Initiative." *The Gerontologist* 43, no. 4 (2003): 532–546.

Gitlin, Laura N., Laraine Winter, Marie P. Dennis, Mary Corcoran, Sandy Schinfeld, and Walter W. Hauck. "A Randomized Trial of a Multicomponent Home Intervention to Reduce Functional Difficulties in Older Adults." *Journal of the American Geriatrics Society* 54, no. 5 (2006): 809–816.

Goffman, Erving. *Asylums: Essays on the Social Situation of Mental Patients and Other Inmates.* Anchor, 1961.

———. *Behavior in Public Place.* Free Press, 1963.

———. *The Presentation of Self in Everyday Life.* Anchor, 1959.

———. *Stigma: Notes on the Management of Spoiled Identity.* Simon and Schuster, 1963.

Golant, Stephen M. "Aging in Place Solutions for Older Americans: Groupthink Responses Not Always in Their Best Interests." *Public Policy and Aging Report* 19, no. 1 (2009): 1–39.

———. *Aging in the Right Place.* Health Professions Press, 2015.

————. "The Changing Residential Environments of Older People." In *Handbook of Aging and the Social Sciences,* 7th ed., 207–220. Academic, 2011.

————. "Commentary: Irrational Exuberance for the Aging in Place of Vulnerable Low-Income Older Homeowners." *Journal of Aging and Social Policy* 20, no. 4 (2008): 379–392.

————. "Conceptualizing Time and Behavior in Environmental Gerontology: A Pair of Old Issues Deserving New Thought." *The Gerontologist* 43, no. 5 (2003): 628–637.

Gold, Deborah T. "Late-Life Death and Dying in 21st-Century America." In *Handbook of Aging and the Social Sciences,* 7th ed., 235–247. Academic, 2011.

Gordon, Chad, Charles M. Gaitz, and Judith Scott. "Leisure and Lives: Personal Expressivity Across the Life Span." In *Handbook of Aging and the Social Sciences,* edited by Robert H. Binstock and Ethel Shanas, 310–341. Van Nostrand Reinhold, 1976.

Gran, Judith, Max Lapertosa, and Ruthie Beckwith. *Olmstead: Reclaiming Institutionalized Lives for the National Council on Disability.* National Council on Disability, 2003.

Granbom, Marianne, Ines Himmelsbach, Maria Haak, Charlotte Löfqvist, Frank Oswald, and Susanne Iwarsson. "Residential Normalcy and Environmental Experiences of Very Old People: Changes in Residential Reasoning over Time." *Journal of Aging Studies* 29 (2014): 9–19.

Green, Sara E. "Convergent Caregiving: Exploring Eldercare in Families of Children with Disabilities." *Journal of Loss and Trauma* 18, no. 4 (2013): 289–305.

Green, Sara, Christine Davis, Elana Karshmer, Pete Marsh, and Benjamin Straight. "Living Stigma: The Impact of Labeling, Stereotyping, Separation, Status Loss, and Discrimination in the Lives of Individuals with Disabilities and Their Families." *Sociological Inquiry* 75, no. 2 (2005): 197–215.

Gretzel, Ulrike, and Kyung Hyan Yoo. "Use and Impact of Online Travel Reviews." In *Information and Communication Technologies in Tourism 2008,* 35–46. Springer, 2008.

Gubrium, Jaber F. *Late Life: Communities and Environmental Policy.* Charles C. Thomas, 1974.

————. *Living and Dying at Murray Manor.* University of Virginia Press, 2012.

————. "Perspective and Story in Nursing Home Ethnography." In *The Culture of Long Term Care: Nursing Home Ethnography,* edited by J. Neil Henderson and Maria D. Vesperi, 23–36. Bergin and Garvey, 1995.

————. *The Social Worlds of Old Age.* Cambridge University Press, 2005.

————. *Speaking of Life: Horizons of Meaning for Nursing Home Residents.* Transaction, 1993.

Guimarães, Renato Maia. "Health Capital, Life Course and Ageing." *Gerontology* 53, no. 2 (2007): 96–101.

Hagestad, Gunhild O., and Bernice L. Neugarten. "Age and the Life Course." In *Handbook of Aging and the Social Sciences,* 7th ed. 35–61. Van Nostrand Reinhold, 1985.

Hahn, Harlan. "Antidiscrimination Laws and Social Research on Disability: The Minority Group Perspective." *Behavioral Sciences and the Law* 14, no. 1 (1996): 41–59.

————. "Introduction: 'Disability Policy and the Problem of Discrimination.'" *American Behavioral Scientist* 28, no. 3 (1985): 293–294.

————. "The Politics of Physical Differences: Disability and Discrimination." *Journal of Social Issues* 44, no. 1 (1988): 39–47.

Haight, Barbara K., Yvonne Michel, and Shirley Hendrix. "The Extended Effects of the Life Review in Nursing Home Residents." *International Journal of Aging and Human Development* 50, no. 2 (2000): 151–168.

Hall, Granville Stanley. *Senescence: The Last Half of Life.* Appleton, 1922.

Hankin, Benjamin L., and John R. Z. Abela. *Development of Psychopathology: A Vulnerability-Stress Perspective.* Sage, 2005.

Harel, Zev, Phyllis Ehrlich, and Richard Hubbard. *The Vulnerable Aged: People, Services, and Policies.* Springer, 1990.

Hareven, Tamara K. *Family Time and Industrial Time: The Relationship Between the Family and Work in a New England Industrial Community.* Cambridge University Press, 1982.

————. "The History of the Family and the Complexity of Social Change." *American Historical Review* 96, no. 1 (1991): 95–124.

————. "The Last Stage: Historical Adulthood and Old Age." *Daedalus* 105, no. 4 (1976): 13–27.

Hartig, Terry, Florian G. Kaiser, and Peter A. Bowler. *Further Development of a Measure of Perceived Environmental Restorativeness.* Institutet för bostadsforskning, 1997.

Haug, Marie R., and Bebe Lavin. "Practitioner or Patient—Who's in Charge?" *Journal of Health and Social Behavior* 22, no. 3 (1981): 212–229.

Hayward, Mark D., and Bridget K. Gorman. "The Long Arm of Childhood: The Influence of Early-Life Social Conditions on Men's Mortality." *Demography* 41, no. 1 (2004): 87–107.

He, Wan, and Luke J. Larsen. "Older Americans with a Disability: 2008–2012." US Census Bureau, American Community Survey Reports. US Government Printing Office, 2014.

Heckhausen, Jutta, and Richard Schulz. "A Life-Span Theory of Control." *Psychological Review* 102, no. 2 (1995): 284.

Heller, Tamar, and Sarah K. Parker Harris. *Disability Through the Life Course.* Sage, 2011.

Helman, Cecil. *Culture, Health and Illness.* CRC Press, 2007.

Henderson, J. Neil. "The Culture of Care in a Nursing Home: Effects of a Medicalized Model of Long-Term Care." In *The Culture of Long-Term Care: Nursing Home Ethnography,* 37–54. Greenwood, 1995.

Henderson, J. Neil, and Maria D. Vesperi. *The Culture of Long Term Care: Nursing Home Ethnography.* Greenwood, 1995.

Henry, Jules. "Culture Against Man." *Science and Society* 29, no. 1 (1965): 116–121.

Henry, William E. "The Theory of Intrinsic Disengagement." In *Age with a Future.* Davis, 1964.

Herbert, Blumer. *Perspective and Method.* Prentice Hall, 1969.

Herd, Pamela, Stephanie A. Robert, and James S. House. "Health Disparities Among Older Adults: Life Course Influences and Policy Solutions." In *Handbook of Aging and the Social Sciences,* 7th ed., edited by Robert H. Binstock and Linda K. George. Academic Press, 2011.

Holstein, Martha B., and Meredith Minkler. "Self, Society, and the 'New Gerontology.'" *The Gerontologist* 43, no. 6 (2003): 787–796.

Horowitz, A., J. P. Reinhardt, and K. Boerner. "The Effect of Rehabilitation on Depression Among Visually Disabled Older Adults." *Aging and Mental Health* 9, no. 6 (2005): 563–570.

House, James S., Karl R. Landis, Debra Umberson, et al. "Social Relationships and Health." *Science* 241, no. 4865 (1988): 540–545.

Howe, Neil, and William Strauss. *Millennials Rising: The Next Great Generation.* Vintage Books, 2009.

Howse, Kenneth, Shah Ebrahim, and Rachael Gooberman-Hill. "Help-Avoidance: Why Older People Do Not Always Seek Help." *Reviews in Clinical Gerontology* 14, no. 1 (2004): 63–70.

Hudson, Robert B. *The Future of Age-Based Public Policy.* Johns Hopkins University Press, 1997.

———. "Politics and Policies of Aging in the United States." In *Handbook of Aging and the Social Sciences,* 8th ed., edited by Linda George and Kenneth Ferraro. Academic Press, 2015.

Hughes, Thomas Parke. *Networks of Power: Electrification in Western Society, 1880–1930.* Johns Hopkins University Press, 1993.

Hurd, Laura C. "'We're Not Old!': Older Women's Negotiation of Aging and Oldness." *Journal of Aging Studies* 13, no. 4 (2000): 419–439.

Idler, Ellen L., and Stanislav V. Kasl. "Self-Ratings of Health: Do They Also Predict Change in Functional Ability?" *Journals of Gerontology Series B: Psychological Sciences and Social Sciences* 50, no. 6 (1995): S344–S353.

Idler, Ellen L., Louise B. Russell, and Diane Davis. "Survival, Functional Limitations, and Self-Rated Health in the NHANES I Epidemiologic Follow-Up Study, 1992." *American Journal of Epidemiology* 152, no. 9 (2000): 874–883.

Iezzoni, Lisa I., and Vicki A. Freedman. "Turning the Disability Tide: The Importance of Definitions." *JAMA* 299, no. 3 (2008): 332–334.

Jaeger, Paul T. *Disability and the Internet: Confronting a Digital Divide.* Lynne Rienner, 2012.

Jefferson, Thomas, and J. Jefferson Looney. *The Papers of Thomas Jefferson, Retirement Series,* vol. 7: *28 November 1813 to 30 September 1814,* edited by J. Jefferson Looney. Princeton University Press, 2011.

Jeppsson Grassman, Eva, Lotta Holme, Annika Taghizadeh Larsson, and Anna Whitaker. "A Long Life with a Particular Signature: Life Course and Aging for People with Disabilities." *Journal of Gerontological Social Work* 55, no. 2 (2012): 95–111.

Jette, Alan M., and Julie J. Keysor. "Disability Models: Implications for Arthritis Exercise and Physical Activity Interventions." *Arthritis Care and Research* 49, no. 1 (2003): 114–120.

Johnson, Malcolm. "Dependency and Interdependency." In *Ageing in Society: An Introduction to Social Gerontology,* 2nd ed., edited by John Bond, Peter G. Coleman, and Sheila Peace. Sage, 1993.

Johnson, Malcolm L., with Vern L. Bengtson, Peter G. Coleman, and Thomas B. L. Kirkwood. *The Cambridge Handbook of Age and Ageing.* Cambridge University Press, 2005.

Johnson, Nan E. "The Racial Crossover in Comorbidity, Disability, and Mortality." *Demography* 37, no. 3 (2000): 267–283.

Kahana, Boaz, Zev Harel, and Eva Kahana. *Holocaust Survivors and Immigrants: Late Life Adaptations.* Springer Science and Business Media, 2007.

Kahana, Boaz, and Eva Kahana. "Changes in Mental Status of Elderly Patients in Age-Integrated and Age-Segregated Hospital Milieus." *Journal of Abnormal Psychology* 75, no. 2 (1970): 177.

Kahana, Eva. "Dreams of Hot Toast and Smiling Nurses: Toward a Model of Patient-Responsive Care in Nursing Homes." In *Research in the Sociology of Health Care,* edited by Jennie Jacobs Kronenfeld, 109. Emerald, 2006.

———. "Emerging Issues in Institutional Services for the Aging." *The Gerontologist* 11, no. 1, Pt. 1 (1971): 51–58.

———. "The Humane Treatment of Old People in Institutions." *The Gerontologist* 13, no. 3, Pt. 1 (1973): 282–289.

———. "Matching Environments to Needs of the Aged: A Conceptual Scheme." In *Late Life: Communities and Environmental Policy,* edited by Jaber F. Gubrium, 201–214. Charles C. Thomas, 1974.

Kahana, Eva, Tirth Bhatta, Loren D. Lovegreen, and Boaz Kahana. "Altruism, Helping, and Volunteering: Pathways to Well-Being in Late Life." *Journal of Aging and Health* 25, no. 1 (2013): 159–187.

Kahana, Eva, David E. Biegel, and May Wykle. *Family Caregiving Across the Lifespan,* vol. 4. Sage, 1994.

Kahana, Eva, and Rodney M. Coe. "Self and Staff Conceptions of Institutionalized Aged." *The Gerontologist* 9, no. 4, Pt. 1 (1969): 264–267.

Kahana, Eva, and Boaz Kahana. "Baby Boomers' Expectations of Health and Medicine." *Medicine and Society* 16 (2014): 380–384.

———. "Conceptual and Empirical Advances in Understanding Aging Well Through Proactive Adaptation." In *Adulthood and Aging: Research on Continuities and Discontinuities,* edited by Vern L. Bengtson, 18–40. Springer, 1996.

———. "Contextualizing Successful Aging: New Directions in an Age-Old Search." In *Invitation to the Life Course: A New Look at Old Age,* edited by Richard A. Settersten, Jr., 225–255. Baywood, 2003.

———. "Effects of Age Segregation on Affective Expression of Elderly Psychiatric Patients." *American Journal of Orthopsychiatry* 38, no. 2 (1968): 317.

———. "On Being a Proactive Health Care Consumer: Making an 'Unresponsive' System Work for You." In *Changing Consumers and Changing Technology in Health Care and Health Care Delivery,* 21–44. Emerald, 2001.

———. "Patient Proactivity Enhancing Doctor-Patient-Family Communication in Cancer Prevention and Care Among the Aged." *Patient Education and Counseling* 50, no. 1 (2003): 67–73.

Kahana, Eva, Boaz Kahana, H. Chirayath, D. Biegel, and A. Blum. "Innovations in Institutional Care from a Patient-Responsive Perspective." In *Innovations in Practice and Service Delivery Across the Lifespan,* edited by David E. Biegel, 249–275. Oxford University Press, 1999.

Kahana, Eva, Boaz Kahana, D. Dannefer, and C. Phillipson. "Stress and Agentic Aging: A Targeted Cancer Adaptation Model." In *The Sage Handbook of Social Gerontology,* edited by Dale Dannefer and Chris Phillipson, 280–293. Sage, 2010.

Kahana, Eva, Boaz Kahana, and Kyle Kercher. "Emerging Lifestyles and Proactive Options for Successful Ageing." *Ageing International* 28, no. 2 (2003): 155–180.

Kahana, Eva, Boaz Kahana, and Jennifer Kinney. "Coping Among Vulnerable Elders." In *The Vulnerable Aged: People, Services and Policies,* edited by Zev Harel, Phylllis Ehrlich, and Richard Hubbard, 64–85. Springer, 1990.

Kahana, Eva, Boaz Kahana, and Jeong Eun Lee. "Proactive Approaches to Successful Aging: One Clear Path Through the Forest." *Gerontology* 60, no. 5 (2014): 466–474.

Kahana, Eva, Boaz Kahana, Loren Lovegreen, Jeffrey Kahana, Jane Brown, and Diana Kulle. "Health-Care Consumerism and Access to Health Care: Educating Elders to Improve Both Preventive and End-of-Life Care." In *Access to Care and Factors That Impact Access: Patients as Partners in Care and Changing Roles of Health Providers,* edited by Jennie Jacobs Kronenfeld, 173–193. Emerald, 2011.

Kahana, Eva, Boaz Kahana, and May Wykle. "'Care-Getting': A Conceptual Model of Marshalling Support Near the End of Life." *Current Aging Science* 3, no. 1 (2010): 71–78.

Kahana, Eva, Boaz Kahana, May Wykle, and Diana Kulle. "Marshalling Social Support: Active Roles in Care-Getting for Cancer Patients Throughout the Life Course." *Journal of Family Social Work* 12 (2009): 168–193.

Kahana, Eva, Jessica Kelley-Moore, and Boaz Kahana. "Proactive Aging: A Longitudinal Study of Stress, Resources, Agency, and Well-Being in Late Life." *Aging and Mental Health* 16, no. 4 (2012): 438–451.

———. "Social Dimensions of Late Life Disability." In *Aging Well: Gerontological Education for Nurses and Other Health Care Professionals,* edited by May L. Wykle and Sarah H. Gueldner, 457–468. Jones & Bartlett, 2011.

Kahana, Eva, Renee H. Lawrence, Boaz Kahana, Kyle Kercher, Amy Wisniewski, Eleanor Stoller, Jordan Tobin, and Kurt Stange. "Long-Term Impact of Preventive Proactivity on Quality of Life of the Old-Old." *Psychosomatic Medicine* 64, no. 3 (2002): 382–394.

Kahana, Eva, Jeong Eun Lee, Jeffrey Kahana, Timothy Goler, Boaz Kahana, Sarah Shick, Erin Burk, and Kaitlyn Barnes. "Childhood Autism and Proactive Family Coping: Intergenerational Perspectives." *Journal of Intergenerational Relationships* 13, no. 2 (2015): 150–166.

Kahana, Eva, Jersey Liang, and Barbara J. Felton. "Alternative Models of Person-Environment Fit: Prediction of Morale in Three Homes for the Aged." *Journal of Gerontology* 35, no. 4 (1980): 584–595.

Kahana, Eva, Loren Lovegreen, and Boaz Kahana. "Long-Term Care: Tradition and Innovation." In *Handbook of Sociology of Aging,* 583–602. Springer, 2011.

Kahana, Eva, Mary Segall, James L. Vosmik, Boaz Kahana, and Kathryn P. Riley. "Motivators, Resources and Barriers in Voluntary International Migration of the Elderly: The Case of Israel-Bound Aged." *Journal of Cross-Cultural Gerontology* 1, no. 2 (1986): 191–208.

Kahana, Eva, Kurt Stange, Rebecca Meehan, and Lauren Raff. "Forced Disruption in Continuity of Primary Care: The Patients' Perspective." *Sociological Focus* 30, no. 2 (1997): 177–187.

Kahana, Eva, and Rosalie Young. "Clarifying the Caregiving Paradigm: Challenges for the Future." In *Aging and Caregiving: Theory and Practice,* edited by David E. Biegel and Arthur Blum, 76–96. Sage, 1990.

Kahana, Jeffrey S. "Reevaluating the Nursing Home Ombudsman's Role with a View Toward Expanding the Concept of Dispute Resolution." *Journal of Dispute Resolution* (1994): 217–233.

Kahana, Jeffrey S., Loren D. Lovegreen, and Eva Kahana. *Expanding the Time Frame for Advance Care Planning: Policy Considerations and Implications for Research.* In *Geriatrics.* InTech, 2012.

Kalish, Richard A. "Death and Dying in a Social Context." In *Handbook of Aging and the Social Sciences,* edited by Robert H. Binstock and Ethel Shanas, 483–507. Van Nostrand Reinhold, 1976.

———. *Death, Dying, Transcending,* vol. 3. Baywood, 1980.

———. *Death, Grief, and Caring Relationships.* Brooks/Cole, 1981.

Kane, Rosalie A., Robert L. Kane, and Richard C. Ladd. *The Heart of Long Term Care.* Oxford University Press, 1998.

Karp, David A. *Speaking of Sadness: Depression, Disconnection, and the Meanings of Illness.* Oxford University Press, 1996.

Kastenbaum, Robert J. *Death, Society, and Human Experience.* Routledge, 2015.

———. "New Thoughts on Old Age." *American Journal of the Medical Sciences* 249, no. 5 (1965): 609.

Katz, Jeanne, Caroline Holland, and Sheila Peace. "Hearing the Voices of People with High Support Needs." *Journal of Aging Studies* 27, no. 1 (2013): 52–60.

Katz, Sidney, Amasa B. Ford, Roland W. Moskowitz, Beverly A. Jackson, and Marjorie W. Jaffe. "Studies of Illness in the Aged: The Index of ADL—A Standardized Measure of Biological and Psychosocial Function." *JAMA* 185, no. 12 (1963): 914–919.

Kaye, Judy, and Senthil Kumar Raghavan. "Spirituality in Disability and Illness." *Journal of Religion and Health* 41, no. 3 (2002): 231–242.

Kayser-Jones, Jeanie, Ellen Schell, William Lyons, Alison E. Kris, Joyce Chan, and Renee L. Beard. "Factors that Influence End-of-Life Care in Nursing Homes: The Physical Environment, Inadequate Staffing, and Lack of Supervision." *The Gerontologist* 43, Suppl. 2 (2003): 76–84.

Kellett, U. M. "Searching for New Possibilities to Care: A Qualitative Analysis of Family Caring Involvement in Nursing Homes." *Nursing Inquiry* 6, no. 1 (1999): 9–16.

Kelley-Moore, Jessica. "Disability and Ageing: The Social Construction of Causality." In *The Sage Handbook of Social Gerontology,* edited by Dale Dannefer and Chris Phillipson, 96–110. Sage, 2010.

Kelley-Moore, Jessica A., and Kenneth F. Ferraro. "The Black/White Disability Gap: Persistent Inequality in Later Life?" *Journals of Gerontology Series B: Psychological Sciences and Social Sciences* 59, no. 1 (2004): S34–S43.

Kelley-Moore, Jessica A., John G. Schumacher, Eva Kahana, and Boaz Kahana. "When Do Older Adults Become 'Disabled'? Social and Health Antecedents of Perceived Disability in a Panel Study of the Oldest Old." *Journal of Health and Social Behavior* 47, no. 2 (2006): 126–141.

Kemp, Bryan J., and Laura Mosqueda. *Aging with a Disability: What the Clinician Needs to Know.* Taylor and Francis, 2004.

Kemper, Peter. "The Use of Formal and Informal Home Care by the Disabled Elderly." *Health Services Research* 27, no. 4 (1992): 421.

Kennedy, Craig H., Robert H. Horner, and J. Stephen Newton. "Social Contacts of Adults with Severe Disabilities Living in the Community: A Descriptive Analysis of Relationship Patterns." *Research and Practice for Persons with Severe Disabilities* 14, no. 3 (1989): 190–196.

Kim, Jinyoung, and Richard Miech. "The Black-White Difference in Age Trajectories of Functional Health over the Life Course." *Social Science and Medicine* 68, no. 4 (2009): 717–725.

Kleinman, Arthur. *The Illness Narratives: Suffering, Healing, and the Human Condition.* Basic Books, 1988.

———. *What Really Matters: Living a Moral Life Amidst Uncertainty and Danger.* Oxford University Press, 2006.

Klinenberg, Eric. *Heat Wave: A Social Autopsy of Disaster in Chicago.* University of Chicago Press, 2015.

Krause, Neal. "Social Relationships in Late Life." In *Handbook of Aging and the Social Sciences,* 6th ed., edited by Robert H. Binstock and Linda K. George, 181–200. Academic, 2006.

Krebs, David E., Donna Moxley Scarborough, and Chris A. McGibbon. "Functional vs. Strength Training in Disabled Elderly Outpatients." *American Journal of Physical Medicine and Rehabilitation* 86, no. 2 (2007): 93–103.

Kudlick, Catherine J. "Disability History: Why We Need Another 'Other.'" *American Historical Review* 108, no. 3 (2003): 763–793.

Kunkel, Suzanne R., and Robert A. Applebaum. "Estimating the Prevalence of Long-Term Disability for an Aging Society." *Journal of Gerontology* 47, no. 5 (1992): S253–S260.

Kutner, Nancy G., and Donna J. Brogan. "Assisted Survival, Aging, and Rehabilitation Needs: Comparison of Older Dialysis Patients and Age-Matched Peers." *Archives of Physical Medicine and Rehabilatation* 73, no. 4 (1992): 309–315.

Kutza, Elizabeth A., and Sharon M. Keigher. "The Elderly 'New Homeless': An Emerging Population at Risk." *Social Work* 36, no. 4 (1991): 288–293.

Land, Kenneth C., and Yang. "Morbidity, Disability, and Mortality." In *Handbook of Aging and the Social Sciences,* 6th ed., edited by Robert H. Binstock and Linda K. George, 41–58. Academic, 2006.

Lane, Harlan. *When the Mind Hears: A History of the Deaf.* Random House, 1984.

Langlois, Jean A., Stefania Maggi, Tamara Harris, Eleanor M. Simonsick, Luigi Ferrucci, Mara Pavan, Leonardo Sartori, and Giuliano Enzi. "Self-Report of Difficulty in Performing Functional Activities Identifies a Broad Range of Disability in Old Age." *Journal of the American Geriatrics Society* 44, no. 12 (1996): 1421–1428.

Lawrence, Renee H., and Alan M. Jette. "Disentangling the Disablement Process." *Journals of Gerontology Series B: Psychological Sciences and Social Sciences* 51, no. 4 (1996): S173–S182.

Lawton, George. *New Goals for Old Age.* Columbia University Press, 1945.

Lawton, M. Powell. "Aging and Performance of Home Tasks." *Human Factors* 32, no. 5 (1990): 527–536.

———. "Environment and Other Determinants of Well-Being in Older People." *The Gerontologist* 23, no. 4 (1983): 349–357.

———. "Environmental Proactivity and Affect in Older People." In *The Social Psychology of Aging,* edited by S. Spacapan and S. Oskamp, 135–163. Sage, 1989.

———. "Residential Environment and Self-Directedness Among Older People." *American Psychologist* 45, no. 5 (1990): 638.

Lawton, M. Powell, and Lucille Nahemow. "Ecology and the Aging Process." In *The Psychology of Adult Development and Ageing.* Edited by Carl Eisdorfer and Lawton M. Powell. American Psychological Association, 1973.

Lawton, M. Powell, Paul G. Windley, and Thomas O. Byerts. *Competence, Environmental Press, and the Adaptations of Older People.* Springer, 1982.

Laz, Cheryl. "Age Embodied." *Journal of Aging Studies* 17, no. 4 (2003): 503–519.

Lebowitz, Barry D., Enid Light, and Frank Bailey. "Mental Health Center Services for the Elderly: The Impact of Coordination with Area Agencies on Aging." *The Gerontologist* 27, no. 6 (1987): 699–702.

Leiter, Valerie. "Bowling Together: Foundations of Community Among Youth with Disabilities." *Disability and Community,* edited by Allison C. Carey and Richard K. Scotch, 3–25, Research in Social Science and Disability. Emerald, 2011.

Lemon, Bruce W., Vern L. Bengtson, and James A. Peterson. "An Exploration of the Activity Theory of Aging: Activity Types and Life Satisfaction Among In-Movers to a Retirement Community." *Journal of Gerontology* 27, no. 4 (1972): 511–523.

Leon, Carlos F. Mendes de, Thomas A. Glass, and Lisa F. Berkman. "Social Engagement and Disability in a Community Population of Older Adults in the New Haven EPESE." *American Journal of Epidemiology* 157, no. 7 (2003): 633–642.

Levy-Storms, Lené, and Dana Miller-Martinez. "Family Caregiver Involvement and Satisfaction with Institutional Care During the 1st Year After Admission." *Journal of Applied Gerontology* 24, no. 2 (2005): 160–174.

Lewis-Beck, Michael S., et al. *The American Voter Revisited.* University of Michigan Press, 2008.

Liao, Youlian, Daniel L. McGee, Guichan Cao, and Richard S. Cooper. "Black-White Differences in Disability and Morbidity in the Last Years of Life." *American Journal of Epidemiology* 149, no. 12 (1999): 1097–1103.

Link, Bruce G., and Jo Phelan. "Social Conditions as Fundamental Causes of Disease." *Journal of Health and Social Behavior* 35, spec. issue (1995): 80–94.

Linton, Ralph. "Age and Sex Categories." *American Sociological Review* 7 (1942): 589–603.

Litvak, Simi, and Alexandra Enders. "Support Systems: The Interface Between Individuals and Environments." In *Handbook of Disability Studies,* edited by Gary L. Albrecht, Katherine D. Seelman, and Michael Bury, 711–733. Sage, 2001.

Litwin, Howard. "Social Relationships and Well-Being in Very Late Life." In *Understanding Well-Being in the Oldest Old,* edited by Leonard W. Poon and Jiska Cohen-Mansfield, 213–226. Cambridge University Press, 2011.

Livingston, Gill, Kate Johnston, Cornelius Katona, Joni Paton, Constantine G. Lyketsos, and Old Age Task Force of the World Federation of Biological Psychiatry. "Systematic Review of Psychological Approaches to the Management of Neuropsychiatric Symptoms of Dementia." *American Journal of Psychiatry* 162, no. 11 (2005): 1996–2021.

Loe, Meika. *Aging Our Way: Lessons for Living from 85 and Beyond.* Oxford University Press, 2011.

Longmore, Paul K. "Uncovering the Hidden History of People with Disabilities." *Reviews in American History* 15, no. 3 (1987): 355–364, http://www.jstor.org /stable/2702029.

Longmore, Paul K. *Why I Burned My Book and Other Essays on Disability.* Temple University Press, 2003.

Lovegreen, Loren D., Eva Kahana, and Boaz Kahana. "Residential Relocation of Amenity Migrants to Florida: 'Unpacking' Post-Amenity Moves." *Journal of Aging and Health* 22, no. 7 (2010): 1001–1028.

Luciani, Andrea, Gilda Ascione, Cecilia Bertuzzi, Desirè Marussi, Carla Codecà, Giuseppe Di Maria, Sarah Elisabetta Caldiera, et al. "Detecting Disabilities in Older Patients with Cancer: Comparison Between Comprehensive Geriatric Assessment and Vulnerable Elders Survey-13." *Journal of Clinical Oncology* 28, no. 12 (2010): 2046–2050.

Magaziner, Jay, Sheryl Itkin Zimmerman, K. M. Fox, and B. J. Burns. "Dementia in United States Nursing Homes: Descriptive Epidemiology and Implications for Long-Term Residential Care." *Aging and Mental Health* 2, no. 1 (1998): 28–35.

Mairs, Nancy. *Waist-High in the World: A Life Among the Nondisabled.* Beacon Press, 1996.

Manton, Kenneth G. "Past and Future Life Expectancy Increases at Later Ages: Their Implications for the Linkage of Chronic Morbidity, Disability, and Mortality." *Journal of Gerontology* 41, no. 5 (1986): 672–681.

Manton, Kenneth G., XiLiang Gu, and Gene R. Lowrimore. "Cohort Changes in Active Life Expectancy in the U.S. Elderly Population: Experience from the 1982–2004 National Long-Term Care Survey." *Journals of Gerontology Series B: Psychological Sciences and Social Sciences* 63, no. 5 (2008): S269–S281.

Manton, Kenneth G., and Beth J. Soldo. "Disability and Mortality Among the Oldest Old: Implications for Current and Future Health and Long-Term Care Service Needs." In *The Oldest Old,* edited by Richard M. Suzman and David P. Willis. Oxford University Press, 1992.

Marmot, Michael. *Status Syndrome: How Social Standing Directly Affects Your Health and Life Expectancy.* Bloomsbury, 2004.

Martin, Diane J., and Laura L. Gillen. "Revisiting Gerontology's Scrapbook: From Metchnikoff to the Spectrum Model of Aging." *The Gerontologist* 54, no. 1 (2014): 51–58.

Maslow, Abraham Harold. "A Theory of Human Motivation." *Psychological Review* 50, no. 4 (1943): 370–396.

Mayer, Karl Ulrich. "Handbook of the Life Course." Review of *Handbook of the Life Course,* edited by Jeylan T. Mortimer and Michael J. Shanahan. *Social Forces* 84, no. 4 (2006): 2364.

———. "New Directions in Life Course Research." *Annual Review of Sociology* 35 (2009): 413–433.

McCreadie, Claudine, and Anthea Tinker. "The Acceptability of Assistive Technology to Older People." *Ageing and Society* 25, no. 1 (2005): 91–110.

Mendes de Leon, Carlos F., Thomas A. Glass, and Lisa F. Berkman. "Social Engagement and Disability in a Community Population of Older Adults: The New Haven EPESE." *American Journal of Epidemiology* 157, no. 7 (2003): 633–642.

Messeri, Peter, Merril Silverstein, and Eugene Litwak. "Choosing Optimal Support Groups: A Review and Reformulation." *Journal of Health and Social Behavior* 34, no. 2 (1993): 122–137.

Meyerhoff, Barbara. "Number Our Days: A Triumph of Continuity and Culture Among Jewish Old People in an Urban Ghetto." *Work and Home (Im) Balance* 15 (1978): 16.

Minkler, Meredith, and Pamela Fadem. "'Successful Aging': A Disability Perspective." *Journal of Disability Policy Studies* 12, no. 4 (2002): 229–235.

Moberg, David O. "Research in Spirituality, Religion, and Aging." *Journal of Gerontological Social Work* 45, nos. 1–2 (2005): 11–40.

Moen, Phyllis, and Mary Ann Erickson. "Chapter 3 Decision-Making and Satisfaction with a Continuing Care Retirement Community." *Journal of Housing for the Elderly* 14, nos. 1–2 (2001): 53–69.

Moon, Marilyn. "Organization and Financing of Health Care." In *Handbook of Aging and the Social Sciences,* 7th ed., edited by Robert H. Binstock and Linda K. George, 295–307. Academic, 2011.

Moos, Rudolf H., and Jeanne A. Schaefer. "The Crisis of Physical Illness." In *Coping with Physical Illness,* 3–25. Springer, 1984.

Morris, Jenny. "Community Care or Independent Living?" In *Independent Lives?* edited by Jenny Morris, 147–172. Macmillan Education, 1993.

Morris, Robert, Robert H. Binstock, and Martin Rein. *Feasible Planning for Social Change.* Columbia University Press, 1966.

Mortimer, Jeylan T., and Michael J. Shanahan. *Handbook of the Life Course.* Springer, 2007.

Murphy, Nancy A., Becky Christian, Deidre A. Caplin, and Paul C. Young. "The Health of Caregivers for Children with Disabilities: Caregiver Perspectives." *Child: Care, Health and Development* 33, no. 2 (2007): 180–187.

Murphy, Robert Francis. *The Body Silent.* Norton, 1987.

Murray, Christopher J. L., Theo Vos, Rafael Lozano, Mohsen Naghavi, Abraham D. Flaxman, Catherine Michaud, Majid Ezzati, et al. "Disability-Adjusted Life Years (DALYs) for 291 Diseases and Injuries in 21 Regions, 1990–2010: A Systematic Analysis for the Global Burden of Disease Study 2010." *The Lancet* 380, no. 9859 (2013): 2197–2223.

Nagi, Saad Z. "Disability Concepts Revisited: Implications for Prevention." In *Disability in America: Toward a National Agenda for Prevention,* edited by the Committee on a National Agenda for the Prevention of Disabilities, 1991.

Nazir, Arif, Kathleen Unroe, Monica Tegeler, Babar Khan, Jose Azar, and Malaz Boustani. "Systematic Review of Interdisciplinary Interventions in Nursing Homes." *Journal of the American Medical Directors Association* 14, no. 7 (2013): 471–478.

Neugarten, Bernice L., and Gunhild O. Hagestad. "Age and the Life Course." In *Handbook of Aging and the Social Sciences,* edited by Robert H. Binstock and Ethel Shanas, with Vern L. Bengtson, George L. Maddox, and Dorothy Wedderburn. Van Nostrand Reinhold, 1976.

Neumann, Peter J., Sally S. Araki, and Elane M. Gutterman. "The Use of Proxy Respondents in Studies of Older Adults: Lessons, Challenges, and Opportunities." *Journal of the American Geriatrics Society* 48, no. 12 (2000): 1646–1654.

Nielsen, Kim E. *A Disability History of the United States,* vol. 2. Beacon Press, 2012.

Nimrod, Galit. "In Support of Innovation Theory: Innovation in Activity Patterns and Life Satisfaction Among Recently Retired Individuals." *Ageing and Society* 28, no. 6 (2008): 831–846.

Nimrod, Galit, and Arie Rotem. "Between Relaxation and Excitement: Activities and Benefits Gained in Retirees' Tourism." *International Journal of Tourism Research* 12, no. 1 (2010): 65–78.

Noelker, Linda S., and Zev Harel. *Linking Quality of Long-Term Care and Quality of Life.* Springer, 2000.

Nuland, Sherwin B. *How We Die: Reflections on Life's Final Chapter.* Vintage Books, 1994.

Odom, Samuel L., and Scott R. McConnell. *Social Competence of Young Children with Disabilities: Issues and Strategies for Intervention.* Paul H. Brookes, 1992.

O'Leary, Timothy J., Jean R. Slutsky, and Marie A. Bernard. "Comparative Effectiveness Research Priorities at Federal Agencies: The View from the Department of Veterans Affairs, National Institute on Aging, and Agency for Healthcare Research and Quality." *Journal of the American Geriatrics Society* 58, no. 6 (2010): 1187–1192.

Oliver, David, and Sally Tureman. *The Human Factor in Nursing Home Care.* Routledge, 2013.

Oliver, Michael. "Fundamental Principles of Disability." In *Understanding Disability: From Theory to Practice,* 19–29. St. Martin's Press, 1996.

———. "The Social Model in Action: If I Had a Hammer." In *Disabling Barriers— Enabling Environments,* 2nd ed., edited by John Swain, Sally French, Colin Barnes, and Carol Thomas, 7–12. Sage, 2004.

———. *The Politics of Disablement: Critical Texts in Social Work and the Welfare State.* Macmillan, 1990.

———. *The Politics of Disablement: A Sociological Approach.* St. Martin's Press, 1990.

———. *Understanding Disability: From Theory to Practice.* St. Martin's Press, 1996.

O'Rand, Angela M. "The Precious and the Precocious: Understanding Cumulative Disadvantage and Cumulative Advantage over the Life Course." *The Gerontologist* 36, no. 2 (1996): 230–238.

———. "Stratification and the Life Course: Life Course Capital, Life Course Risks, and Social Inequality." In *Handbook of Aging and the Social Sciences,* 6th ed., edited by Robert H. Binstock and Linda K. George. Academic Press, 2006.

Orelove, Fred P., Dick Sobsey, and Rosanne K. Silberman. *Educating Children with Multiple Disabilities: A Collaborative Approach.* ERIC, 2004.

Ornstein, Katherine A., Bruce Leff, Kenneth E. Covinsky, Christine S. Ritchie, Alex D. Federman, Laken Roberts, Amy S. Kelley, Albert L. Siu, and Sarah L.

Szanton. "Epidemiology of the Homebound Population in the United States." *JAMA Internal Medicine* 175, no. 7 (2015): 1180–1186.

O'Shaughnessy, Carol. "Aging and Disability Resource Centers (ADRCs): Federal and State Efforts to Guide Consumers Through the Long-Term Services and Supports Maze." Background Paper No. 81, National Health Policy Forum, Washington, DC, November 2010.

Oswald, Frank, and Hans-Werner Wahl. "Dimensions of the Meaning of Home in Later Life." In *Home and Identity in Late Life: International Perspectives,* edited by Graham D. Rowles and Habib Chaudhury. Springer, 2005.

Packer, Tanya L., Bob McKercher, and Matthew K. Yau. "Understanding the Complex Interplay Between Tourism, Disability and Environmental Contexts." *Disability and Rehabilitation* 29, no. 4 (2007): 281–292.

Palmore, Erdman Ballagh. *Normal Aging,* vol. 2: *Reports from the Duke Longitudinal Studies, 1970–1973.* Duke University Press, 1974.

Parr, Joyce, and Sara Green. "Systemic Characteristics of Long-Term Care in Residential Environments: Clinical Importance of Differences in Staff and Resident Perceptions." *Clinical Gerontologist* 25, nos. 1–2 (2003): 149–171.

Parsons, Talcott. "The Sick Role and the Role of the Physician Reconsidered." *Milbank Memorial Fund Quarterly: Health and Society* 53, no. 3 (1975): 257–278.

Pastelan, Leon, and D. Carson. *Spatial Behavior of Older People.* Institute of Gerontology, University of Michigan, 1970.

Pearlin, Leonard I. "The Sociological Study of Stress." *Journal of Health and Social Behavior* 30, no. 3 (1989): 241–256.

Perrin, James M. "Health Services Research for Children with Disabilities." *Milbank Quarterly* 80, no. 2 (2002): 303–324.

Phoenix, Cassandra, Brett Smith, and Andrew C. Sparkes. "Narrative Analysis in Aging Studies: A Typology for Consideration." *Journal of Aging Studies* 24, no. 1 (2010): 1–11.

Piachaud, David. "Disability, Retirement and Unemployment of Older Men." *Journal of Social Policy* 15, no. 2 (1986): 145–162.

Pollack, Otto, and Glen Heathers. "Social Adjustment in Old Age: A Research Planning Report." *Sociological Practice* 11, no. 1 (1993): 33–39.

Poon, Leonard W., and Jiska Cohen-Mansfield. *Understanding Well-Being in the Oldest Old.* Cambridge University Press, 2011.

Poon, Leonard W., Yuri Jang, S. G. Reynolds, and Erick McCarthy. "Profiles of the Oldest-Old." In *The Cambridge Handbook of Age and Ageing,* edited by Malcolm L. Johnson, 346–353. Cambridge University Press, 2005.

Poulshock, S. Walter, and Gary T. Deimling. "Families Caring for Elders in Residence: Issues in the Measurement of Burden." *Journal of Gerontology* 39, no. 2 (1984): 230–239.

Priestley, Mark. "Childhood Disability and Disabled Childhoods Agendas for Research." *Childhood* 5, no. 2 (1998): 207–223.

Pritchard, Jacki. *Male Victims of Elder Abuse: Their Experiences and Needs.* Jessica Kingsley, 2001.

Pursell, Carroll. *The Machine in America: A Social History of Technology.* Johns Hopkins University Press, 2007.

Putnam, Michelle. *Aging and Disability: Crossing Network Lines.* Springer, 2007.

———. "Conceptualizing Disability: Developing a Framework for Political Disability Identity." *Journal of Disability Policy Studies* 16, no. 3 (2005): 188–198.

————. "Moving from Separate to Crossing Aging and Disability Service Networks." In *Aging and Disability: Crossing Network Lines,* edited by Michelle Putnam, 5–16. Springer, 2007.

Rantanen, Taina, Erja Portegijs, Anne Viljanen, Johanna Eronen, Milla Saajanaho, Li-Tang Tsai, Markku Kauppinen, et al. "Individual and Environmental Factors Underlying Life Space of Older People—Study Protocol and Design of a Cohort Study on Life-Space Mobility in Old Age (LISPE)." *BMC Public Health* 12, no. 1 (2012): 1.

Reed, Christie M. "Travel Recommendations for Older Adults." *Clinics in Geriatric Medicine* 23, no. 3 (2007): 687–713.

Reinharz, Shulamit. *Observing the Observer: Understanding Our Selves in Field Research.* Oxford University Press, 2010.

Riddell, Sheila, and Nick Watson. *Disability, Culture and Identity.* Routledge, 2014.

Rier, David A. "The Patient's Experience of Illness." In *Handbook of Medical Sociology,* edited by Chloe E. Bird, Peter Conrad, Allen M. Fremont, and Stefan Timmermans, 163–178. Vanderbilt University Press, 2010.

Rosow, Irving. *Socialization to Old Age.* University of California Press, 1974.

Roszak, Theodore. *The Making of an Elder Culture: Reflections on the Future of America's Most Audacious Generation.* New Society, 2009.

Roulstone, Alan, and Simon Prideaux. *Understanding Disability Policy.* Policy Press, 2012.

Rowe, John W., and Robert L. Kahn. "Human Aging: Usual and Successful." *Science* 237, no. 4811 (1987): 143–149.

————. "Successful Aging." *The Gerontologist* 37, no. 4 (1997): 433–440.

————. *Successful Aging.* Random House, 1998.

Rowles, Graham D. "Evolving Images of Place in Aging and 'Aging in Place.'" *Generations* 17, no. 2 (1993): 65–70.

Rowles, Graham D., and Habib Chaudhury. *Home and Identity in Late Life: International Perspectives.* Springer, 2005.

Ruff, George E. *Aging and Rehabilitation: Advances in the State of the Art,* Vol. 1. Springer, 1986.

Russell, Heather, and Peter E. Foreman. "Maintaining a Relationship with a Family Member in a Nursing Home: The Role of Visitor." *Journal of Family Studies* 8, no. 2 (2002): 147–164.

Ryan, Richard M., and Edward L. Deci. "Self-Determination Theory and the Facilitation of Intrinsic Motivation, Social Development, and Well-Being." *American Psychologist* 55, no. 1 (2000): 68–78.

Savishinsky, Joel S. *Breaking the Watch: The Meanings of Retirement in America.* Cornell University Press, 2000.

————. *The Ends of Time: Life and Work in a Nursing Home.* Praeger, 1991.

Schafer, Markus H., and Tetyana Pylypiv Shippee. "Age Identity in Context: Stress and the Subjective Side of Aging." *Social Psychology Quarterly* 73, no. 3 (2010): 245–264.

Schwabbauer, M. L. "Use of the Latent Image Technique to Develop and Evaluate Problem-Solving Skills." *American Journal of Medical Technology* 41, no. 12 (1975): 457–462.

Scotch, Richard K. "Disability Policy: An Eclectic Overview." *Journal of Disability Policy Studies* 11, no. 1 (2000): 6–11.

————. *From Good Will to Civil Rights: Transforming Federal Disability Policy.* Temple University Press, 2009.

Scotch, Richard K., and Kay Schriner. "Disability as Human Variation: Implications for Policy." *ANNALS of the American Academy of Political and Social Science* 549, no. 1 (1997): 148–159.

Scott-Maxwell, Florida. *The Measure of My Days*. Knopf, 1968.

Seplaki, Christopher L., Emily M. Agree, Carlos O. Weiss, Sarah L. Szanton, Karen Bandeen-Roche, and Linda P. Fried. "Assistive Devices in Context: Cross-Sectional Association Between Challenges in the Home Environment and Use of Assistive Devices for Mobility." *The Gerontologist* 54, no. 4 (2014).

Settersten Jr., Richard A. "Aging and the Life Course" In *Handbook of Aging and the Social Sciences,* 6th ed., edited by Robert H. Binstock and Linda K. George. Academic Press, 2006.

———. "Linking the Two Ends of Life: What Gerontology Can Learn from Childhood Studies." *Journals of Gerontology Series B: Psychological Sciences and Social Sciences* 60, no. 4 (2005): S173–S180.

Settersten Jr., Richard A., and Jon Hendricks. *Invitation to the Life Course: Toward New Understandings of Later Life*. Baywood, 2003.

Seymour, Wendy. *Remaking the Body: Rehabilitation and Change*. Routledge, 1998.

———. "Time and the Body: Re-embodying Time in Disability." *Journal of Occupational Science* 9, no. 3 (2002): 135–142.

Shakespeare, Tom. *Disability Rights and Wrongs*. Taylor and Francis, 2007.

———. *Disability Rights and Wrongs Revisited*. Routledge, 2013.

———. "Disability Studies Today and Tomorrow." *Sociology of Health and Illness* 27, no. 1 (2005): 138–148.

Shanas, Ethel. *The Health of Older People: A Social Survey*. Harvard University Press, 1962.

Shanas, Ethel, and George L. Maddox. "Aging, Health, and the Organization of Health Resources." In *Handbook of Aging and the Social Sciences,* edited by Robert H. Binstock and Ethel Shanas, 592–618. Van Nostrand Reinhold, 1976.

Shapiro, Joseph P. *No Pity: People with Disabilities Forging a New Civil Rights Movement*. Three Rivers Press, 1994.

Sheets, Debra. "Aging with Disabilities: Ageism and More." *Generations* 29, no. 3 (2005): 37–41.

Sherry, Mark. *Disability Hate Crimes: Does Anyone Really Hate Disabled People?* Ashgate, 2010.

———. "Overlaps and Contradictions Between Queer Theory and Disability Studies." *Disability and Society* 19, no. 7 (2004): 769–783.

———. "A Sociology of Impairment." *Disability and Society* 31, no. 6 (2016): 729–744.

Shield, Renée Rose. *Uneasy Endings: Daily Life in an American Nursing Home*. Cornell University Press, 1988.

Shock, Nathan Wetherill. *Aging: Some Social and Biological Aspects*. Association for the Advancement of Science, 1960.

———. *Trends in Gerontology*. Stanford University Press, 1951.

Shuey, Kim M., and Andrea E. Willson. "Cumulative Disadvantage and Black-White Disparities in Life-Course Health Trajectories." *Research on Aging* 30, no. 2 (2008): 200–225.

Shumway-Cook, Anne, Marcia A. Ciol, Kathryn M. Yorkston, Jeanne M. Hoffman, and Leighton Chan. "Mobility Limitations in the Medicare Population: Prevalence and Sociodemographic and Clinical Correlates." *Journal of the American Geriatrics Society* 53, no. 7 (2005): 1217–1221.

Simkin, Penny. "Birth Plans: After 25 Years, Women Still Want to Be Heard." *Birth* 34, no. 1 (2007): 49–51.

Simon-Rusinowitz, Lori, and Brian F. Hofland. "Adopting a Disability Approach to Home Care Services for Older Adults." *The Gerontologist* 33, no. 2 (1993): 159–167.

Solé-Auró, Aïda, Hiram Beltrán-Sánchez, and Eileen M. Crimmins. "Are Differences in Disability-Free Life Expectancy by Gender, Race, and Education Widening at Older Ages?" *Population Research and Policy Review* 34, no. 1 (2014): 1–18.

Solimeo, Samantha. *With Shaking Hands: Aging with Parkinson's Disease in America's Heartland.* Rutgers University Press, 2009.

Spillman, Brenda C., and Liliana E. Pezzin. "Potential and Active Family Caregivers: Changing Networks and the 'Sandwich Generation.'" *Milbank Quarterly* 78, no. 3 (2000): 347–374.

Starr, Paul. *The Social Transformation of American Medicine.* Basic Books, 1982.

Stewart, Moira. *Patient-Centered Medicine: Transforming the Clinical Method.* Radcliffe, 2003.

Stone, Deborah A. *The Disabled State.* Temple University Press, 1986.

———. *The Samaritan's Dilemma: Should Government Help Your Neighbor?* Nation Books, 2008.

Stone, Robyn I. "The Direct Care Worker: The Third Rail of Home Care Policy." *Annual Review of Public Health* 25 (2004): 521–537.

Stone, Robyn, Gail Lee Cafferata, and Judith Sangl. "Caregivers of the Frail Elderly: A National Profile." *The Gerontologist* 27, no. 5 (1987): 616–626.

Stone, Robyn I., and Pamela Farley Short. "The Competing Demands of Employment and Informal Caregiving to Disabled Elders." *Medical Care* 28 (1990): 513–526.

Strauss, William, and Neil Howe. *Generations: The History of America's Future, 1584 to 2069.* William Morrow, 1991.

Teresi, Jeanne A., Douglas Holmes, and Marcia G. Ory. "The Therapeutic Design of Environments for People with Dementia: Further Reflections and Recent Findings from the National Institute on Aging Collaborative Studies of Dementia Special Care Units." *The Gerontologist* 40, no. 4 (2000): 417–421.

Tibbitts, Clark. *Handbook of Social Gerontology: Societal Aspects of Aging.* University of Chicago Press, 1960.

Titchkosky, Tanya. *The Question of Access: Disability, Space, Meaning.* University of Toronto Press, 2011.

Tobin, Sheldon S. *Preservation of the Self in the Oldest Years: With Implications for Practice.* Springer, 1999.

Tornatore, Jane B., and Leslie A. Grant. "Family Caregiver Satisfaction with the Nursing Home After Placement of a Relative with Dementia." *Journals of Gerontology Series B: Psychological Sciences and Social Sciences* 59, no. 2 (2004): S80–S88.

Torres-Gil, Fernando M. *The New Aging: Politics and Change in America.* Auburn House, 1992.

Trouillet, Raphaël, Kamel Gana, Marcel Lourel, and Isabelle Fort. "Predictive Value of Age for Coping: The Role of Self-Efficacy, Social Support Satisfaction and Perceived Stress." *Aging and Mental Health* 13, no. 3 (2009): 357–366.

Ulicny, Gary R., Glen W. White, Barbara Bradford, and R. Mark Mathews. "Consumer Exploitation by Attendants: How Often Does It Happen and Can Anything Be Done About It?" *Rehabilitation Counseling Bulletin* 33, no. 3 (1990): 240–246.

Umberson, Debra, and Jennifer Karas Montez. "Social Relationships and Health: A Flashpoint for Health Policy." *Journal of Health and Social Behavior* 51, no. 1 (2010): S54–S66.

U.S. Department of Health and Human Services. "Summary Health Statistics: National Health Interview Survey, 2014." 2014. https://ftp.cdc.gov/pub/Health _Statistics/NCHS/NHIS/SHS/2014_SHS_Table_A-10.pdf.

Van Kraayenoord, Christa. "The Media's Portrayal of Mothers with Disabilities." *International Journal of Disability, Development and Education* 49, no. 3 (2002): 221–224.

Vasunilashorn, Sarinnapha, Bernard A. Steinman, Phoebe S. Liebig, and Jon Pynoos. "Aging in Place: Evolution of a Research Topic Whose Time Has Come." *Journal of Aging Research* (2012).

Verbrugge, Lois M. "Survival Curves, Prevalence Rates, and Dark Matters Therein." *Journal of Aging and Health* 3, no. 2 (1991): 217–236.

Verbrugge, Lois M., and Alan M. Jette. "The Disablement Process." *Social Science and Medicine* 38, no. 1 (1994): 1–14.

Verbrugge, Lois M., Kenzie Latham, and Philippa J. Clarke. "Aging with Disability for Midlife and Older Adults." *Research on Aging*, Special Issue (2017): 1–37.

Vermeire, Katrien, Jan P. L. Brokx, Floris L. Wuyts, Ellen Cochet, Anouk Hofkens, and Paul H. Van de Heyning. "Quality-of-Life Benefit from Cochlear Implantation in the Elderly." *Otology and Neurotology* 26, no. 2 (2005): 188–195.

Victor, Christina. "The Epidemiology of Ageing." In *The Cambridge Handbook of Age and Ageing*, edited by Malcolm L. Johnson, with Vern L. Bengtson, Peter G. Coleman, and Thomas B. L. Kirkwood. Cambridge University Press, 2005.

Vladeck, Bruce C. *Unloving Care: The Nursing Home Tragedy.* Basic, 1980.

Wahl, Hans-Werner, Agneta Fänge, Frank Oswald, Laura N. Gitlin, and Susanne Iwarsson. "The Home Environment and Disability-Related Outcomes in Aging Individuals: What Is the Empirical Evidence?" *The Gerontologist* 49, no. 3 (2009): 355–367.

Wahl, Hans-Werner, Susanne Iwarsson, and Frank Oswald. "Aging Well and the Environment: Toward an Integrative Model and Research Agenda for the Future." *The Gerontologist* 52, no. 3 (2012): 306–316.

Watson, Nick. "Theorising the Lives of Disabled Children: How Can Disability Theory Help?" *Children and Society* 26, no. 3 (2012): 192–202.

———. "Well, I Know This Is Going to Sound Very Strange to You, but I Don't See Myself as a Disabled Person: Identity and Disability." *Disability and Society* 17, no. 5 (2002): 509–527.

Weiner, Audrey S., and Judah L. Ronch. *Culture Change in Long-Term Care.* Routledge, 2003.

White, Patience H. "Access to Health Care: Health Insurance Considerations for Young Adults with Special Health Care Needs/Disabilities." *Pediatrics* 110, no. 6, Pt. 2 (2002): 1328–1335.

Whittier, Stephanie, Andrew Scharlach, and Teresa S. Dal Santo. "Availability of Caregiver Support Services: Implications for Implementation of the National Family Caregiver Support Program." *Journal of Aging and Social Policy* 17, no. 1 (2005): 45–62.

Whittington, Frank J. "Well-Being of the Oldest Old: An Oxymoron? No!" Review of *Understanding Well-Being in the Oldest Old,* edited by Leonard W. Poon and Jiska Cohen-Mansfield. *The Gerontologist* 52, no. 6 (2012): 871–880.

Wiles, Janine L., Annette Leibing, Nancy Guberman, Jeanne Reeve, and Ruth E. S. Allen. "The Meaning of 'Ageing in Place' to Older People." *The Gerontologist* 52, no. 3 (2011): 357–366.

Williams, David R., and Pamela Braboy Jackson. "Social Sources of Racial Disparities in Health." *Health Affairs* 24, no. 2 (2005): 325–334.

Wilson, Laura. *Civic Engagement and the Baby Boomer Generation: Research, Policy, and Practice Perspectives.* Routledge, 2006.

Wolf, Douglas. "Late-Life Disability Trends and Trajectories." In *Handbook of Aging and the Social Sciences,* 8th ed., edited by Linda George and Kenneth Ferraro. Academic Press, 2016.

Wolinsky, Fredric D. *Health and Health Behavior Among Elderly Americans: An Age-Stratification Perspective.* Springer, 1990.

Wolinsky, Fredric D., Douglas K. Miller, Elena M. Andresen, Theodore K. Malmstrom, and J. Philip Miller. "Further Evidence for the Importance of Subclinical Functional Limitation and Subclinical Disability Assessment in Gerontology and Geriatrics." *Journals of Gerontology Series B: Psychological Sciences and Social Sciences* 60, no. 3 (2005): S146–S151.

Wright, Beatrice A. *Physical Disability: A Psychosocial Approach.* HarperCollins, 1983.

Wrosch, Carsten, and Richard Schulz. "Health-Engagement Control Strategies and 2-Year Changes in Older Adults' Physical Health." *Psychological Science* 19, no. 6 (2008): 537–541.

Wykle, May L., Eva Kahana, and Jerome Kowal. *Stress and Health Among the Elderly.* Springer, 1992.

Yoshinaga-Itano, Christine, Allison L. Sedey, Diane K. Coulter, and Albert L. Mehl. "Language of Early- and Later-Identified Children with Hearing Loss." *Pediatrics* 102, no. 5 (1998): 1161–1171.

Zarb, Gerry, and Mike Oliver. *Ageing with a Disability: What Do They Expect After All These Years?* University of Greenwich London, 1993.

Zola, Irving Kenneth. *Missing Pieces: A Chronicle of Living with a Disability.* Temple University Press, 1982.

———. "Self, Identity and the Naming Question: Reflections on the Language of Disability." *Social Science and Medicine* 36, no. 2 (1993): 167–173.

———. "Toward the Necessary Universalizing of a Disability Policy." *Milbank Quarterly* 67, no. 2, Pt. 2 (1989): 401–428.

Index

About the Book

What is the lived experience of previously healthy older adults as they face disability in late life, and how is disability assimilated in their identity? How do prevailing practices facilitate—or limit—options for elders living with new disabilities?

To address these questions, Jeffrey Kahana and Eva Kahana uniquely synthesize disability and gerontological perspectives to explore both the unfolding challenges of aging and the practices and policies that can enhance the lives of older adults.

Jeffrey S. Kahana is associate professor of history and codirector of the Center on Aging and Policy at Mount Saint Mary College. **Eva Kahana** is Distinguished University Professor and Pierce T. and Elizabeth D. Robson Professor of the Humanities at Case Western Reserve University, where she also is director of the Elderly Care Research Center.